4/21

Doris A. Fuchs, Friedrich Kratochwil (eds.)

# Transformative Change and Global Order

D1373806

# Fragen politischer Ordnung in einer globalisierten Welt

herausgegeben von

Prof. Dr. Friedrich Kratochwil
(Universität München)

Band 2

LIT

Doris A. Fuchs, Friedrich Kratochwil (eds.)

# Transformative Change and Global Order

## Reflections on Theory and Practice

Withdrawn

LIT

JZ
1318
.T73
2002

**Bibliografic information by Die Deutsche Bibliothek**
Die Deutsche Bibliothek lists this publication in the Deutsche Nationalbibliografie; detailed bibligraphic data are available in the Internet at http://dnb.ddb.de abrufbar.

© LIT VERLAG Münster – Hamburg – London

Grevener Str./Fresnostr. 2 48159 Münster
Tel. 0251-23 50 91 Fax 0251-23 19 72
e-Mail: lit@lit-verlag.de http://www.lit-verlag.de

Distributed in North America by:

**Transaction Publishers**
New Brunswick (U.S.A.) and London (U.K.)

Transaction Publishers
Rutgers University
35 Berrue Circle
Piscataway, NJ 08854

Tel.: (732) 445 - 2280
Fax: (732) 445 - 3138
for orders (U. S. only):
toll free (888) 999 - 6778

# Contents

## Acknowledgments

Numerous people have in one way or another influenced this book. First of all, we are grateful to the *Volkswagen Foundation* for her generous financial support. Moreover, we have benefited from the discussions with our colleagues in the research network politics-law-philosophy (PRP) at the University of Munich and participants of the "Globalization and Justice" workshop in Bad Reichenhall in June 2001. Illustrations in this book, except for those in the Müller chapter, have been provided by Chris Light Artworks, Munich, and we owe Christian Leithaeuser particular gratitude for those. Finally, Janet Retseck and Anne Elsen deserve thanks for their editorial assistance and assembling of the final typescript, as do Julia Pollok and Norbert Grauvogel for their assistance with references and literature.

September 2002 D. F. and F. K.

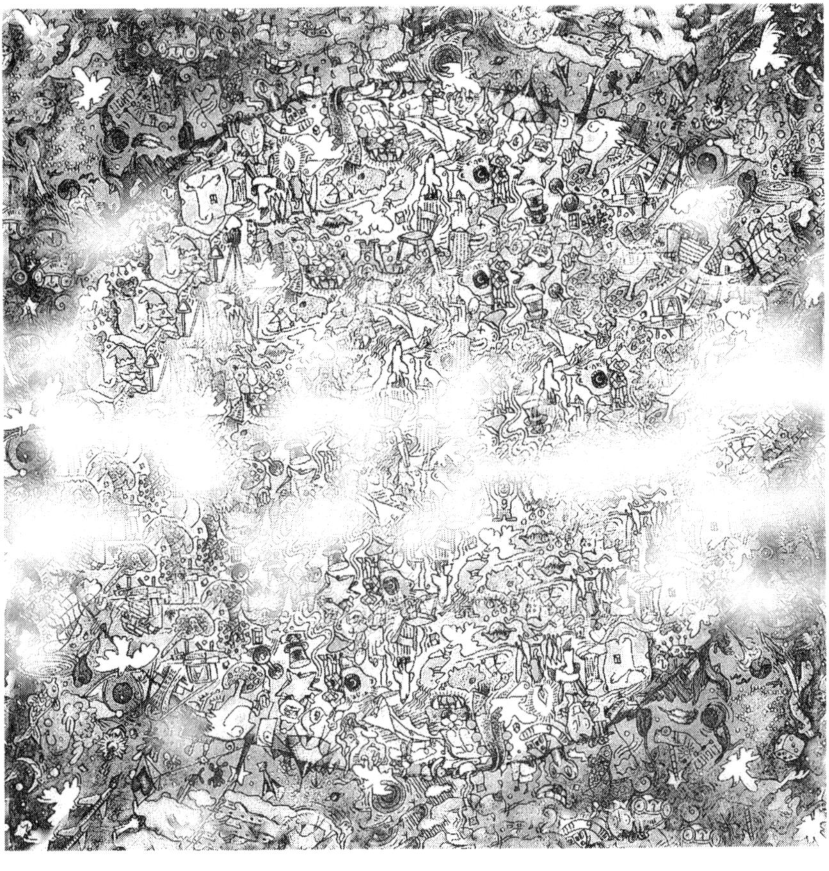

# Globalization and Global Governance: Discourses on Political Order at the Turn of the Century

Doris A. Fuchs

The world at the beginning of the 21st century is fundamentally different from what it was only 50 years ago – or so it seems. At the global, national, local, and individual levels, observers report dramatic transformations in the economic, social, and ecological environments. Likewise, political decision-makers and scholars identify deep changes in political organization and apply new concepts to describe and explain them. What then are the new institutions and qualities of political order? To be sure, a significant number of observers reject "newness" claims, arguing that the present situation merely reflects trends that started anywhere from 50 to more than a thousand years ago.

Debates on new (or not so new) structures and qualities of international affairs have utilized references to two related concepts in particular: globalization and global governance. In the popular and academic discussions, globalization has come to stand for new opportunities and challenges for political organization. Likewise, among practitioners and scholars, global governance has been used to describe new forms of transnational political decision-making and regulation. Using these two concepts as entrance points, therefore, the present book explores theory and practice of political organization in a transformed/ing world.

Our objective in this endeavor is to shape the post-globalization discussion. To this end, we want to delineate what we can learn from the strengths and weaknesses of globalization and global governance arguments and debates. In particular, the book emphasizes the need to consider both discourse and material phenomena. Thus, the book highlights developments regarding the theory of globalization and global governance. At the same time, however, it stresses the existence of material consequences of changes in the world. In regard to both aspects, the globalization and global governance debates have had considerable problems. Pressure to specify and conceptualize objects of analysis adequately came too little and too late. Without explicit communication on these matters, a productive exchange is difficult. Subsequent debates focusing on theoretical questions sometimes reduced questions of social realities to irrelevance, however. Clearly, we should be careful not to depict all arguments about transformative changes in the world and their respective labels as pure discourse and forget about the people affected. This book, therefore, aims to do both: to consider theoretical and conceptual aspects of the transformative changes generally captured under the terms of globalization and global governance, but to inquire into the implications of these changes as well.

The first part of the book stresses theoretical and conceptual aspects of the globalization and global governance debates.[1] Thus, the remainder of this introduction dissects the conceptual foundations of globalization and, in particular, global governance arguments and examines their consequences for assessments of the nature and extent of these "phenomena." The second group of chapters places more emphasis on empirical aspects, then, before the final section of the book tries to link the two dimensions.

## The Theory of Globalization and Global Governance

Globalization and global governance have become buzzwords. Globalization is a frequent referent in popular, political, and academic discussions. While more limited to the scholarly and political communities, global governance has reached a similar level of popularity within those groups, with an exponentially growing number of publications on the topic. In spite of the ongoing attention globalization and global governance receive, however, it would appear that we know very little about them at first glance. Discussions on both concepts are highly controversial. Participants in these debates disagree about the nature, extent, and implications of each of the two "phenomena," if not their mere existence. How can such disagreements be explained after more than a decade or two of intensive research and

[1] Globalization and global governance are related concepts, of course. Both refer to changes taking place at the global or transnational level but reaching down to the individual. The debate sometimes is vague and undecided about their relationship. Some would argue that global governance is the political response to economic globalization, created with the intent to tame globalization or shape it in the interest of specific actors. Others would contend that global governance is the unavoidable consequence of globalization and shifts in political capacity among actors caused by it. Probably, both are right to some extent, and we can best view global governance as a combination of automatic consequence of and intentional response to globalization.

debate? One possible answer to this question is, of course, that the changes described are ongoing and globalization is not a finished stage of the world nor global governance a completion of political (re)organization. Thus, time and further research may contribute to clarity.

To a substantial extent, however, these disagreements arise from the convolution of discourse and empirical description present in communication and the use of fundamentally different conceptualizations, assumptions, and foci by participants. Statements about globalization and global governance are not "objective" descriptions, but a combination of material phenomena, subjective views, and argumentation. Discourse and empirical phenomenon cannot be easily separated, of course. Likewise, conceptualizations and assumptions frequently are not explicit. Critical analyses of globalization and global governance, however, need to be aware of the existence of these dimensions of the debates and to scrutinize conceptualizations and assumptions in order to identify sources of disagreement. Such analytical measures do not end disagreements on the nature and implications of globalization and global governance. To some extent, disagreements arise from different ideological beliefs and frames of participants in the debates, which are not easily modified by reasoning. However, knowing the sources of disagreement allows observers a better understanding of the debates and their objects.

## Globalization

One prominent source of the disagreements about the nature and extent of globalization as well as its implications is the range of phenomena captured with this term. Scholars and practitioners use the term 'globalization' to refer to various quantitative and qualitative developments ranging from a dramatic increase in international transactions, especially in finance, to the international and spatial reorganization of production, the global harmonization of tastes and standards, liberalization, deregulation, privatization, the arrival of new information technologies, the global diffusion of information, values, and ideas, massive population transfers, trends towards a universal world culture, the spread of a worldwide preference for democracy, and the erosion of the nation state (Friedman 1999, Woods 2000). Differences in foci, however, will lead to fundamentally different assessments of globalization and its characteristics.

One way to approach the globalization debate, then, is to categorize globalization accounts according to their substantive focus. Thus, we can differentiate between exchanges in goods, exchanges in money and finance, exchanges in information and ideas, exchanges in people, exchanges in authority, and exchanges in ecological goods and bads (Clark 1999). Depending on which focus observers choose, they will notice very different aspects and characteristics of globalization. A concentration on exchanges in goods (and, to a lesser extent, services), for instance, would underline developments such as the quantitative increase in the flow of goods around the globe, decreasing barriers to trade, and the entry of more and more countries in world markets. Likewise, it would turn the spotlight on changes in the organization of business activities such as supraterritorial sourcing and distribution strategies, the increasing global subsidiarization of business activities, the deterritorialization of the labor markets, and the resulting almost complete detachment of business from territorial space (Bartlett and Goshal 1998). Similarly, a focus on exchanges in money and finance would highlight round-the-clock instantaneous foreign exchange transactions in round-the-world markets, highly mobile capital floating around the globe in search of good investment opportunities anywhere and the corresponding volatility of financial markets, the lack of connection to "real" economic activity and employment, as well as the deterritorialization of national currencies (Eichengreen 1996).

A systematic assessment of globalization based on such categories of activities would demonstrate the variety of globalization trends, allow a better differentiation between characteristics of these various facets of globalization, and force participants to be more explicit in their use of the term globalization. The categories identified above highlight, for instance, sources of fundamental disagreement about the extent of globalization. Thus, exchanges in people are still much less developed than exchanges in capital or goods (Sassen 1996). While controls on the movement of goods and capital have been greatly reduced around the world since the Second World War, a number of developed countries have recently strengthened their controls on the movement of people by imposing tougher immigration laws.

As a second step in a systematic assessment of the globalization debate, we need to differentiate between the geographic foci and perspectives applied by participants. Similar to substantive foci, geographic foci have fundamental implications for the perceived characteristics of globalization. Their importance becomes particularly clear when evaluating the current extent of globalization. Globalization has spread very unevenly across regions, countries, and social groups. While the tentacles of globalization may reach everywhere in this world in one way or another, the experience clearly is different in downtown London, New York, or Munich than in a village in rural Chad. Arguments about a fully globalized world tend to focus on the former rather than the latter (Langhorne 2001). The dominance of such claims in the globalization debate should not come as a surprise, if one considers the origins of the majority of participants: "Protagonists of the globalization debates are disproportionately urban, white, middle-class, Judaeo-Christian, English-speaking men resident in the North " (Scholte 2000a, p. 40).

In consequence, the extent and role of globalization frequently are exaggerated in the popular debate (especially if this serves the argumentative objectives of the participant). From the perspective of developing countries, the world clearly is not fully globalized.[2] More than 95% of the world population lack access to the Internet. Transnational exchanges in capital, communication, and even goods are much more concentrated on industrialized countries than developing countries (Thomas 2000). (Global) civil society is primarily a Western phenomenon. Developing countries do feel the impact of globalization in one way or another, for instance in the form of constraints on some policy choices. The majority of the characteristics of "their reality," however, are not global.

Differences in geographic focus and perspective thus are a second source of disagreement in the globalization debate. Claims about globalization and its characteristics need to be scrutinized for their explicit or implicit application of a particular geographic focus. Moreover, observers should question their own convictions on this basis.

The application of such a differentiated assessment to the globalization debate in terms of substantive and geographic foci then provides superior insights into its multiple facets and characteristics. It allows a better understanding of each individual focus as well as an opportunity to learn across foci. Having realized a lack of globality of globalization in terms of the movement of people, i.e. the restriction of the new mobility to social and economic elites residing predominantly in developed countries, for instance, we may conclude that we need to be careful with claims about the extent of globalization in exchanges in goods and finance. From a discursive perspective, such a differentiated approach

[2] Even within developed as well as developing countries, wealthier sectors of society are much more integrated in the globalizing world than poor and marginalized groups.

also provides the opportunity to examine the position and interests of given commentators on globalization and their potential reasons for choosing a particular focus.

Another option to shed some light on the complex matter of globalization is to explore the various theoretical notions scholars utilize to conceptualize perceived developments. These concepts include internationalization, liberalization, universalization, westernization/ modernization, and deterritorialization (Scholte 2000a). Again, differences in concepts will lead to differences in observed trends and in assessment of the extent and qualities of globalization. The internationalization lens highlights the increase in transborder relations between countries, in particular the growth of interdependence and communication and the movements of goods, capital, people and ideas around the globe. In contrast, the liberalization frame points to the removal of barriers to the movement of goods and capital between countries and to attempts to create a borderless world economy. Universalization draws attention to the spatial diffusion of experiences and objects across the world, while westernization-modernization emphasizes the spreading of certain social structures as well as lifestyles and governance styles, in particular the "Americanization" of the world and the associated threat to traditional cultures. Finally, deterritorialization stresses the aspect of spreading supraterritoriality, the reconfiguration of "social geography" (op.cit., p. 46).

These concepts illustrate well how participants in the globalization debate can arrive at fundamentally different assessments of globalization. The temporal dimension, i.e., the "starting date" of globalization, for instance, is a particular source of controversy. Such a debate may seem irrelevant at first glance. However, the discursive nature of globalization renders it quite important. Assessments of the newness of the globalization phenomenon, for instance, may be used to argue for the need for dramatic changes in politics, carried by claims of an inability to learn from history. Likewise, identifications of a long history of globalization tendencies may be used for depictions of globalization arguments as "globalony" and associated claims of the benefits of continuing business (i.e., politics) as usual or making marginal adjustments only.

In consequence, it matters whether a given observer conceptualizes globalization as universalization, i.e., the diffusion of cultures and values that, according to some scholars, can be traced back to ancient history (Gamble 1994), or as a long linear development of "internationalization" that started some 100 to 500 years ago (Hirst and Thompson 1996). Even the latter view, which tends to be associated with arguments that interdependence and exchange in the late 19th century are comparable to the present situation, will arrive at fundamentally different results than "deterritorialization" lenses suggesting that globalization is a relatively new phenomenon that emerged a few decades ago at most (Scholte 2000a).

The use of different conceptual lenses will lead to similarly diverging results with respect to evaluations of the extent of globalization. If we conceptualize globalization as internationalization, we may consider it almost complete, as some transborder interaction in terms of goods, ideas, people, or money does take place in all regions of the world. Likewise, the Westernization framework will suggest a rather extensive stage of globalization as even tribal villages in Africa and slums in India have access to TVs and are watching American soaps and sitcoms. In contrast, the deterritorialization lens will highlight that there are substantial regions in the world where people are still firmly embedded in the logic of local relations, in particular those left behind by the digital revolution. Even production and consumption activities often depend on specific localities, and environmental degradation, for instance, strongly matters at the local level. A fully globalized world economy based on supra-territorial economic relations does not yet exist, much less a globalized world society based on supra-territorial social relations.

Clearly, then, arguments made in the globalization debate need to be scrutinized for the underlying conceptualization of globalization. Such critical assessments will bring to light the bases for claims made, as well as the facets of globalization neglected by the argument. Ideally, the debate would converge on a particular conceptualization. Such a result is rather unlikely, of course, given the number of participants in the debate and their various lenses and objectives. Still, an increasing focus on the deterritorialization lens appears to be taking hold, at least in the academic community. This trend results from a reversal in the direction of inquiry. Rather than ask what globalization is and whether it is new or not, scholars have started to ask if there is anything fundamentally new here that deserves to be called globalization instead of increasing interdependence, liberalization, modernization, or any of the other traditional concepts.

In this perspective, deterritorialization is the significant and novel trait of the globalizing world. Numerous scholars have argued that territorial location, distance, and borders have lost their determining influence (Held, McGrew, Goldblatt, and Perraton 1999). Territory still matters, but territoriality is no longer the key aspect in defining identities, activities, and relationships (Ruggie 1993b). Globalization as deterritorialization means the ability to conduct affairs across the world irrespective of time and place, and without reference to nationality or the territorial jurisdiction of governments. The core aspect of globalization, according to this conceptual lens, is the collapse of space-time relations.

Even the spread of supra-territoriality has longer term dimensions, of course. For centuries, world religions have incorporated notions of the planet as a single space. The enlightenment philosophy of the 18th century decidedly considered the fate of "humanity" as such (even though conceptualizations of this "humanity" may have carried certain regional biases). Similarly, observers have reported the decreasing significance of territory and borders in exchanges in goods, finance, and information for a while (Ohmae 1990).

As advocates of the deterritorialization lens convincingly argue, however, recent changes in the role and function of territory are much more striking than in the other typical conceptualizations of globalization. In the latter part of the 20th century, supra-territoriality has achieved a different quality due to an increased pace and scale of developments for which territorial dimensions are irrelevant. The size, speed, and reach of global communications, capital mobility and investment decisions, business strategies and activities, and the diffusion of ideas and values all exemplify the role of supra-territoriality in the complex and multi-faceted phenomenon of globalization.

In sum, the controversies regarding the nature, extent, and, as the final chapter of this book will demonstrate, implications of globalization can be attributed to three factors in particular. One reason for controversies is the range of phenomena and processes lumped together under the term of globalization. Thus, participants in the globalization debate are applying different substantive foci. A second cause of disagreements is the use of different geographic foci, and, in particular, an insufficient level of differentiation between the situation in developed and developing countries. The third source of controversies about the nature and extent of globalization is the utilization of different theoretical conceptualizations of globalization.

These differences in substantive and geographic foci and theoretical conceptualizations automatically will lead to corresponding divergences in assessment of globalization. They strongly influence whether globalization leads us to paradise or is the road to hell. In consequence, critical analyses need to scrutinize globalization accounts for explicit and implicit choices of focus and conceptualization in order to identify facets and characteristics emphasized and, more importantly, facets and characteristics neglected.

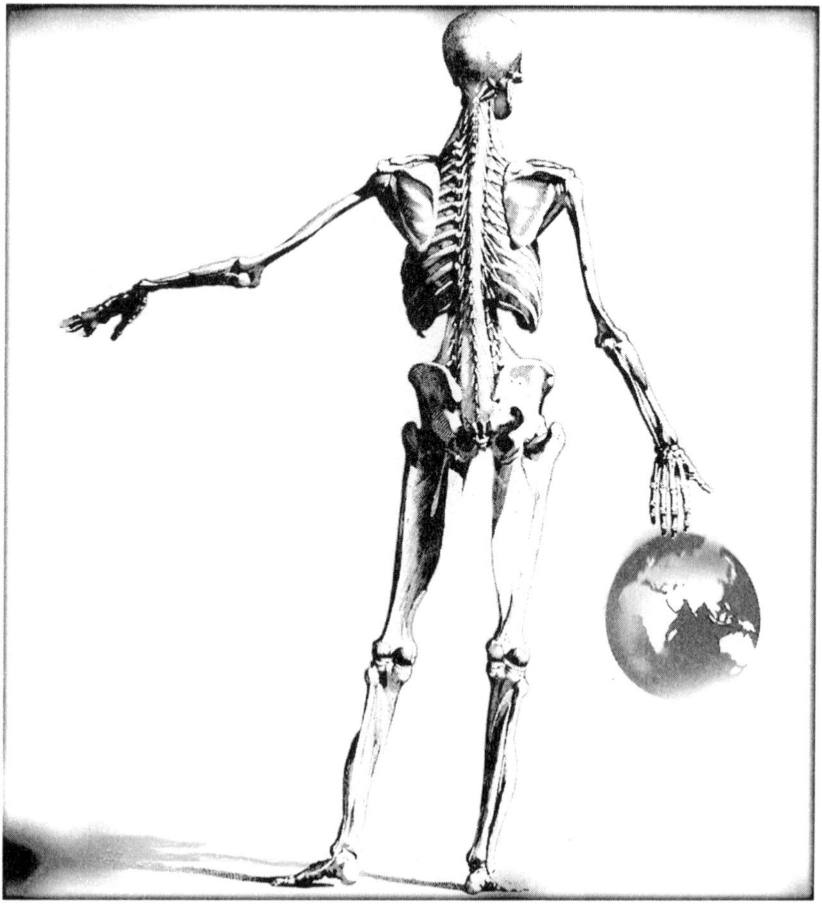

## Global Governance

With respect to global governance, conceptualizations of the "phenomenon" as such do not diverge as much as in the case of globalization. However, assessments of its actual and potential extent as well as its implications are highly controversial, due to differences in conceptualizations of the actors in global governance, underlying ideological beliefs and assumptions about the nature of the world, and, again, differences in foci.

On a very general level, scholars conceptualize global governance in a similar way, as a move toward multi-actor, multi-level decision-making in world politics. They point to the development of new forms of problem-solving structures and processes with a growth in regulatory initiative and control by sub-state, supra-state, and non-state actors (Cutler, Haufler, and Porter 1999, Rosenau and Czempiel 1992). Thus, scholars describe a change of the international system from a state-centric to a multi-centric one with multiple sources of power and loci of authority (Väyrynen 1999). The architecture of global governance, then, is composed of states, international regimes, regional blocs, the United Nations and other IGOs, civil society, transnational business, the media, and local politics. Shrinking distances, shifting boundaries, and relocations of authority are all fostering a disaggregation of loci of governance. As territorial boundaries are becoming porous and political power and activity increasingly extend across the boundaries of nation states, political options and roles of actors are being defined anew (Held and McGrew 1993).

The core of the global governance argument concerns the acquisition of authoritative decision-making capacity by non-state and supra-state actors. These actors now have the "capacity to get things done without the legal competence to command that they be done" (Czempiel 1992, p. 250), a capacity which results from a "form of authority rather than jurisdiction" (Lipschutz 1999, p. 260). This redistribution of authority to multiple actors and levels and the corresponding creation of multiple new loci of authority render global governance a highly disaggregate system of many "overlapping spheres of authority (SOAs)" distinguished by actors, activities, and exercise of authority (Rosenau 1999, p. 295).

Furthermore, scholars and practitioners agree for the most part that global governance does not mean global government due to perceptions of its undesirability and infeasibility (see, for instance, Commission on Global Governance 1995, p. xvi). Arguments for undesirability underline both the threat of a (world) tyranny and bureaucratic nightmare[3] and a lack of democratic legitimation due to the necessary distance between a world government and its civil society (Messner and Nuscheler 1996a). Arguments for unfeasibility refer to an insufficient level of uniformity in values and beliefs and a lack of social cohesion among the global population, the impossibility of reaching agreement on the details of constitutional design, economic gaps, forces of nationalism, and ideological conflicts, as well as the likelihood that the rich and powerful countries would reject the idea of a democratic world government in fear of losing power. A small number of practitioners and scholars argue that world government is not only desirable and feasible, but also the best strategy to pursue democratic ideals and improve the fate of the world population (Harris and Yunker 1999). However, the dominant underlying framework in the global governance debate is a liberal belief in the benefits of individualism, decentralization, and voluntary cooperation (Falk 1999). Generally, then, the reigning conceptualization of global governance identifies the establishment of social institutions and decision-making procedures and practices without requiring the material elements and police power generally considered characteristics of governments.

Disagreements in the conceptualization of global governance arise mainly in terms of its political or apolitical nature. They result from different definitions of the term "governance" and diverging assumptions about the nature of world politics. In the *New English Dictionary*, governance is defined as "the action or manner of governing, controlling, directing or regulating influence, ...; discreet or virtuous behavior; wise self-command." In some interpretations, then, governance is attributed an a priori positive nature. Some of the definitions given by scholars exhibit a similar tendency, delineating governance as "mechanisms for steering social systems toward their goals" (Rosenau 1999, p. 296, [emphasis added]). Politics seem irrelevant in such a definition. The tendency to define global governance apolitically is related to the assumption of a rather harmonious world (Mürle 1998). In the case of the Commission on Global Governance, such an assumption may not be that surprising, given that the Commission met in the hope and euphoria immediately following the end of the Cold War, suggesting the promise of improved international cooperation. Arguments for an intensification of cooperative and consensual international decision-making based on common interests and the

---

[3] Interestingly, the same arguments were raised against the creation of a federalist United States of America (Griffin 1999).

increasing importance of norms and institutions emphasizing cooperation over unilateral action, however, are frequent in the general literature (Langhorne 2001).

Increasingly, however, scholars are pointing out that global governance is not necessarily virtuous and should not be viewed as an apolitical problem-solving exercise (Hewson and Sinclair 1999). They question the premise of harmony in the world and are skeptical toward the willingness of countries to engage in international cooperation. These scholars emphasize the continued dominance of national interests and orientations, which is further strengthened by internal disintegration tendencies (Stairs 1999). Fundamentally, they argue that global governance has clear political dimensions that need to be assessed. Recent studies, therefore, have started to highlight the power relations underlying global governance and to question their political implications (Brand, Brunnengräber, Schrader, Stock, and Wahl 2000). The currently emerging understanding of global governance is a focus on steering (of something by someone), of the establishment and operation of rules of conduct, and the creation and modification of practices, entailing a purposive though not necessarily socially beneficial behavior.

In contrast to a relatively broad conceptual agreement on global governance as such, significant disagreements regarding its actual and potential extent do exist. These disagreements are a function of divergent conceptualizations of the core actors in global governance and the ideological beliefs and assumptions underlying these conceptualizations, as well as of differences in foci.

Those scholars and practitioners arguing for a large actual and even larger potential extent of global governance tend to follow the premise of a high level of cooperative and consensual international decision-making described above as well as the capacity of various actors to contribute substantially to (global) governance (Rosenau and Czempiel 1992, Messner and Nuscheler 1996a). Global governance optimists base their hope especially on civil society (Anheier, Glasius, and Kaldor 2001). They claim that civil society has successfully established itself as a political agent whose activities have a significant effect on international and domestic politics. According to this argument, civil society actors fulfil tasks not covered by the state in some areas, while drawing influence from cooperation with the state, IGOs, or business actors in others. Scholars arguing that global civil society is an influential actor in global governance point to the existence of some 20,000 NGOs world-wide and the existence of transnational collaborations, affiliations, networks, and collective efforts in pursuit of common goals (Wapner 1997). They stress the sources of power of non-state actors, such as the ability to provide specialized local knowledge and technical expertise, increasingly global NGO networks and activities, and the ability to take advantage of new possibilities of public participation due to the global diffusion of telecommunication technologies[4]. Moreover, scholars contend that the influence of non-state actors is growing in areas other than the traditional ones of social and environmental policy, such as economic and even security policy. Moreover, they argue that non-state actors have benefited from the legitimacy crises of IGOs and the state and international sensitivities to activities of the latter.

In addition, scholars arguing for a substantial extent of global governance highlight that supra-national actors have significantly expanded their political capacity in scope and depth and therefore their potential to contribute to global governance. These scholars point out that networks of IGOs span the planet. The large and prominent ones, like the United Nations and the Bretton Woods organizations, are each associated with numerous affiliated institutions and complemented by a large amount of independent ones. Furthermore, formal IGOs with bureaucracies and legal statutes are complemented by institutionalized cooperation between countries and informal decision-making "clubs," for instance in the form of the G7 (G8) meetings taking place since 1975. Additional layers of institutionalized supranational public governance are provided by regional agreements, in particular the EU, as well as semi-state-controlled institutions such as the Basle Committee on Banking Supervision. Moreover, scholars highlight the contribution of IGOs to global governance through their reach into "sovereign" countries and influence on domestic policy.[5]

In contrast to optimistic assessments of the extent of global governance and the potential of various actors to contribute to it, pessimistic assessments are increasingly surfacing (Grande 2001). A substantial number of scholars are highly sceptical regarding the

---

[4] Examples of such new forms of public participation include, for instance, Internet websites such as "Scorecard", allowing the public relatively easy access to relevant information (in this case information about the environmental quality in the neighborhood) as well as tools for participation (such as draft letters to political representatives).

[5] The WTO with its Trade Policy Review Mechanism fortified by a strengthened Dispute Settlement Mechanism and the IMF with its detailed comprehensive surveillance of the economic performance of its member states and corresponding adjustment proposals, according to some scholars, have the creeping undermining of national sovereignty written into the statutes (Brand et al. 2000).

potential extent of global governance. They claim that regime development and effectiveness tends to fall short of its ambitions, with the international regime on human rights as a case in point (Brand et al. 2000). Moreover, they highlight a persistent enforcement gap in international politics due both to the weakness of ethical constraints and social pressure and to an insufficient scope and quality of legal institutions crossing state, ethnic, and religious borders. Finally, they reject notions of steering competence and common pursuit of technical solutions as illusionary and perceive a dominance of haphazard agenda setting and decision-making in the context of global crises such as Yugoslavia, AIDS, or climate change (Björklund and Berglund 2001). In particular, the failures of UN missions, for instance, in Somalia, have increased scepticism towards the potential extent and effectiveness of international cooperation and problem solving.

Most importantly, critical observers raise doubts about the capacity of the "new" actors to contribute substantially to global governance. They question both the existence of a global civil society as well as the extent of its influence, for instance (Kratochwil 1997, O'Brien, Goetz, Scholte, and Williams 2000). Thus, scholars argue that a lack of access by large sectors of the global population prevents the development of societal structures known at the national level. Furthermore, they contend that categorization and large numbers of NGOs do not constitute a collective actor, due to a substantial heterogeneity of members and a lack of common goals and ability to cooperate in pursuit of political goals (Brand et al. 2000). Moreover, studies have shown that NGOs fail to achieve policy goals if they do not conform with the dominant discourse and ideological belief system, even in cases where IGOs depend on them for democratic legitimacy (O'Brien et al. 2000). Thus, scholars argue that global civil society will not be able to exert the expected influence in global governance until its participation is sufficiently supported by international law.

Likewise, pessimistic assessments of the potential for global governance emphasize the dependence of IGOs on state support and the prevalence of national interests among states. States determine the budgets of IGOs as well as their policies and organizational structures. Thus, domestic political contexts and expert consensus on issues influence what IGOs can achieve. The United Nations is the most prominent example of this dependence of IGOs on state support, as perceptions of its incapacity and weakness due to uncooperative members prevail.

Such variance in the assessment of the political capacity of supposedly core actors in global governance and therefore the potential for global governance itself is a function of divergences in conceptualizations of the actors and foci of analysis. In particular, scholars use dramatically different concepts of civil society. In addition, they arrive at very different evaluations depending on whether they focus on the situation in developed or developing countries.

With respect to civil society, scholars disagree about the political nature of its members. Using a broad definition of civil society, some scholars include actors and groups without an explicit political objective.

> Civil society is that domain of associational life situated above the individual and below the state. It is made up of complex networks based on interest, ideology, family, and cultural affinity through which people pursue various aims. Churches, unions, movements, political parties, and clubs of all sorts are examples of such networks, and the host of these together constitutes civil society (Wapner 1997, p. 65).

Others, however, define civil society as non-state, non-market actors pursuing activities that involve a deliberate attempt to shape policies, norms, and/or deeper social structures (Scholte 2000b). In consequence, scholars arrive at rather different estimates of the extent of a global civil society, as the majority of NGOs are not intentionally pursuing politics, in particular not across national borders.

Likewise, differences in foci cause huge variances in the political capacity of (global) civil society as well as IGOs. Highly optimistic evaluations tend to generalize from the situation in Western liberal democracies. The underlying (frequently inexplicit) conceptualization of civil society is based on the Western liberal model of society, romanticized by ideas of local participation and networks, emphasizing mobility and permeability, as well as cooperative relations. In developing countries, however, political traditions differ and individuals and groups do not have the resources and corresponding ability to make themselves heard even in their own countries, much less at the global level. Rather than being empowered by globalization and global governance, these societies increasingly tend to lack opportunities for meaningful participation.[6]

---

[6] Associated with this difference in focus is a difference in scope. Pessimistic assessments of the potential of global civil society to contribute to global governance point out that the global heterogeneity of values and divergence in welfare, as well as

With respect to IGOs, the situation is almost the opposite. IGOs clearly have much more governance capacity from the perspective of developing countries than from the perspective of developed ones. The latter are much less dependent on IMF loans and the associated establishment of their creditworthiness, for instance. Similarly, the WTO's dispute settlement mechanism, with its tool of retaliatory compensation, is much more powerful when used by the US or EU against a developing country than when employed by the latter against the former. Weighted voting in the Bretton Woods institutions further contributes to this difference in the political capacity of IGOs with respect to developed and developing countries.[7] Thus, scholars questioning the capacity of IGOs to contribute successfully to global governance tend to focus on their dependence on developed country support, while those arguing the opposite frequently cite examples from developing countries.

Finally, assessments of the potential extent of global governance also differ in their evaluation of the role of the state. A number of scholars argue that there are significant limits to global governance because the state would need to play a crucial role but does not have the capacity to do so. Scholars point out that the state is necessary to provide the order and stability that make governance feasible and to create the opportunities for agency by non-state actors (Latham 1999). In addition, the state is the primary if not only actor legitimately able to raise resources for global governance through taxation and to implement collectively binding decisions. Moreover, global markets need the state to protect property rights and reduce transaction costs.

However, one of the core claims of the global governance debate has been the decline of the state. Numerous scholars have highlighted constraints imposed on the state by the global markets and supra-national policy decisions, as well as institutional and technological developments facilitating international surveillance (Ohmae 1995, Strange 1996, Zürn 1998). Furthermore, participants in the debate report the state's loss of

---

the lack of access and marginalization of large parts of the global population, are in stark contrast to the "small, peaceful, orderly, and inviting residential area in which people live together in serene and mutually supportive harmony" implied by the title of the Commission's report "Our Global Neighborhood" (Yunker 1999, p. 142).

[7] This dynamic is further strengthened by an increasing tendency to marginalize IGOs with unweighted voting in the global governance architecture. UNCTAD, for instance, was almost dissolved while the WTO is acquiring more and more competencies. Similarly, international legislation on intellectual property has been placed in the WTO's jurisdiction rather than that of the World Intellectual Property Organization (WIPO), which uses unweighted voting.

its monopoly over the provision of public goods, of its abilities to provide political integration and balance the needs of the individual with the freedom of the whole. Further in this line of argument, the persistence of low growth rates, rising unemployment and inflation, and experiences of personal economic and physical insecurity and everyday "hypercompetitiveness" are causing a legitimacy crisis for the state (Sinclair 1999a). In the end, scholars see the welfare state as stuck in the expectation gap between an increasing need to regulate and a decreasing capacity to do so, between rising costs of the welfare system and a decreasing capacity to adopt and enforce a corresponding tax level.

Another group of scholars rejects such pessimist assessments of the fate of the state, however, arguing that the state retains substantial governance capacities. They claim that the state still contributes substantially to social cohesion and the organization of social and redistributive policies, safeguards interests related to the common good, and functions as a control on particularist interests (Jessop 1997). Scholars even claim that the state remains the dominant regulatory agent in highly globalized economic sectors (Helleiner 1998) and identify it as the key actor in the steering of IGOs, especially in times of crisis (Zacher 1999).

A third group of scholars accepts the idea of decline in some of the traditional capacities of the state, but emphasizes a strengthening of other capacities. According to this perspective, the state has become a "competition state"[8] rather than a welfare state, providing it with a pivotal role in the setting of economic and political frameworks allowing the attracting of investment and the reaping of maximum economic benefit while maintaining social content (Garrett 2000). Important tasks in this respect are the protection of property and enforcement of contracts, as well as investments in education and infrastructure. The competition state produces social capital, facilitates efficient factor and product markets, and guards the legal and commercial institutions underpinning markets.

These variances in assessment of the capacity of the state to some extent reflect the need for further research. To a substantial amount, however, they originate in differences in conceptualization of the state and its role. Different ideological frameworks attribute different core tasks to the state. In the eyes of many observers, the competition state does not fulfill its core tasks, for instance, due to its inability and

---

[8] Jessop (1997) speaks of a shift from a Keynesian welfare state to a "Schumpeterian workfare state."

unwillingness to provide welfare guarantees for its population. Others, however, are more sympathetic to a restriction of state intervention to the provision of institutions and infrastructure necessary for the individuals' pursuits of their (economic) interests, and they do not perceive any threats to state capacity as long as the state can and does fulfill this role. Here, scholarly assessment meets discourse, and research fails to lead to agreement.

Even if one were to argue that the move towards the competition state does not mean a decline in state capacity, and that this competition state theoretically can fulfill the tasks necessary for its role in global governance, differences in foci would still lead to differences in assessment of the potential extent of global governance. The competition state may be a new model for many developed countries. In some regions of the world, however, the state does not really exist. Warlords are the only "authority" and old tribal arrangements are redeveloping in some areas in Africa (Teztlaff 1998). In some areas of Asia, especially parts of the former Soviet Union, "authority" takes the form of organized crime syndicates and private security forces (Volkow 2000). In these areas, the state has hardly any internal and external negotiation and enforcement capacity and clearly cannot fulfill the tasks required for global governance (Grande 2001). Moreover, neither markets nor civil society can contribute the missing governance capacity in these situations. Accordingly, entire regions are left out of global governance, and a focus on these regions will lead to an extremely skeptical assessment of the actual and potential extent of global governance.

In sum, differences in global governance accounts, like those in globalization accounts, can be linked to differences in focus of analysis, conceptualizations adopted, and underlying ideological frames. In particular, conceptualizations of actors and assumptions about their appropriate roles are powerful determinants of the nature and extent of global governance perceived by individual observers. The question to what extent civil society exists at the global level and what its credentials are has a decisive influence on evaluations of global governance. Likewise, ideological stances on the appropriate role of the state matter dramatically when "describing" potential shifts in political authority. In addition, choices in geographic focus make a huge difference in observers' assessments of the nature, as well as the actual and potential extent of global governance. The geographic bias in the debate, i.e. the predominant focus on the experience of industrialized countries, which is a function of the origins of the vast majority of participants in the global governance debate, leads to a neglect of the meaning of global governance for a large part of the world. As the final chapter will show, such differences in conceptualization, focus, and underlying ideological belief system also play a crucial role in assessments of the implications of global governance.

## Outlook

This chapter has demonstrated the pivotal function substantive and geographic foci, theoretical conceptualizations, and underlying ideological belief systems play in shaping globalization and global governance accounts. Thereby, the chapter has highlighted some of the fundamental difficulties of the globalization and global governance debates in terms of theory and discourse. The material implications have been left to the side for now. They will be the focus of the second half of the book, and the concluding chapter in particular will integrate findings on theory and practice of globalization and global governance on the basis of the individual contributions. The next four chapters, then, will explore the theory- and discourse-related difficulties with respect to the globalization and global governance discourses in more depth.

In the following chapter, Friedrich Kratochwil scrutinizes the globalization debate. He exposes globalization as a discursive formation that lumps together a variety of processes and functions as a shorthand providing a framework for orientation and the attribution of meaning that can be compared and contrasted with other shorthands such as the "end of history." Examining globalization from this angle puts the spotlight on the claims and justifications generally associated with references to globalization, which Kratochwil then compares with empirical evidence concerning the nature of the ongoing processes of transformative change.

In his contribution, Philipp Müller adopts a Wittgensteinian therapeutic approach to examine the term globalization and its uses. In his endeavor, he employs a four step procedure; he challenges globalization dogmas, exposes the pictures standing behind them, proposes alternative pictures, and attempts to deflect anxiety regarding them. His primary aim in this effort is to increase the understanding, accountability and freedom of policy makers. Specifically, Müller "therapetizes" usages of globalization suggesting a wave, an independent or dependent variable, the paradox of glocalization, and a Darwinist selection process.

Developing a counterfactual account of globalization, its nature, and consequences, Richard Ned Lebow and Janice Stein, then, challenge the globalization discourse from another angle. By imagining what the world would look like today, if the First World War had not occurred, they arrive at surprising findings regarding inevitable and changeable characteristics of globalization. Globalization still would have occurred in their alternative world, and would, in fact, have taken off earlier. Yet, the alternative globalized world would have looked fundamentally different, according to Lebow and Stein, regarding some of the characteristics of globalization that we now take for granted, such as "Americanization."

Finally, David Kennedy adds to these more theoretically and conceptually focused explorations of globalization an extensive and multifaceted inquiry into global governance. In his endeavor, he is particularly concerned with developing the ability of scholars and practitioners, especially humanitarian oriented and progressive ones, to assess global governance more pragmatically. In pursuit of this objective, Kennedy draws our attention to common ways of evaluating global governance that locate the politics of global governance outside the policy vocabulary, suggests alternative foci and strategies, and lays out general ideas about the politics of the common policy making vocabularies.

The following chapters place more emphasis on the implications of globalization and global governance. In his contribution, Matthias Finger delineates the instrumentalization of the state in developing countries by public services trans-national corporations (TNCs), thus adding an important piece of the mosaic to the debate on the fate of the state. He lays out how these TNCs have simultaneously used several strategies to obtain lucrative contracts and achieve the dependency of the state on their skills and resources. In particular, public services TNCs have obtained support from the World Bank for their objectives and fostered transfers of authority from the national to the sub-national level in the countries of their interest. Finger delineates similar although adjusted strategies by these TNCs for their "real" targets, the public services markets in developed countries.

In the next chapter, Corneliu Dan Berari examines the roles played by the International Monetary Fund and the World Bank in the management of the world economy. He argues that the influence of these institutions varies dramatically between developed and developing countries. Berari speaks of two tiers of economic governance in this context, highlighting a fundamental imbalance in authoritative decision making capacity in the management of the world economy. Thus, he finds that the International Financial Institutions (IFIs) have acquired an extraordinary influence on the policies of many transition and developing countries, while ultimate decisions in matters of international economic governance are still taken by the G7 under the leadership of the US.

While Finger and Berari, thus, delineate specific implications of globalization and global governance, Heike Brabandt highlights the absence of "expected" consequences in her contribution. Using arguments about globalization's positive implications for the global diffusion of human rights norms as a starting point, Brabandt shows that even developed countries, which support these norms in international negotiations and are generally viewed as drivers behind diffusion dynamics, fail to implement them. In her analysis of the (lack of) implementation of international women's human rights norms, specifically those relating to Female Genital Mutilation, in Germany, Brabandt shows that implementation was hampered by concerns about financial and political costs in spite of NGO activism and support for the latter from the global level.

Finally, Markus Lederer's contribution links the more empirically focused part of our inquiries back to conceptual questions and, most importantly, implications for scholarly analysis. Looking at the example of stock-exchanges, Lederer argues that the traditional analytical dichotomy of "states" versus "markets" is not appropriate for analyzing the transformative changes associated with globalization and global governance. He points out four specific problems with this framework; the interdependence between states and markets, a structural bias associated with the term market, a national bias associated with the term state, and a general liberal bias of the framework. Lederer suggests using the categories of "exchange" and "regulation" instead, to better be able to inquire into new and important questions focusing on instruments, agents, and political spaces.

In the final chapter, Friedrich Kratochwil and I attempt to pull together some of the strings developed by the contributions to this volume and scholars participating in the globalization and global governance debates. Focusing on the implications of globalization and global governance, we argue that practitioners and scholars need to disaggregate trends described by shorthands like globalization and global governance, if they want to identify intervention points and opportunities for action. Highly aggregate analyses situated at the macro level may serve well to initially identify general trends. However, they fail to reveal the opportunities for intervention and levers for action necessary for strategic political efforts to shape the ongoing changes in the global order. In support of our argument, we highlight conceptual and substantive, and ideological determinants of differences in evaluations of the implications of globalization and global governance and assessments in terms of (in)equity, (in)security), and (a lack of) democratic legitimacy and try to identify a bottom line of understanding of political and research needs.

Throughout the book, the reader will find a number of illustrations of different views of globalization and global governance. These illustrations were provided by Chris Light Artworks, Munich. Please note that the views reflected in these illustrations are not necessarily those of authors of the respective preceding or following chapters.

# Globalization: What It Is and What It Is Not. Some critical reflections on the discursive formations dealing with transformative change

Friedrich Kratochwil

## Introduction

It is surprising how the events of September 11 seem to have eclipsed the preoccupation with globalization. While only yesterday globalization was celebrated in public discourse[9] as the virtually universal "explanation" for a variety of phenomena, the terrorist attacks have placed security concerns back on the front burner, and fears of a potential clash of civilizations seem to have displaced notions that globalization, working inexorably behind our backs, is fundamentally transforming our world (Huntington 1996). Within the context of the attacks, "globalization" is at best accorded a subsidiary status in that the attacks themselves are being interpreted as one of the manifestations of "globalization". A variety of versions of such interpretations can be distinguished here. There is first the apparently globally active network of terrorist cells whose attacks show the fragility of the order that we have taken for granted. Second, precisely because of their symbolic significance, the attacks on New York and Washington can also be interpreted as both a result and a manifestation of resistance to the global dominance of the US and Western culture. Finally, the vile destruction of the World Trade Center is seen as a protest by the "losers" of globalization.

Whatever the appropriateness of these interpretations may be - and indeed the privileged status of the planners and organizers of the attack makes the explanation of underprivileged "losers of globalization" hard to sustain - the great variety of explanations and their contradictory implications demonstrate that globalization is hardly a good candidate for a powerful *explanans*. For one, its rather amorphous character cannot

---

[9] For a general discussion of the globalization *problematique* in sociology and political science see for example Ulrich Beck 1999a, Ulrich Beck (ed.) 1998b, Ulrich Beck (ed.) 1998a, Manuel Castells 1996, Roland Robertson 1992, John Baylis, Steve Smith 2001, Ian Clark 1999, Martin Shaw 2000, Andrew Hurrell, Ngaire Woods 1999, David Held, Anthony McGrew, David Goldblatt, Jonathan Perraton 1999, Robert Gilpin 2001a, Robert Gilpin 2001b, Paul Hirst, Grahame Thompson 1999.

be made much more precise by definitional exercises. It is simply a discursive formation that lumps together a variety of processes of change, each one being propelled by its own complex causal chains and interactions. Second, precisely because it is a discursive formation, "globalization" can hardly be conceived of as an actor or an antecedent cause that engenders certain phenomena.

It thus might be useful to approach the problem not via a clarification of the empirical referent, nor by means of the construction of unequivocal "definitions", but by examining the *use* and *function* of the term in discourse. The simple "referential" understanding of concepts is still beholden to a mirror theory of truth in which reality on the one hand is appropriately depicted by the theoretical concepts on the other. Whatever the arguments about the problematic nature of such a theory of "truth" are, one thing is certain: in the case of social reality, the international system, the state, or whatever are not simply out "there" like furniture or a black dog that awaits its naming by such a matching operation. Instead, they are constituted by the very concepts we use in referring to them (e. g. Searle 1995).

In addition, as is the case with many of our terms in our political vocabulary, such as "sovereignty" or the "social contract", the concept of "globalization" does not refer to a fixed "thing" in the outer world, but to an assembly of phenomena and practices that are lumped together on the basis of some presumed resemblance. The term thus has "fuzzy boundaries." The world we encounter in the social sciences is not simple, neatly packaged in "natural kinds"–although that understanding might be problematic even in the natural sciences - but "reality" is being created by the practices of actors and the underlying understandings constituting their practices and interactions. We had therefore better not follow any advice to exclude those phenomena for which no clear and distinct properties can be found that would allow for an unequivocal attribution of meaning to a concept. Instead, as stated above, we had better examine the *function of these terms* in our vocabularies[10] even if they turn out to be not simply descriptive in nature but serve as *signals for actions* and as *justifications* and not merely as labels for "things".

Given this orientation, I propose in this chapter to address the issue of globalization in the following terms. In the next section, I investigate the various themes that are lumped together by this term and contrast it with other instances of global shorthands such as "modernity" or "end of history," terms that usually provide the widest conceptual grid within

---

[10] For a discussion of the differences such a view makes in respect to traditional issues concerning conceptualizations see Rorty 1989, chap. 1.

which we attempt to orient ourselves and understand transformative change. In section three, I contrast the themes and their subsidiary assertions with some of the evidence we in the meantime have assembled concerning the nature of the ongoing and deep-seated changes. In section four, I then attempt to assess some of the initial arguments and suggest further avenues for research.

## Phenomena and Themes

How do we talk about globalization? To a significant extent, the experience of "acceleration" to which the historian Koselleck (1985) called attention a few decades ago figures prominently in this discourse. Not only do we experience a high volume and ubiquity of transactions, but we also have the feeling that things are happening faster and faster, virtually overwhelming us. In a way, globalization picks up on a theme that had been part of the modernization discourse. When the future began to resemble the past less and less because of the intensity of change, "history", particularly as understood as the exemplary teacher for life (*historia magistra vitae*), was no longer able to instruct us in the "right" way (Koselleck 1985). As Toqueville (1970) so aptly put it, "the past has ceased to throw its light upon the future"(p. 396). The discourse of modernity of course tried to calm such fears by simply recasting the problem of history, moving it away from the exemplary past, from notions of a natural or original order, and by attempting to install "progress" as the loadstar.[11] Here, change no longer induced anxiety since in a "historicist" reading of the human world, the present could be understood in its radical novelty, as a "stage" of an unfolding historical development, as in the speculations of Hegel or Marx and their many acolytes.

Globalization, on the other hand, faces a more complicated world. There is first the problem that instead of the slow but perceptible spirit moving through the epochs and displacing one with the other - modernity emerging from the shackles of the dark ages - no such optimistic interpretation of developments seems possible. Instead of the utopian hope for a more cosmopolitan order that would substitute for the outmoded particularisms of yesteryear[12], the overall development is not one of homogenization and progress. Instead, we encounter both tendencies of integration and disintegration, and we have to notice the

[11] For a good discussion of these problems see Arendt 1966.

[12] See for example the optimist expectations in Held 1995.

surprising insistence on particularisms that often are not even reassertions of things past, but, as is the case in former Yugoslavia, results of modern, or better, of contemporary circumstances (Lapid, Kratochwil 1996). In this case, interpretations of primordialism seem to be as mistaken as the notions of universal progress that the Enlightenment once postulated as the hidden plot of history (Connor 1994). Both the notion of an epoch and the order and sequence of epochs in a scheme called (universal) history fail to convey precisely that meaning that the original invention of "history" in the collective singular promised. Instead of the grand plot, we see now only the ups and downs that have managed to be recorded in *histories* of this or that historical individual entity - be it a city, region, party, whatever - but that no longer fit all together into one overarching narrative that contains its own meaning and justification.

Second: whatever differences we might have concerning the phenomenon of globalization, we all seem to agree that we are dealing here with several, albeit probably connected, processes, although we seem particularly unsure of whether they are all conceptualized at the same level of generality or are only manifestations of one fundamental change that drives the other processes. On the most general level, in the globalization discourse we come to terms with the implications of the *communications revolution* and probably also with that aspect that made the increasing speed and volume of transactions possible: *digitalization* (Drake 1995). This explains modern organizational forms such as multinational firms, which would not have been feasible without the possibility of controlling enormous streams of information, ranging from financial data to designs and marketing decisions. Thus the *globalization of production* can hardly be interpreted as a simple response to "cheaper labor" abroad - particularly since modern production methods rely on human capital and not on a largely unskilled labor force in most industries. The discussion of post-Fordism as the dominant form of production reinforces these points (Lipietz 1992). In the same vein, one must examine critically the links between the growth of trade in services and communications, even though frequently service providers are moved by traditional forms of transport - consultants have to be flown in, for example - rather than procured by electronic transmission.

Similarly, the development of *financial markets* and thus of credit creation on a global scale (but also of the annihilation of monetary resources on a global scale) would not have been possible without linking the various markets by extensive communication links that let them operate as close to *one market* and on a 24-hour basis (Cerny 1993,

Cowhey, Richards 2000, Cohen 2000). True, there were substantive amounts of money floating around in the former Euro-dollar market that played their role in subverting the traditional means of national monetary policies, i.e. strict capital controls, but there is no doubt that these markets developed hand in hand with the informational infrastructure. To what extent financial markets have overwhelmed other parts of the economy is a theme that has been discussed since the studies of Hilferding (Lenin 1939) who pointed to different patterns of economic development of individual economies, depending on the role of financial institutions (and now perhaps of sectors of the world economy, particularly since financial institutions also have increasingly become global players) (Reinicke 1995, Cerny 2000, Willets 2000). It is precisely the links between the financial sectors and other parts of the economy on the one hand, and the links that connect the market with the state on the other hand, (since even the "freest" markets need the state as guarantor of property rights and contract enforcement) that create the new and substantial controversies in the field (Evans 1997).

Finally, we also subsume a variety of cultural phenomena under the term globalization. Without new electronic media and their link to digitalized transmission and on-line communication, the explosive force of "ideas" and their influence on notions of legitimacy, rights, and cultural forms are hardly imaginable. The sociologists John Meyer and others of the Stanford school have correctly pointed out that public as well as "private" organizational structures have been diffused throughout the globe not because of local needs or functional superiority but largely because these organizational forms represent legitimate versions of social and political projects (Thomas, Meyer, Ramirez and Boli 1987, Boli and Thomas 1999, Meyer and Rowan 1977). Similarly, notions of accountability of governments, of minimum standards, and of human rights are having their impact in virtually all societies, even if many show serious objections to the propagation of "Western" values and counter with strategies of affirming identities and of confronting this cultural imperialism by inventing "traditions" or simply controlling access to these media.[13] Nevertheless, cultural optimists hope for the emergence of new "public spaces" in the internet in which communities form not on the basis of territory or origin but on the basis of common concerns, as "movements" that spring up everywhere, establish global networks, and engage in new forms of collective actions (e. g. Wapner 1995). The link between the territorial state and democracy, which also

---

[13] See for example the interesting discussion of the differing strategies China and Cuba have used in order to "regulate" access to the Internet in Kalathil, Boas 2001.

implied the paradox that universalist political aspirations could only be realized in the particularity of a given state, seems to have been severed (Walker 1993). The era of cosmopolitanism - until now limited perhaps to certain elite strata - appears to be the logical conclusion of the democratic revolutions that previously needed nationalism to integrate societies.

Confronted with this dizzying variety of developments it is not surprising that we are prone to experience a certain loss of orientation. One can no longer hope or pretend to be able to characterize "the whole process", that is, know the "end of history"(Fukuyama 1992). Precisely at the moment we seemed to have reached this "end," all hell seemed to break loose. Yesterday still triumphant since the formidable competitor had fallen by the wayside, the dismal record for making a liberal democratic system and a capitalist economy work in the former Soviet Union gave cold comfort to those who believed that indeed history had a *telos* and that we possessed the adequate knowledge and strategies for realizing it.[14] The anxiety was by no means assuaged by the fact that many of those who were supposed to be on the side of the "winners" in this global contest were equally displaced by economic restructuring and therefore had the feeling that with such victories, who needed defeats?

Two gambits in dealing with the understandable anxieties engendered by these changes were now available. One was to seek orientation again in the past by pointing to phenomena that resembled the present density of interaction and exchange. Presumably, by showing that the phenomena associated with globalization were not new, one could not only give the novelty a name but also at least implicitly suggest that this storm could be weathered, as were those changes in similar periods of the past. Thus the denial of globalization's uniqueness provided the assurance that fundamentally nothing had changed and that the shocks experienced were but the surface phenomena of some deep-seated but more or less permanently operating equilibrating mechanisms that soon would bring things back to "normal".[15] The other strategy was to insist on the unprecedented character of this transformative change, which did not leave us much room for action and choice because of its fundamental nature and

---

[14] See for example the collection of essays written by political scientists who tried to figure out why none of their theories was able to "predict" the collapse of the Soviet Empire in Lebow, Risse-Kappen (eds.) 1995.

[15] See Milton Friedman´s surprising statement in 1989: „The world is less internationalized in any immediate, relevant, pertinent sense today than it was in 1913 or in 1929," as quoted in Ruggie 1996, p. 145.

necessity. We either had to adjust or perish. Here elements of the social Darwinist discourse of yesteryear made their surprising reappearance.

Despite their diametrically opposed evaluations of the "surface" phenomena, both responses were essentially conservative in nature. The first one, exemplified perhaps best by the work of Kenneth Waltz (1970), not only denied the novelty of the experience by pointing to the far greater interdependence of the world market in the end of the 19th century. In this regard, the experiences following the great Depression and WWII were the exception that was slowly being corrected by recent events. It also suggested that these changes were hardly of relevance for international politics, as no systemic transformation had occurred and anarchy prevailed now as it did before. By rigorously focusing on only aggregate data on trade, for example, and by neglecting new organizational forms (such as the multi-national corporation (MNC) which conducted trade now mainly as intra firm trade and not as arms length trade) Waltz's perspective failed to identify properly the change in the recipient of the benefits that accrue from a free trade regime. To that extent, the symmetry between the old world and the present was more a result of the optics chosen than of the similarity of the environments themselves.[16]

Waltz's thesis was also surprising in that it neglected to pay attention to the changes in the goals of states as they emerged from the shambles of the Great Depression and from the consensus concerning goals and means for establishing an "embedded" liberal order in the post-WWII era (Ruggie 1982). More astonishingly, it gave short shrift to the argument for the "lack of control" that virtually all decision-makers seemed to have experienced since the end of the 70s, a problem which even some fellow (neo)-realists such as Gilpin (1975) and Strange (1994b) did not tire in pointing out. Nevertheless, the international institutional order showed surprising resilience even though the decision-makers often felt that they were pushing instead of pulling strings.

The second interpretation, perhaps much less articulated by academics than by proponents of "liberalization" from Reagan to Thatcher, emphasized on the one hand the fundamental novelty of the phenomena associated with globalization but on the other suggested that reasserting control *should not* be done (even if possible by some concerted actions of states), since such interventionist strategies would only waste resources and since one "could not fool with the market" (to quote Lady Thatcher). This is not the place to examine this assertion in greater detail, particularly since such statements fail to address the

[16] For a good criticism of these arguments see Ruggie 1996 chap. 6.

necessary preconditions of markets - as if the entire literature about market failure had made no contribution to our understandings about the limits of markets - and since the apodictic nature of such statements is also on the level of such insights that "states" do not go bankrupt, which might be technically true but is cold comfort to those people who must use wheelbarrows of bank-notes to buy bread in times of hyper-inflation.

From this point of view, the market has now taken on the role of "history" as the ultimate justification. This stance also systematically aborts the inquiry into which particular decisions (and their unintended consequences) led to the cascade-like changes that characterize the dire "necessities" connected with globalization. The ideological nature of this perspective is of course not difficult to fathom. By depicting something as being akin to "natural" necessity, questions of policy, of responsibility, and of (re)distributing gains and losses cannot be systematically raised. The problem of global change is simply one in which "the market" and its logic of boundary-transcending exchanges overwhelm the logic of the state as a boundary-maintaining form of organization. Even critics of the "necessity" argument who like Susan Strange (1994c) have devoted considerable efforts and research to showing that globalization was the result of particular political choices and their interaction effects, however, take a pessimistic tone when they address issues of how to redress some of the externalities of these changes. Representative of this position is the following assertion:

> The impersonal forces of world markets are now more powerful than the state to whom the ultimate political authority over society and economy is supposed to be-long. Where states were once masters of markets, now it is the markets, which, on many crucial issues, are the masters over the governments of the states (Strange 1996 p. 4).

In this regard, states do not seem to possess many options, and despite the denial of a historical necessity, the logic of the market seems to be ready to displace the logic of the territorial state. Thus it is not surprising that in Strange's work, for example, the classical systems theory in which the "units" (states) and their arrangement play a practically exclusive role, is replaced by several interacting structures (security, production, credit, and knowledge) in order to capture the dynamics of change (Strange 1994b Part II, 2nd ed.). While such innovation in theory-building is in a way to be welcomed, it nevertheless first has to answer two questions: one, whether the original diagnosis on which the newly proposed structures rest was correct, and two, whether a new conceptualization of the international system requires not only the introduction of additional structures, but even more the additional conceptual innovations proposed by Luhmann (1999) and his radically different systems theory, for example. Since answering both questions would go far beyond the scope of the present chapter, I want to focus below solely on the former by first drawing out some of the most obvious implications of this argument and second by confronting them with the available evidence.

## Presumptions and Evidence

Although we speak of globalization because we want to emphasize the "total" character of change, we should not be misled by our rhetoric. Whatever the impact of the forces identified is, we should be aware that this impact varies tremendously. The "market" might be global for the Organization for Economic Cooperation and Development (OECD) countries, but other regions, such as Africa, might now be less systematically connected to this world market than before. When we adhere to the technology-driven argument that globalization is the result of the communications revolution, for instance, we should e.g. not forget that in the mid-90s all of sub-Saharan Africa had only as many telephone numbers as Manhattan alone[17], and there is, unfortunately, no reason to suspect that this imbalance has been corrected. This does not mean of course that certain effects of the globalizing economy will not be felt by those countries, and it does not mean that those countries will have all the options that former states had when the interdependencies were lower. But it does mean that our analysis has to be a bit more fine-grained for an assessment than simply working on the basis of an image of a tidal wave. As a matter of fact, the sad truth seems to be that the problems of colonialism and exploitation, the dominant fears of yesterday, are increasingly replaced by practical irrelevance of entire parts of the globe for the "global" economy.

Similarly, the lack of access to the important networks of global communications in a time when the traditional ones in these societies are decaying or have disappeared does not bode well for the future of political order. Hopes for a global community that builds around the

[17] See the remarks by South Africa's then Deputy President Mbeki at the G7 meeting in February 1995, as quoted in Everard 2000, p. 34.

nodes of transnational networks and creates in internet chat rooms places of open discussion and democratic participation seem utterly utopian given the lack of access of most of the world population.[18] Whatever the failures of nationalism have been – from war to racism and intolerance – at least one aspect deserves attention: it gave "status" to the individual as a member of a community and thus at least opened the door for later claiming the rights attendant to citizenship (Kratochwil 2000 chap. 8). Modern networks might select their "members" differently than previous groups - here place and origin do not play a role, as opposed to interests and affinities - but these networks select nevertheless and perhaps even more decisively so. The old French joke that the modern state guaranteed to the rich and the poor an equal right to sleep under the bridges of Paris has a new twist: by the magic wand of a PC we now can make those under the bridges voiceless and even invisible.

But even when we have recognized that most of the phenomena associated with globalization are more or less limited to the OECD world, several other presumptions need to be examined. There is for example the fear that the increase of the pressures from free trade will sooner or later lead to visceral reactions of protectionism, which in turn would lead to not only a depressed economy but also serious conflict.[19] The analogon here is obviously the interwar period. During our time, however, the challenges to a free trading order have been rather limited

---

[18] Raymund Werle and Volker Leib, who investigated the governance of the internet, come to the following conclusion, which has little to do with the exalted hopes of those expecting "direct democracy": "The differences between the older governmental and the new private organizations notwithstanding, we find substantial organizational similarity in the field of technical standardizations in telecommunications and related areas of information technology...Organizations rather than individuals predominate. Individuals are regarded as "delegates" of the organizations.... When ...the internet assumed an international dimension, and increasingly overlapped and interfered with technical areas which were traditionally controlled by actors outside the Internet complex, this provided opportunities for the Internet Society (ISOC) as a corporate actor to establish itself as a player...Individual membership and the predominance of the individual over the collective have been typical of the Internet community, whereas corporate membership and the priority of corporate before individual interest characterize the telecommunications domain. The ISOC has tried to integrate both elements under one roof and, in doing so, has maneuvered itself into a somewhat marginal position with regards to both organizational fields." Raymund Werle, Volker Leib, The Internet Society and its Struggle for Recognition and Influence", in Ronit, Schneider (eds.) 2000, chap. 5, quote at p. 120f.

[19] For a critical discussion of this point and the differences between the present and the inter-war period see Milner 1988.

despite some serious tensions and the introduction of Voluntary Export Restraints, unilateral retaliatory measures (Sec 301 procedures in the US), and other trade-distorting political measures such as the pronouncement of a strategic trade policy. Even the emergence of trade blocs such as NAFTA and the enlarged EU with its preference system are not likely to bear out the fears engendered by the interwar example. Two reasons seem to account for this apparent anomaly. One has to do with the impact of the globalization of production on "interests", the other with the apparent ability of existing institutions to prevent states from unilateral visceral reactions, so characteristic of the interwar period. Both deserve some brief discussion.

As Helen Milner has shown, protectionist measures are unlikely to be in the interest of firms that operate globally, and thus the globalization of production by the biggest and most important firms has lessened the incentives for traditional measures of protection. Not only are the different sectors of industry increasingly differentiating into national and international producers, but it also turns out that usually those enmeshed in global production are more competitive than those producing only locally. There is not only no longer a "national industry," but even firms within the same sectors have different interests, and competitive enterprises have little to gain from classical protective measures. Similarly, the emergence of blocs in a trading order need not necessarily lead to conflict as long as the relations across these blocs remain relatively free or can be consensually managed. Here obviously the legacy of the "multilateralism"[20]of the post-WWII era matters in that it provided for some consensual principles, as does the commitment to dispute resolution that was transformed from a more or less negotiated mode of settlement in GATT to a much more judicially-oriented binding decision procedure under the current WTO regime. The jury is of course not in yet whether this new mode will be as effective as it was hoped, but as in the case of the problematic conditionality of the IMF, states have accepted certain limits on their freedom of action that, together with the cooperation of non-state actors, provide at least a chance for resolving conflicts by de-politicizing them and transferring them to special arenas.

The most heated debate centers, of course, around the problem of the welfare state and its loss of steering capacity. Given that the experiments of re-instituting capital controls in the 70s and early 80s to stem the tide of speculative flows engendered by the formation of global financial

---

[20] For a fundamental discussion of multilateralism as a distinct organizational form see Ruggie 1993b.

markets ended in failure, the prospects of dealing with domestic employment problems by classical Keynesian means are dim indeed (for a brief discussion of the historical record see Helleiner 1994). The fear not only that states would lose one (even though important) instrument for managing the economy, but also that a race to the bottom would ensue was rather pronounced. Capital flight seemed unavoidable, as foreign direct investment would now go to those countries with low wages and a small public sector (which meant low taxes).[21]

The actual record is less alarming. Although states have indeed lost part of their economic "sovereignty" in monetary matters through the emergence of global financial markets that function practically as one due to their linkage, many of the other fears have been exaggerated. Most investment goes, as every statistic shows, not to countries with low wages and small public sectors, but to countries within the OECD, which presents a rather different picture from that one could expect if the "race to the bottom" had materialized. Thus, to take but one example, despite the decrease in taxes on capital gains in the US (about 2.7%), other countries were not automatically forced to steer the same course. In Japan, Sweden, and Finland, they actually increased substantially (up to 10%) (Garrett). Similarly, the public sector has not shrunk over all, even in those countries like England that preached "liberalization" and privatization, although expenditures have been allocated differently. Instead of welfare programs (demand side), expenditures moved to programs on the supply side (education, human capital, and so on). Thus, despite the largely ideological argument that "the market" should take care of things, it is clear to investors and other business people that in order to have a functioning market one needs a strong rather than a weak state. As the experiences with "liberalizations," such as those in Latin America, also show, deregulation is only possible when the lock on the economy by vested interests can be broken. And if one needed any further proof, Singapore's success has resulted precisely from its "strong" state and its bureaucrats that provide for an efficient and non-corrupt business environment.

As to the problem of capital flight, since the mid-80s when France as the last hold-out reversed course and abolished capital controls, the record has hardly substantiated the original fears. Thus Swank's (1998) and Quinn's (1997) studies suggest there is virtually no correlation between corporate taxes and capital flight. Furthermore, according to

---

21 For a discussion of the conditions that result in races as opposed to new governance structures see Spar, Yoffie, "A Race to the Bottom, or governance from the top", in Prakash, Hart 2000 chap. 1.

Garret (1998), there exists only a slight correlation between low taxes and internationalization of the economy as measured by the proportion of export/import balance to GNP, which would be impossible if indeed low taxes were the most important factor for the foreign direct investment decisions. Since actually neither low wages in general (but productivity, which in turn is highly dependent on the availability of human capital) nor low taxes per se explain FDI activity, we had better give up on the idea that foreign workers are taking away our jobs. This might be so in certain sectors of the economy that rely on unskilled labor (basic textiles is here probably the best example) but certainly does not explain the overall picture.

If any further proof for the mythical character of the "loss of jobs" to low wage competition theory is needed, then Fritz Scharpf´s et al. (2000) study has provided it. Basing his argument on a large comparative examination of the trends attributed to globalization, Scharpf found that a "lack of jobs" does indeed exist in Germany, for example, but not in those sectors that are subject to international competition. Instead, and at first somewhat surprisingly, a significant gap in jobs exists in *those sectors that are virtually sheltered from international competition*, such as services. Here, obviously the inflexibility of wage-policies, the rather high costs not relating to production, over-regulation for small service-oriented enterprises, and so on, are the most likely candidates for explaining this gap. But again making the necessary adjustments in order to correct this record does not necessarily amount to a dismantling of the welfare state or to a move towards the lowest common denominator, as suggested by the race to the bottom metaphor. As the same study makes clear, different countries have found different niches, belying the argument of a race to the bottom. The picture ranges from countries in which high taxes are coupled with traditionally high welfare expenditures (Sweden), to those with some minimal welfare function that basically provides a safety net for catastrophic disabilities and old age (such as GB and the US), to those which increasingly package public and private measures, a solution which is probably emerging in the German case (Scharpf 2000).

That globalization is not simply a set of causal factors that can explain the changes that are taking place is also borne out by the fact that the assumed homogenization in the organizational structures of firms, for example, is disproved by empirical studies. To be sure, multi-national corporations might represent a new species of organization, and they might also have gotten more "international" in their staff, especially in the leading positions, than they were even a couple of decades ago, but so far they have not shown the "sameness" one would expect if organizational structures were simply the result of environmental pressures. Thus, Siemens is still "German" in structure and organizational culture, quite distinct from IBM or Fujitsu (Pauly, Reich 1997). One reason for this stickiness of institutional structures is that organizations are responses to environmental challenges. These environmental conditions, however, may allow for a variety of roughly equivalent solutions (as multiple equilibria may exist) and any one chosen will then quickly "lock in". This effect, in turn, makes changes costly and often undesirable, given the "codes" that develop within a firm (Arrow 1974). In addition, this argument also suggests the "winners" in a Darwinian struggle for survival are not those who wait for the random changes characteristic of biological mutations, but those who quickly innovate instead of simply adjusting or copying someone else's "solution". Far from being "forced" by the environment, leaving no room for decisions and choices - after all, the social realm consists not simply of a fixed "nature" but of other organizational forms that are also changing - rapid change calls for cognitive evolution, that is, innovation and decisive action.

**Moralité**

Our brief discussion has, in a way, reached the point of departure as the "ideological" character of the globalization debate comes to the fore again. This ideological character is by no means accidental, even though the Marxist notion of "wrong consciousness," that is, some conceptual distortions that mystify and cover up the inconsistencies in the existing "real" facts, claims too much, as we have seen. It pretends to know where the history is going, as only from this absolute vantage point can the "distortions" of the "wrong consciousness" be assessed. The problem is that "history" is not going anywhere and thus the narrative structure that created the optic of "progress" has its own ideological blinders. Nevertheless, one need not be a Marxist when one notices inconsistencies in the discursive formations that are not simply wrong descriptions of the facts at hand, that is, errors, but that are rather *self serving* errors. It is this justificatory (mis)-use of the globalization discourse that deserves attention and scrutiny. On the one hand, the globalization argument relies on the plot of natural necessity. Globalization is in its effect likened to an enormous wave that cannot be resisted, as is so aptly depicted in Müller's contribution to this volume.

On the other hand, the very same persons who just told their employees that they could not do anything for them because of the dire necessities induced by global competition let themselves be celebrated as "innovators", leaders, and strategists who recognized the right moment and selected a "winning" strategy.

At least the above discussion should have driven home the fact that the story line of necessity in whatever form is hardly persuasive. Not only is the present the outcome of yesterday's choices - and here the technological argument that globalization is simply the result of technological innovation, that is, the manifestation of the communications revolution (digitalization) - is as problematic as the self-serving accounts of the "logic of the market" that Strange rightly criticized. Both are the result of a simple causal optic that connects two "facts" (as complex as they are) with one another, without bothering to "fill in " the picture. However, as we all know, we can always draw a straight line through any two chosen points, and as long as we do not give this procedure a causal interpretation, everything is fine. It becomes problematic only when one fact (that is, availability of a particular technology) is connected to a certain social state of affairs and then tendered as an "explanation". What was at best an enabling condition has now become a causal account that connects the "before" and "after". Never mind that different social states would have been reached, given different choices at different intervening steps, even though unintended consequences might have led to additional surprises. The mystifying nature of explaining fundamental social transformation in such a fashion hides not only the question of responsibility for the choices made - which is still part and parcel of our concerns and our political vocabulary - but it also shows the incoherent nature of conceptual gambits that virtually eliminate choice entirely and assume that some strange system is working itself out behind the actor's back. After all, it should be obvious that unintended consequences can only be parasitic upon intentional action and that models emphasizing unintentional outcomes, therefore, cannot dispense with a framework of intentionality.

As we have seen, the best evidence available does not support such a construct. Choices were and are possible even though some of the previous strategies to steer processes of change are no longer effective or even available to us[22]. Nevertheless, the welfare state is not simply to be

---

[22] Here Hirst´s and Thompson´s account (Globalization in Question, op. cit) might be a bit too optimistic as it does not take the fundamental changes in the nature of public goods and of politics into account. For this alternative view see Cerny 1995, Cerny 1999.

replaced by the competition state even if a definitive shift from the demand side to the supply side has been made. However, that certain cut backs in social welfare programs had to be made was clear to anyone who cared to look at the population statistics as far back as the 70s. The benign neglect with which this problem was treated in virtually all countries is a glaring example of the tendency not to address issues in time by putting a taboo on them and covering them up with partisan slogans. Similarly, the lack of preparedness of large segments of even our younger generation for employment in a rapidly changing society was known in Germany long ago, and thus the PISA study should not have come as a surprise.[23] Whatever we might think about this or that result, it has become quite clear that it is mainly we, ourselves, and not some cheap laborers in the developing world who are "taking away" the jobs.

The bitter truth seems also to be that the phenomenon of the growing gap between the developing and the developed world that we watched with such detachment during the last half-century now has come home to us too. Similar phenomena are now observable in our countries, between regions as well as between different sectors of society and even within the same occupational groups. Here obviously the states - even though they are no longer more or less autonomous nation states but deeply embedded in international regimes and challenged by transnational networks - will have to act and provide some solutions to the pressing problems. They can no longer be addressed by simple programs of "priming the pump" when unemployment is on the rise again, instead of paying constant attention to questions of productivity, R&D, and the formation of human capital.[24]

However, solutions to these problems are difficult to find since we no longer possess some of the traditional steering mechanisms, and we also do not seem to possess the adequate theoretical tools to deal with these complex interactions of systems that challenge our "normal" causal thinking. Finally, we do not seem to have a good grasp of politics, as the boundaries between the "us" for whom collectively binding decisions are made, and "others," who might be affected and have thereby some claims against us, are not clear, and neither are the domains in which

---

[23] The Pisa assessment compared student achievement in OECD countries. See PISA Study at www.PISA.oecd.org

[24] For a cautious note on quick fixes to improve the "competitiveness" of states see Krugman 1994.

political action can still intervene[25]. The former problem is often hotly debated in terms of duties to others who are not citizens as well as in terms of the criteria by which citizenship shall be bestowed. As we have seen, despite the hopes for the emergence of a cosmopolitan form of democracy based on technological networks, this is hardly realistic, given the discrepancies in access. Besides, precisely because the "packaged imagery of the visionary global culture is either trivial or shallow, a matter of mass commodity advertisement," the reactions to these trends have been affirmations of (often imaginary) identities that are in the process of undoing former stabilizations such as were achieved by nationalism (Smith 1995, p. 23).

Before we simply consider such reactions as irrational throwbacks to a time passed, we had better remember that a political community as an ongoing and trans-generational concern addresses more than merely irrational needs. Conceiving of a community as something that unites all its members is important precisely because it provides the means of ascribing responsibilities and of indicating the levers for political action. Thus persons who are excluded from the "normal" means of exerting influence because they cannot participate in the networks and in the market owing to their lack of resources, are still part of the "public" to which decision-makers and bureaucrats have to answer. In other words, the point I want to make here is not so much that functioning markets and networks need regulators - although this is a genuine problem when national regulation has been outflanked and no international equivalent is yet in place. The point is rather: to whom do these regulators have to answer? Is it only to shareholders, inventors, and marketing agencies that have acquired (intellectual) property, or is it to the public at large? But *which public*, since networks are characterized by the disappearance of publics?[26]

A similar case can be made for the non-economic sectors as well by transferring Pauly's (1997) provocative question of "who elected the bankers" to other issue areas: who elected Greenpeace, or Amnesty International for that matter, even if we happen to agree with their goals? In short, what is strangely missing from the discourse of globalization in general and from the debates about the alleged eclipse of the state and the ascendancy of the market, in particular, is politics plain and simple. Yet, by identifying politics with government and

---

[25] Aside from the exploding literature on citizenship, see a good discussion of the problems of drawing and redrawing borders for purposes of governance: Albert, Jacobson, Lapid (eds.) 2001.

[26] For a further discussion of this point see Kratochwil 1997, chap. 4.

governmental structures and by pointing to the important function of these structures even under contemporary conditions of complex interdependencies, the advocates of the strong state thesis submit to the neo-Weberian vision of bureaucratic efficiency and rationality. They might score some points against those utopian liberals that believe in "frictionless" markets and the freedom of "consumer choice" as the ultimate yardstick, but they do so at a heavy price by limiting their field of vision largely to problems of efficiency.

Politics is, as we all know, something more complicated. It is about representative choices *and* their legitimization; in modern times it is about gaining the consent of the governed. Precisely because the present transformations deeply affect our accustomed ways of dealing with problems, rules for shaping our way of life need to be buttressed by a broad-based consensus and not only by some thin notions of legality. Administrative rationality is frequently insufficient to deal with those problems, as has been demonstrated by Beck (1995). Similarly, years ago Habermas (1973) pointed to the legitimization crisis of the modern state in which administrative procedures overwhelm efforts at building effective political consensus. These pressures have increased, and it is cold comfort to hear that strong bureaucracies and administrative structures are not going to wither away under the impact of globalization.

The argument certainly does not imply that nothing significant has changed in the international arena or that the states with which we are familiar will persist. Rather, it raises the question on which basis the "units" or parts of the system will be differentiated and what new organizational forms, located between hierarchy and anarchy, are going to evolve. That politics will increasingly revolve around membership questions is suggested by the brief discussion above. In this regard, we also should perhaps ponder more carefully Benedict Anderson´s (1983) astute observation, made long before the dissolution of the Soviet empire, that there is in virtually every country a tomb of the unknown soldier, but none of the unknown Marxist. There is apparently some force to nationalist ideologies that other forms of ideology have difficulty in matching, even though nationalism has little to do with some primordial sentiments or roots, but is rather a response to the changes introduced in stratified societies by the transformations of "modernity". After the death of God – the traditional guarantor of order – "the people" remains the only source of legitimacy. By joining pre-modern ties and sentiments characteristic of traditional ethnic communities with modern ideas of popular sovereignty, nationalism provided a partial answer to the crisis of meaning engendered by modernity.

In this respect, notions of world society and of the victory of universalism against the assertions of more particular identities seem rather anemic, as do the strangely technocratic visions of network societies and of "private ordering" that are to replace those public spaces in which public order gets articulated[27]. This was after all also the concern of one of the founders of the field of international relations, E.H Carr (1946), who tried to warn us about the utopian ring of many organizational proposals while very much insisting that every conception of politics has to have an utopian element in it.[28] Since politics is about projects which are never complete and which constantly move between the is and the ought, its analysis cannot be reduced to the logic of the law or of the market, to structural constraints, to the economy of force, or to a course of history. That much a critical examination of the discourse on globalization should have shown.

---

[27] For a good discussion of the problem see Biersteker, Hall (eds.) forthcoming 2002.

[28] See also the anthology edited by Dunne, Cox, Booth (eds.) 1998.

# Imag[in]ing Globalization
# Therapy for Policy Makers[29]

Philipp Müller

> *The point is not to show that metaphysical uses of words are grammatical mistakes, but rather to persuade an interlocutor that he has no good reasons for making them, that he can simply drop them and thereby eliminate certain disquiets or dissatisfaction [PPI § 99]. Getting rid of metaphysical questions is voluntary, an exercise of an individual's freedom (Baker 2000, 25).*

## Overture

There are many ways of approaching Globalization. I am interested in addressing policy makers. Addressing the understanding of policy makers matters in the Globalization debate because Globalization is an emergent phenomenon in which recursivity between theory and policy impacts the phenomenon. Also, by increasing the understanding of policy makers, we increase their accountability. The approach I propose is (a) grammatical, i.e., asks the question *How do we use the concept?* and (b) therapeutic, i.e., it offers a local clarification of the use of words achieved through *cooperative deliberation with an interlocutor.* The interlocutors in the therapy are policy makers.

My approach is based on Wittgenstein's philosophical therapy. It is an approach that makes visible the images underlying our use of concepts, showing in what ways they are problematic and offering alternative images. I will describe it as a four-step procedure that has the goal of reducing anxiety about Globalization and increasing the freedom of policy makers to make decisions. By increasing their freedom, we force them to take responsibility for their policies. In this paper, I will outline the procedure and then apply it, focusing on our usage of the term Globalization from four perspectives.

---

[29] I want to thank Doris A. Fuchs, Markus Lederer, and Jörg Friedrichs for their substantial substantive critiques, Gordon Baker for introducing me to Wittgenstein, Friedrich Kratochwil and David Kennedy for their feedback on the argument, and David Singer for letting me present the material at the Correlates of War Project.

**Procedure**

During World War II, Ludwig Wittgenstein was working as an assistant nurse for two doctors at a hospital in Newcastle that were writing a book on wound shock and found that the symptoms they were looking at in their patients with wound shock were very dissimilar. He suggested that because the term 'wound shock' described a syndrome that included disparate symptoms and therefore referred not to a naturally given category but to a conventionally established one, it should be printed upside down to remind the reader constantly of its problematic nature. In the end, the publisher decided against this idea because it would have been too costly.[30] Even in this age of computers, it has not become cheaper to play this type of game. So imagine Globalization writ upside-down!

In the next section, I sketch an approach that aims not to define or redefine Globalization but to clarify the usage of language and to dissolve some of the discomforts we have with the term Globalization and thereby increase the freedom of decision makers. This dissolution consists of making the meaning of the words used when analyzing Globalization so clear to ourselves that we are released from the spell the term globalization casts on us. Friedrich Waismann (1968) argues that in philosophy, the real problem is not to find the answer to a given question but to find a sense for it:

> We are trying to catch the shadows cast by the opacities of speech. A wrong analogy absorbed into the forms of our language produces mental discomfort (and the feeling of discomfort, when it refers to language, is a profound one) (p. 7).

The procedure I am proposing is called 'Philosophical therapy'. It offers a family of methods--clarification, dissolution, and the shifting of metaphors--to deal with 'philosophical problems'.[31] It is not a language-cleaning algorithm, to clear language of misuses once and for all, but an individualized therapy with the goal of the <u>local</u> clarification of the usage of language and the construction of alternative plausible images in

---

[30] I thank Gordon Baker for telling me the story (at Manuels Baccharo on Sanipolo in Venice), March 2000. Observations on the General Effects of Injury in Man: With Special Reference to Wound Shock. Medical Research Council, Special Report No. 277, London, England by Grant, R. T., and Reeve, E. B. is still regarded as the seminal work on the topic of wound shock.

[31] The family concept is based on Wittgenstein's picture of familiarities as interlocking fibers forming a rope. Philosophical Investigations, § 67.

order to increase the freedom of the thinker. By increasing the freedom of the thinker, we recapture moments of decision, i.e., moments of politic, in which policy makers can change the course of events and we as constituents can hold them accountable.

Philosophical therapy has some interesting features. The interlocutor is not forced to comply; instead, he is left free to select, accept, or reject any way of using his words. The only thing that one has to insist upon is that the interlocutor use words consciously. The aim is not to confirm or invalidate any ahistorical truth. 'Philosophical therapy' aims to describe, not to 'explain':

> An explanation, in the sense of a deductive proof, cannot satisfy us because it pushes the question 'Why just these rules and no other ones?' only one stage back. In following that method, we do not *want* to give reasons. All we do is to describe a use or tabulate rules. In doing this, we are not making any discoveries: there is nothing to be discovered in grammar. Grammar is autonomous and not dictated by reality. Giving reasons, bound as it is to come to an end and leading to something which cannot further be explained, *ought* not to satisfy us. In grammar we never ask the question 'why?' (Waismann 1968, p. 12)

The tactic in the procedure of 'philosophical therapy' is to bring a challenge to a dogma, to expose a picture that stands behind this dogma, to propose an alternative picture of concept-application, and to deflect anxieties about this new model (Baker 2000, p. 32).

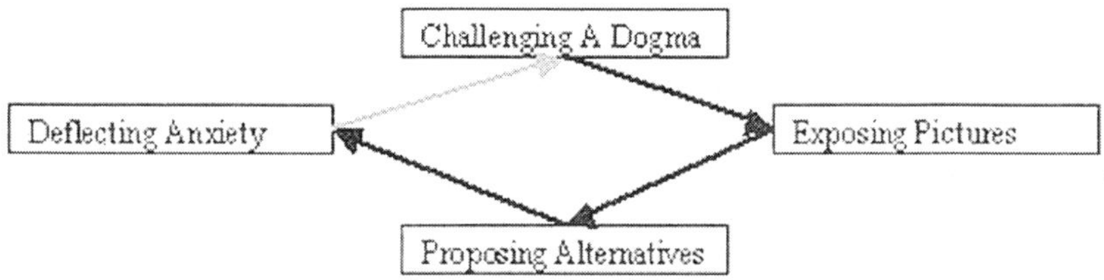

This is a personalized endeavor, similar to psychoanalytical therapy.[32] This understanding of 'philosophical therapy' is not shared by all Wittgenstein scholars. Kenny, Hacker, or Kripke would argue that 'philosophical therapy' aims to solve philosophical problems "once and for all" (Kenny 1984, Stern 1995, Hacker 1999). 'Philosophical therapy' seen from this perspective aims to expose the misuses of words (mistakes in grammar) by simply confronting the discourse with descriptions of how words are correctly used (linguistic facts). This perspective is based on paragraph II, § 133 of the Philosophical Investigations: *For the clarity that we are aiming at is indeed complete clarity.* An example of this way of seeing Wittgenstein's philosophy is in G.P. Baker and P.M.S. Hacker's *Wittgenstein: Rules, Grammar and Necessity*:

> Philosophy... is a grammatical investigation (§90) on which philosophical problems are resolved and misunderstanding eliminated by describing our use of words, clarifying *the grammar* of expressions and tabulating rules (WWK 184). .... If someone ... claims that colours are sensations in the mind or in the brain, the philosopher must point out that this person is *misusing* the words 'sensation' and 'colour'. Sensations in the brain, he should remind his interlocutor, are called 'headaches', and colours are not headaches; one can have (i. e. it makes sense to speak of) sensations in the knee or in the back, but not in the mind. It is, he must stress, extended things that are coloured. ... It is a grammatical observation, viz. that the grammar of colour licenses predicating 'is coloured' (primarily) of things of which one may also predicate 'is extended'. And minds and sensations are not extended, i. e. it *makes no sense to say* 'This pain is 5cm long' ... [In this way we correct] the wayward interlocutor ... (Baker and Hacker 1985, p. 52-3) [Emphasis added]

This dogmatic perspective on Wittgenstein informs his reception in international relations theory. Viewing Wittgenstein's theory from this perspective, we can understand the importance that the analysis of rule-following has had for international relations theory. This is seen in Habermas' (1984, p. 65) and Kratochwil's (1989) writing. They read Wittgenstein as a philosopher offering solutions to problems once and

---

[32]For the Freudian approach see: Sigmund Freud: Die analytische Therapie, 28. Vorlesung (Vorlesungen zur Einführung in die Psychoanalyse). Frankfurt, 1991. Psycho-analytical therapy aims for empathetic understanding of the interlocutor, while philosophical therapy poses stronger consistency requirements.

for all. This has been a common and very useful approach to Wittgenstein.

Wittgenstein has been well-known for the dissolution and conceptual shifting of philosophical problems: e.g., rule-following as a practice (Wittgenstein 1958, § 202) or thinking as 'the activity of operating with signs.' He has been much less known for the method of 'philosophical therapy' that he demonstrates with these examples. A close reading of § 133 seems to suggest that it is not the resolution of problems once and for all that he is interested in:

> The real discovery is the one that makes me capable of stopping doing philosophy when I want to. -- The one that gives philosophy peace, so that it is no longer tormented by questions which bring in question. -- Instead, we now demonstrate a method, by examples; and the series of examples can be broken off. -- Problems are solved (difficulties eliminated), not a single problem.
>
> There is not a philosophical method, though there are indeed methods, like different therapies.

It even suggests that he does not offer a strict method to solve these problems, i.e., philosophical therapy, but only offers an idea that can be the basis of a number of methods. Gordon Baker (2000) describes this with the picture of an argument with an interlocutor who has to be persuaded:

> The crucial move must be to persuade an individual interlocutor to renounce the prejudice expressed by statements featuring the words 'must' and 'cannot' [cf V.201-2]; or better, persuading another to rid his thinking of these deeply entrenched notions (Denkgewohnheiten) [BT 423]) and of deep desires to see things in certain ways [GT 406 = CV 17]. The therapy focuses on bringing to another's consciousness neglected possibilities; on winning sincere acknowledgement of possibilities which he had previously excluded [§144, 244: BB 43, 85-7]. Nothing else can liberate an individual from various forms of prejudice or change his way of looking at things [§ 144] (p. 27).

In one example of philosophical therapy, Wittgenstein dissolves our understanding of categories as boxes into which we put things that have common characteristics by asking what it is that lets us distinguish what games are. By categorizing his method into a four-step procedure, we lose some of the flexibility that Wittgenstein introduces into philosophy, but gain an understanding of the approach.[33] It should be seen more as an example of a method than an ideal-type. We have to keep in mind that the tactic in the procedure is first to bring a challenge to a dogma, next to expose a picture that stands behind this dogma, then to propose an alternative picture of concept-application, and finally to deflect anxieties about this new model. He is challenging the dogma by arguing in § 66 of the Philosophical Investigations:

> Consider for example the proceedings that we call "games". I mean board-games, card-games, ball-games, Olympic games, and so on. What is common to them all? -- Don't say: "There must be something common, or they would not be called 'games'"-but look and see whether there is anything common to all.

He exposes the picture we have of categorizing things by asking, "There must be something common, or they would not be called 'games'" and clarifies the problem.

> For if you look at them you will not see something that is common to all, but similarities, relationships, and a whole series of them at that. To repeat: don't think, but look!
> Look for example at board-games, with their multifarious relationships.
>
> Now pass to card-games; here you find many correspondences with the first group, but many common features drop out, and others appear.
>
> When we pass next to ball-games, much that is common is retained, but much is lost.-- Are they all 'amusing'? Compare chess with noughts and crosses. Or is there always winning and losing, or competition between players? Think of patience. In ball games there is winning and losing; but when a child throws his ball at the wall and catches it again, this feature has disappeared. Look at the parts played by skill and luck; and at the difference between skill in chess and skill in tennis.

---

[33] In the following chapters we will apply the framework less stringently.

> Think now of games like ring-a-ring-a-roses; here is the element of amusement, but how many other characteristic features have disappeared! sometimes similarities of detail.
> And we can go through the many, many other groups of games in the same way; can see how similarities crop up and disappear.

In the next step he proposes an alternative picture.

> And the result of this examination is: we see a complicated network of similarities overlapping and criss-crossing: sometimes overall similarities.
> I can think of no better expression to characterize these similarities than "family resemblances"; for the various resemblances between members of a family: build, features, colour of eyes, gait, temperament, etc. etc. overlap and cries-cross in the same way.- And I shall say: 'games' form a family (p. 67).

And deflects our anxiety about it by arguing:

> "But if the concept 'game' is uncircumscribed like that, you don't really know what you mean by a 'game'." -- When I give the description: "The ground was quite covered with plants" --do you want to say I don't know what I am talking about until I can give a definition of a plant? My meaning would be explained by, say, a drawing and the words "The ground looked roughly like this". Perhaps I even say "it looked exactly like this."-Then were just this grass and these leaves there, arranged just like this? No, that is not what it means. And I should not accept any picture as exact in this sense (p. 70).

By walking us through the process of challenging a dogma, exposing a picture that stands behind this dogma, proposing an alternative picture of concept-application, and deflecting anxieties about this new model, Wittgenstein leads us through a procedure in which we learn to give up long-held misunderstandings that have caused anxiety to us. It is highly personalized philosophy, and it has the potential to expose political decisions, i.e. situations where somebody decided something. Someone who never felt that members of a category need to share at least one characteristic will not find the argument persuasive or even interesting. Philosophical therapy is a personalized endeavor, similar to psycho-analytical therapy.

This means the types of questions about Globalization such an approach can ask are different. This means the thrust of my argument will not be to offer a new definition of Globalization but to put some of the discomfort policy makers have about it to rest and thus to increase their freedom. Increasing their freedom reintroduces politics and a discourse about accountability and responsibility. I will do this by observing Globalization in its natural habitat, language. One might ask, why language? After all, things are being transported, investments are being made, and human beings are being moved about by airplanes and trains. However, if we look at the distinctness of the things that are being transported and the ideas we subsume under the concept "Globalization," it becomes clear that it is a linguistic category, not a natural one.

Different scholars and policy makers as well as the public conceptualize Globalization in different ways (Cox 1997, Keck and Sikkink 1998). However, the mainstream discourse shares one common feature: conceptualizing Globalization by reifying it into a causal variable (Sassen 1996, Barber 1995, Bauman 1998, Friedman 1999).

This can be an independent variable (Globalization leading to integration/disintegration) or a dependent variable (technological/ cultural change leading to Globalization), but this differentiation between Globalization as an independent or dependent variable is underspecified. I will argue that the reification of Globalization into a variable has to do with the images we use to understand the concept. These images are normally in the background. Gilles Fauconnier (1997) claims that

> Our conceptual networks are intricately structured by analogical and metaphorical mappings, which play a key role in the synchronic construction of meaning in its diachronic evolution. Parts of such mappings are so entrenched in everyday thought and language that we do not consciously notice them; other parts strike us as novel and creative. The term metaphor is often applied to the latter, highlighting the literary and poetic aspects of the phenomenon. But the general cognitive principles at work are the same, and they play a key role in thought and language at all levels.

Dealing with these mental images is an important aspect of thinking about Globalization because our beliefs about Globalization shape Globalization.

## Surfing the Wave

Beneath the understanding of Globalization as a reified variable lurks the imagery of a natural force or more concretely, a wave.[34] The following examples by policy makers show how internalized the reified variable metaphor of Globalization as a natural force is in the policy-making discourse:[35]

[34] E. g. Kristof, Nicholas D. Experts Question Roving Flow of Global Capital. *New York Times*, September 20, 1998, Sunday. Cohen, Roger. The Cries of Welfare States Under the Knife. *New York Times*, September 19, 1997.

[35] Comments from policy-makers made at the World Economic Forum in Davos 2001 have been selected because the forum offers a good perspective on the non-academic globalization discourse.

As globalization sweeps the world, many areas, Africa especially, wonder if this tidal wave is good or bad for them.[36]

Faced with popular demands for greater self-determination, national governments around the world are under pressure to devolve power to the local level. In this context, globalization is like a giant wave that can either capsize nations or carry them forward on its crest.[37]

Like a great natural force, Globalization offers major opportunities for and perils to the possibilities for human flourishing. Characterized by the rapid spread of market systems, the extraordinary advances in science and technology, continuing urbanization, and changing demographics, Globalization can become a positive unifying bond for humanity; or it can pose a major threat to human relations, cultural traditions, and a sense of personal identity.[38]

A tide of economic liberalization has swept across the world over the past two decades. It is creating vast opportunities. But the question arises whether today's integrating world economy will be more durable than that of a century ago.[39]

"But it cannot and must not be allowed to override all other natural forces," he said. He likened Globalization to a river, which can bring substantial economic, social and environmental nourishment to those who are in a position to benefit from it. "But it can erode, devastate and overwhelm if it rushes too fast or spreads too far," he said.[40]

---

[36] Adam Dieng, assistant secretary-general of the United Nations, in International Herald Tribune, August 21st, 2001, 6.

[37] Shahid Yusuf, senior economic adviser at the World Bank, in: International Herald Tribune, September 17th, 1999.

[38] Globalization and the Human Condition. An Introduction. Aspen Institute 50th Anniversary Symposium, August 19-22., 2000, Aspen, CO.

[39] Martin Wolf. The dangers of protectionism, in *Financial Times*, November 8th, 2000, 21.

[40] Julian Disney, President, International Council of Social Welfare, Australia, What Model for 21st Century Capitalism? World Economic Forum, Davos (2001).

> "But trends have a nasty habit of reversing. There can be a flywheel effect when momentum takes things too far," he said. He pointed to the recent Asian economic crisis, and the stringent measures taken to correct it, as a warning. "It doesn't necessarily mean the pendulum is swinging back, but we would be prudent to watch out for straws in the wind."[41]

These and other comments expose the image informing discourse on Globalization and the dissatisfaction with the Globalization debate. This seems to be where the 'philosophical problem' of Globalization is located.

If one were able to show that the image underlying mainstream Globalization discourse is troubling and if one could offer a more compelling image that is acceptable to an audience, the Globalization discourse could be re-politicized. And maybe, new policy options would emerge. Let us engage in therapy!

The challenge to the dogma in this example is to the common conception of Globalization. Can we really understand the phenomenon by asking what is caused by Globa-lization? Or what is causing Globalization? This seems doubtful.

In the next step one has to persuade the interlocutor of the problematic nature of the concept by exposing a picture that informs this dogma. The dogma of seeing Globalization as a reified variable is based on Globalization as a natural force, a tidal wave sweeping across the world, destroying welfare states and introducing sport utility vehicles to the world. Even though this description is an exaggeration, the imagery of Globalization as a natural force is constantly with us. Whenever we argue about Globalization and are not careful, this can happen even to the best of us. We sometimes will rely on the imagery of the wave when thinking about Globalization. Gordon Baker (2000) argues that

> Bringing to consciousness this whole set of interlinked pictures belongs to the therapeutic activity of exploring the motives for falling into philosophical confusion (p. 33).

In a third step we need to propose an alternative picture of concept-application. In the case of Globalization, this can be the picture of a discourse. Globalization does not take place outside of language. If there were no word for it, we would not cluster together such distinct

---

[41] Francis Finlay, Chairman, Chief Executive Officer and President, Clay Finlay, USA, ditto.

phenomena as the global spread of Microsoft WindowsXP, nationalism, and Britney Spears. Globalization is a concept that is utilized to make claims (claims about the truth and political claims). By making them, we aim to persuade, to argue, to threaten, and to charm. An image of Globalization as a discourse of heterogeneous groups that are making arguments can replace the image of Globalization as a natural force.

But can we deflect the anxieties about this new model? What does a discourse do? How can it help us understand Globalization? How does it influence the real world? Has our therapy been successful? No, it cannot be this easy. If we are asking these questions, we are showing that we have not yet left the imagery of cause-and-effect. This shows how deeply ingrained this conception is. Understanding Globalization as a discourse should lead to questions like: Who is accountable? Why is group A making this argument? What is the legitimating claim of this argument? But also, what is the content of the discourse? If we smuggle the reified variable back in by analyzing a 'discourse about a reified variable,' we fall back into our old position. Therefore, we need to look closely at the specific instances in which the usage of Globalization is problematic. To insure that our therapy is successful and that our policy makers do not fall back into the old state of imag[in]ing Globalization as a wave, we need to tackle it from more than one side.

## Duck-Rabbit

We use Globalization in active form and in passive form. The dictionary definition exemplifies this ambiguity:

> Globalization: the act of globalizing or condition of being globalized (Webster's 1993).

Globalization read in active form is an independent variable, while read in passive form is a dependent variable. How we understand the concept and how we use it have important repercussions on how we see the politics of Globalization. We can switch between the two perspectives; however, we have a preference for one or the other. This vexing moment is described by Wittgenstein (1969) in the Philosophical Grammar.

> I shall call the following figure, derived from Jastrow, the duck-rabbit. It can be seen as a rabbit's head or as a duck's.

> And I must distinguish between the 'continuous seeing' of an aspect and the 'dawning' of an aspect. The picture might have been shown to me, and I never have seen anything but a rabbit in it (p. 194).

Globalization is perceived by policy makers as an event taking place that impacts lives (in the active form) or as a result of a development (in the passive form). A protester at the World Economic Forum in Davos will see it differently from a participating politician. One can, by concentrating, or by pure coincidence, see the other aspect. However, one must distinguish between the aspect one sees steadily and the aspect that suddenly flashes up.

This aspect-changing quality of the concept of Globalization is not caused by deficient thinking but is a situation in which the grammar of the concept is indeterminate. By accepting this indeterminacy, we become aware of the fact that some questions concerning Globalization cannot be answered sensibly.

## Glocaligration

James Rosenau introduced the concept of fragmegration, a combination of Integration and Fragmentation, into the Globalization discourse (Rosenau 1997).

> We are in a new epoch. It is an epoch that is based on contradictions, on uncertainties, on what I call "fragmegration." That's a combination of fragmentation and integration.[42]

Glocalization, i.e., Globalization+Localization, became the en vogue explanation for the dynamic of Globalization.[43] This practice of coining words enables us to express Globalization as a paradoxical phenomenon (Naisbitt 1994).

By accepting a contradiction in terms as a component of Globalization, we feel that we describe a concept that defies our normal linear logic. The image of an Escher-esque world appalls and attracts us. The power of Globalization is manifested in its paradoxical nature. What type of phenomenon is this that can actually transcend normal logic?

To a large extent, what we perceive as paradox is just muddled thinking. When we argue that Globalization leads to homogenization and disintegration at the same time, we compound two different phenomena that are taking place on different conceptual levels.

> A way to understand the world today is to understand that, not only are there forces at work that are in the direction of fragmentation, localization, decentralization on the one-hand, and forces at work towards Globalization, centralization, and integration on the other hand, but most importantly these are interactive and causally related.[44]

A reconstruction of the argument, therefore, dissolves the paradox.

> It's almost the case that every increment of integration gives rise to an increment of fragmentation and vice-versa. The way to understand the world: it's not chaos, but it is complexity; it's a world of endless feedback. It's a mistake to think in narrow time frames in terms of cause and effect within a particular time frame because every effect becomes a cause in the next stage of time.

---

[42] http://www.csis.org/ics/dia/introsen.html.Interview with James N. Rosenau University Professor of International Affairs George Washington University August 4, 1997

[43] Parker, B. 1996. Evolution and revolution: from international business to globalization. In S.R. Clegg, C. Hardy & W.R. Nord (Eds). *Handbook of organization studies*. London: Sage.

[44] http://www.csis.org/ics/dia/introsen.html.Interview with James N. Rosenau University Professor of International Affairs George Washington University August 4, 1997

> What fragmegration does or involves is the close interaction between distant events and very local events.[45]

The module Nationalism spreads globally and when implemented, leads to disintegrative acts by political actors. By breaking the argument down into two steps, the dissemination of the module nationalism and the effect of the module nationalism, we dissolve the paradox.

The same can be done for Glocalization. Globalization, again defined as a driver, leads to the dissemination of products, information, and ideas. On the local level these are accepted. However, after a threshold level is reached, local products, information, and ideas are perceived as more valuable. Therefore, in order to increase dissemination of global products, they have to be localized. The argument here is not very sophisticated; however, it is interesting that when reconstructed step-by-step, the glocaligration paradoxes lose their paradoxical attractiveness.

## Selection Bias

Policy makers often have a Darwinesque understanding of Globalization. They feel that Globalization selects the fittest organizations and destroys the rest. This evolutionary image of Globalization evokes a vocabulary in which they talk about selection, adaptation, regulatory races to the bottom, and the competition state.

This image is very deeply-entrenched in mainstream thinking, and by relying on this image, policy makers forget that evolution is only a metaphor, and that the logic of social life functions differently. Anthony Giddens (1984) argues in *The Constitution of Society* that

> Biology has been taken to provide a guide to conceptualizing the structure and the functioning of social systems and to analyzing processes of evolution via mechanisms of adaptation (p. 1).

---

[45] http://www.csis.org/ics/dia/introsen.html.Interview with James N. Rosenau University Professor of International Affairs George Washington University August 4, 1997

In the chapter "Change, Evolution, and Power," he deconstructs the usage of biological metaphors in social theories (Giddens 1994, pp. 229-263). The logic of evolutionary biology posits that unconscious random changes in the DNA of living beings lead to differentiations, which are selected by the environment. If one of the random changes fits the environment well, then this living being can potentially reproduce more often.

In social life we assume that actors have the ability to reflect on and decide on strategies. These are moments of freedom in which they can choose.

However, when we see growing homogeneity in the international system, e.g., similar economic, social, and environmental policies in developing and developed countries, we intuitively feel that selection is at work. However, homogeneity does not have to be explained by the imagery of evolution but may be better described by the alternative image of kids in the schoolyard that emulate their 'leader of the pack'. Governments emulate policies in order to legitimize their position in the international community. This means that processes we imagine as selection processes can often be better described as emulation processes (Meyer et al. 1997).

By proposing an alternative image, we can offer alternative strategic options to policy makers. When imagining Globalization as an evolutionary selection process, the responsible policy maker has to adapt, whereas if Globalization is imagined as an emulation process, a responsible policy maker can reflect consciously on his or her decisions. The inevitability of Globalization loses its power and we increase the freedom of choice for the policy makers.

## Conclusion

Globalization is a social phenomenon and theories about Globalization flow directly into the policy-making process. This recursive relationship between theory and policy makes it important to address the policy makers. As long as policy makers understand Globalization through the imagery of a wave, it will create restraints on state capacity. They will aim to adapt to Globalization. Therefore, there is an important political element to theorizing about Globalization.

By challenging the mainstream understanding and offering an alternative image of Globalization as a discourse, the grammatical and therapeutic approach enables us to help policy makers ask new questions and develop different policies. Approaching the imagery underlying Globalization from four different sides (Wave, Duck-Rabbit, Glocaligration, and Evolution) made it clear how deeply rooted conceptions of Globalization as a natural force are.

The very individual and local project of the grammatical and therapeutic approach is of general importance, insofar as it offers a way to increase the freedom of policy makers to make important decisions about our future. By ascribing freedom to policy makers, we change the discourse from a discourse of necessity to a discourse on ethics.

# Globalization and Security: An Alternative World History

Richard Ned Lebow and Janice Gross Stein

At first glance, it may seem counter-intuitive to begin an analysis of the underlying trends driving security with a discussion of globalization. Yet in the last twenty-five years, globalization has had important consequences for the global environment, for the autonomy of the state and its capacity to provide security, for the pattern of inequality both within and between states, for the diffusion of science and technology, and for the growth of a networked world.

According to the International Monetary Fund (2000), globalization is a historical process, referring "to the increasing integration of economies around the world, particularly through trade and financial flows." But it also describes "the movement of people (labor) and knowledge (technology) across international borders." The volume and speed of these flows have been greatly facilitated by modern information technology and spread of English to the point where it has become the working language of world business, science and transportation. As might be expected, the IMF offers an upbeat assessment of globalization as a world historical process, and describes it as "the result of human innovation and technological progress." But there is also a downside. As critics have noted, globalization facilitates the export of problems as well as solutions, it links together conflicts in ways that make them more intense and far-reaching in their effects than they formerly were, and it provides the same opportunities to crime and opponents of order as it does to legitimate business and proponents of order.

On September 11th, we witnessed the first large-scale violent attack against post-industrial society, using its signature form of organization: the network. The network has become the most pervasive organizational image and the dominant form of social organization in post-industrial society.[46] "As a historical trend," observes Manuel Castells (1996), "dominant functions and processes in the information age are increasingly organized around networks. Networks constitute the new social morphology of our societies, and the diffusion of networking logic

---

[46] For an analysis of knowledge networks, see Janice Gross Stein, Richard Stren, Joy Fitzgibbon, and Melissa MacLean, *Networks of Knowledge: Collaborative Innovations in International Learning* (Toronto: University of Toronto Press, 2001).

substantially modifies the operation and outcomes in processes of production, experience, power, and culture" (p. 469). Networks also shape processes of terror and violence.

A network is a collection of connected points or nodes, generally designed to be resilient through redundancy. It can be one terminal, connected to the Internet, or one expert communicating with another in a common network devoted to a shared problem. Networks, in other words, can be both technological and social. The design of the network determines its resilience, its flexibility, its capacity to expand, and its vulnerability.

The first and still archetypal electronic network is, of course, the Internet. Its central feature is a distributed form of communication without central control (Baran 1964, Hafner 1996). In a distributed network, messages are broken into individual "packets" that then take multiple different paths to reach their destination. Such a mode of transmission allows communication exchanges to continue even if parts of the node are destroyed or inoperative. The network is resilient because of its built-in redundancy; the more nodes are added to the network, the more resilient the network as a whole becomes. Built upon principles antithetical to centralized broadcasting modes of communication, the Internet builds strength through dispersion and multiplication of individual nodes. It is precisely for this reason that centralized forms of political authority find the task of monitoring and censoring Internet communications so difficult. With the Internet, there is no single node from which all information emanates or passes through. Removing a single node, or even several, will not destroy the network. The network adjusts, reroutes, and reforms. In the pure model of a network, such as the Internet, eliminating one node of a network does not imperil other nodes.

Social networks mirror their electronic counterparts in important ways. They too are highly decentralized, with different leadership branches that operate with a large degree of autonomy. Unlike the tight pyramids of command-and-control political structures, the hallmark of industrial society, networks are "flat," with leaders who are empowered to act under a minimum of direction and supervision. Using advanced electronic forms of communication, global networks of every kind have multiplied in the last decade: businesses, civil society networks, journalists, scientists, physicians, lawyers, scholars, and environmentalists. These networks differ in how they are organized and, consequently, in their flexibility and resilience.

Most networks generally do not approximate the pure form. The most advanced can be found in the financial sector, where capital flows relatively seamlessly around the world through integrated electronic trading networks. Another can be found at the opposite end of the political spectrum, among so-called "anti-globalization" activists (Deibert 2000). Linked through thousands of websites, emails lists, and Internet relay chats, citizen activists from around the world have been able to co-ordinate mass protests at major international events without a hierarchical mode of organization. The network form of organization allows direction without hierarchy.

Such pure network models are rare, however. A study of global knowledge networks found, for example, that the most successful networks require a center or a "hub," financial support, and a secure environment for the "host" which serves as the temporary organizational focus. There is an element of "place," even if that place is temporary, with which almost all successful networks work (Stein, Stren, Fitzgibbon, and MacLean 2001). Even among global financial networks, major urban centers act as crucial central nodes where financial expertise and personnel are located. It is for this reason that the city of London, for example, occupies such a central role in the global financial economy (Thrift 1994).

Most social networks build some elements of a "web" into their design, even ones that have major nodes within them. Analysts have suggested, for example, that one of the reasons why complex financial networks were able to resume operations so quickly after the attack on September 11th was that the "corporate headquarters" of many of the firms had been moved off site after the first attack in 1993. Within hours, many had resumed operations because of the redundancy they had built into their information systems. Such redundancy also explains why email traffic continued to move unimpaired on September 11th, while telephone traffic ground to a halt in the northeast United States. In the pure model of a network, eliminating one node of a network does not imperil other nodes.

Global networks of terror and crime bear an uncanny resemblance to their generally benign and productive counterparts. Unlike legitimate global networks, of course, they work in secrecy and through illegitimate practices and violence to advance their political purposes. Often with life-cycles of decades, networks of terror thrive on the openness, flexibility, and diversity of post-industrial society, crossing borders almost as easily as do goods and services, knowledge and cultures. They have global reach, particularly when they can operate within the fabric of the most open and multicultural societies, and through post-industrial organizational forms.

Global networks of terror are enabled by conditions characteristic of this phase of globalization. They are conceivable only in a world that is tightly interconnected. Without global markets and communications, the widespread mobility of people, and multicultural, diverse societies, these networks of terror could not survive, much less succeed.

Many hosts of networks of terror, although not all, cling to weak states that can provide a secure environment for the infrastructure and resources that they need. They often depend on states for infrastructure, logistics, and training sites. In exchange for the shield provided by a state, a network delivers complex political and financial rewards that help a regime to stay in power. An ideal environment for a "host" of a network of terror is a weak or fractured state where a network can provide critically needed assets in exchange for the capacity to operate "in place." Even without a secure physical environment, however, networks can survive; a host can use mobile headquarters, but training, operations, and recruitment become more difficult.

Global networks have enabled new kinds of economic, political, and social activities that go around, under, and over states. Drawing on new information technology, which is itself a distributed network, they have thickened and enriched the global economy, and created conditions for global political and social action. At the same time, networks enable international crime, terror, and violence. These too go around, over, and around the state.

This analysis suggests that networks of terror, violence, and crime will not disappear, for they are drawing on the form of social organization which is uniquely enabled by the current global environment. If anything, they are likely to thicken and deepen over the next decade. They pose new kinds of challenges to the security of citizens and governments, and require fundamental changes in the way states and other key actors think about and manage security.

## Globalization in Context

One of the problems in assessing the consequences of globalization for security is the fact that it is occurring at the same time as a number of other domestic and international processes and transformations. These include rapid decolonization and demise of the British, French, Spanish and Portuguese empires, the end of the Cold War and the break-up of the Soviet Union, and enduring regional conflicts, especially between countries that were partitioned in the aftermath of colonialism. The last half century has also witnessed a striking range of outcomes in economic growth and state-building in Latin America, Africa and Asia. All of these developments interact with globalization, often in non-linear ways, and shape its complex implications for regional and international security. To further complicate the picture, these outcomes and their implications depend in large part on how they are understood by actors.

The first wave of decolonization was in the late eighteenth and early nineteenth century, when wars of liberation led to independence for most of North and South America. A second wave of decolonization followed World War I and the breakup of the Austrian, Russian and Ottoman Empires. By far the largest wave broke in the late 1950s and early 1960s, and resulted in a large number of newly independent states, mostly in Africa and Asia.

The political and economic record of the ex-colonial countries, and those few non-European states that escaped colonialism (e.g., Ethiopia, Thailand and Korea) has been mixed. Many of the countries along the Pacific Rim experienced extraordinary economic growth in the second half of the twentieth century and developed, or are in the process of consolidating democratic institutions. Other states have experienced sustained growth, but have not yet made a transition to democracy. Thailand, Indonesia and Mexico have all made tentative progress in this direction. Other countries, especially in the Middle East and North Africa, have made some economic progress, but are governed by corrupt, authoritarian and highly repressive regimes, many of them with very limited popular support. Worse still, are the state failures; countries like Somalia, Zaire, Burundi, Rwanda, where government and civil society have collapsed as the result of kleptocratic regimes, zero economic growth, communal conflict and population growth. These factors - and the consequences of HIV infection - put a score of other countries at risk.

For reasons that we noted, it is difficult to determine the extent to which globalization is responsible for any of these diverse outcomes. This has not prevented scholars, government officials and NGOs from making strident claims in both directions. Proponents of globalization single out foreign investment, co-production and the transfer of technology of manufacturing techniques it enabled, and the education and training on location and abroad of large numbers of scientific, professional and managerial cadres, as the foundations for rapid growth in the Pacific rim, and in other countries like Thailand and India.

Opponents of globalization tend to focus on Africa, where growth in many countries has been marginal to non-existence, and where the gap between the small rich elite and the mass of the still poor population is dramatic. They also describe globalization as a great cultural leveler, replacing local companies, practices and tastes with imported goods and ways of doing business that are reshaping cultures at the most fundamental level. In countries like the former Soviet Union, the consequences of globalization are often sufficiently diverse and uncertain as to provide both sides with ample evidence for their respective arguments.

The second important development that interacted with globalization was the Cold War, running from roughly the de facto division of Central Europe in 1947 to the reunification of Germany in 1991, quickly followed by the breakup of the Soviet Union. Liberals have, on the whole, attributed the collapse of communism to its inability to compete with democracy and capitalism. In this explanation, globalization plays an important role. It forged synergistic links among the developed democracies, and made the peoples of the Soviet Union and Eastern Europe more aware of the growing gap between their lives and the freedom and life styles of the West.

There has been less discussion about the consequences of the Cold War and its demise for globalization, and here the record might fairly be said to be mixed. The Cold War slowed globalization by insulating the communist world from its most important economic consequences. The Soviet bloc, China, Cuba, North Korea and North (then united) Vietnam remained largely, if not resolutely, outside the world economy, and most of their trade consisted of barter among themselves. China and Vietnam aside, communist economies performed badly -- pitifully in cases of Cuba and North Korea - and indicate that autarchy can be self-destructive. But this judgment must be tempered by recognition that Cuba and North Korea were the objects of Western sanctions and embargos. China and Vietnam were economically more successful, but it is also true their growth rates accelerated dramatically after they joined the world economy.

If the Cold War slowed down the effects of globalization in the third of the world that was communist, it probably accelerated them elsewhere. The Marshall Plan gave Western Europe's war-devastated economies and Greece an enormous boost. In the absence of the Cold War, it is unlikely that the U.S. Senate would have approved such an extensive aid program, or that the Truman and Eisenhower administrations would have pushed economic integration on the

Europeans. Germany might well have been left divided for some time in four occupation zones, each with its own currency. In the Far East, a lot of the initial investment - and most, if not all, of the foreign aid - that went to countries like Japan, South Korea, the Philippines and Taiwan, was a response to the Cold War.

Some of the nastiest and most enduring conflicts in our world are the result of the breakup of the Ottoman, Austro-Hungarian, Russian, British and Soviet empires. Many of their successor states were destabilized by acute communal cleavages, often exacerbated by territorial disputes with their neighbors. The war between Greece and Turkey in the aftermath of World War I, Yugoslavia's fragmentation and the series of wars it triggered, and the war between Armenia and Azerbaijan, are all cases in point. Communal conflict was so acute in some colonies (e.g., Ireland, India, Palestine) that they were partitioned on the brink of independence. Partition failed to prevent violence, and may have exacerbated it in all these cases. Post-independence violence led to the *de facto* partition of Cyprus between Greeks and Turks. None of these conflicts have been resolved; the Irish conflict, which had made the most progress, has nevertheless been with us in its present form since 1921.

These contextual factors interact with each other and globalization in complex and often non-linear ways. This is most evident in the Middle East, where all the sources of conflict we have described have come into confluence. Well before the partition of Palestine in 1947, traditional Arab elites encouraged popular antagonism against the Jewish settlement as a way of deflecting it from themselves. This tradition was inherited by their modernizing successors, and led to multi-state wars in 1956, 1967 and 1973, and an Egyptian-Israeli war in 1970. Israel's successive victories expanded its territorial control, making accommodation more imperative, but also more difficult for its Arab neighbors and Palestinians. In key Arab states - Syria, Iraq and Egypt, development is stalled, or overtaken by population growth, governments are corrupt and unpopular and fearful of appearing weak. In Egypt and Saudi Arabia, a fundamentalist opposition is well organized and financed, and has made significant inroads among disenchanted or disadvantaged segments of the population. For most of the last five decades, Arab governments and their domestic opponents have engaged in the politics of outbidding to see which of them could position itself as the most hostile to Israel and its American ally. And on those occasions, where political compromise was a possibility, Israeli and Arab extremists have carried out acts of violence with the express intent of polarizing public opinion and pulling the carpet out from underneath more moderate leaders.

The Arab-Israeli regional conflict became internationalized by virtue of the Cold War, and the way it drew in the superpowers, initially in support of Israel, but soon on opposite sides. American support for Israel was key to its decisive military superiority, maintained over five decades. Soviet support for its Arab clients attempted to redress this balance, and provided the military and political support that triggered the 1967, 1970 and 1973 wars, and the superpower crisis that followed the last of these wars. Since the Cold War, internationalization has taken a different form: a terror campaign against the United States. This reflects the widespread view in the Middle East that Israel is a colonial interloper supported by the United States, which is implacably hostile to Islam. Suicide bombers sent against Israel have received funding and material support from the Palestinian authority, Iraq and Iran, and terrorists dispatched against the United States or American targets overseas have received extensive support from private and state sources.[47] A principal political effect of globalization in the Middle East has been to forge unholy alliances between nationalism and fundamentalism, and national liberation and gangster regimes (Qadaffi and Saddam Hussein). Their violence, in turn, prompted American (and some allied) military intervention in Afghanistan. The violence is unlikely to end here.

If Soviet military support for Egypt and Syria made the 1967, 1970 and 1973 Middle East Wars possible, American support for Mujahadeen in Afghanistan is a contributing cause to the current cycle of violence. American funds, weapons and support for training camps in Pakistan, created trained cadres of guerrilla fighters that have subsequently been active in military and terror campaigns against Israel, the United States, India and some of the Central Asian successor states of the Soviet Union. As we write this chapter, India and Pakistan stand poised on the brink of war in a crisis provoked by terrorist attacks against the Indian presence in Kashmir and the Indian parliament in New Delhi. Regional experts worry that the Pakistani army and government, which trained and supported terrorist and guerrilla units to put pressure on India, may not be in a powerful enough position to rein them in.

---

[47] Saddam Hussein has supplied Mahmoud Besharat of the Arab Liberation Front with money to reward the families of suicide bombers. Alan Philips, *National Post* (Wellington, NZ), 30 May 2002, A. 15.

**Alternative Worlds**

Even if we could identify all of the processes and developments that influence the consequences of globalization, we would still need to unravel them for one another (and everything else that influences them) and study them in isolation and in interaction with each other. But the world is not a laboratory that offers us a large number of comparable cases of globalization with adequate variation on dependent and independent variables. The best we can do is engage in counterfactual thought experiments. Such flights of imagination make no pretense of being scientific, in the sense of rigorously controlling for the presence and absence of relevant variables. But thought experiments are a wonderful tool for helping us work our way through a problem; by adding or removing parameters we think might be important, and thinking about likely interactions and outcomes in their presence or absence, we can reach novel conceptual understandings, and possibly generate propositions that are amenable to empirical research. Globalization, by its very nature, seems an ideal candidate for such a counterfactual analysis.

Given limitations of space, we are going to dispense with the usual methodological discussion. There is a good emerging literature, to which we have contributed, on the analytical utility of counterfactuals, protocols for their rigorous use, and specific applications to historical and international relations' controversies. Readers interested in the method are urged to consult this literature (Lebow 2000, 2000/2001, Tetlock and Belkin 1996, Tetlock, Parker, and Lebow forthcoming). Let us note only that counterfactuals come in two flavors: minimal rewrite and miracle counterfactuals. The former introduce small, credible changes in reality (e.g., Hitler dies on the Western Front in 1916) and infer large consequences from them (no Holocaust). The latter make major, even unrealistic interventions history (e.g., China's principal coal and iron deposits are adjacent, not 2500 km apart) to develop or evaluate theories (i.e., would an industrial revolution have been any more likely in eighteenth century China?). In the thought experiment that follows we limit ourselves to minimal rewrite counterfactuals, and use them to change key features of the present international environment. The point of the exercise is not to show that alternative worlds were possible, perhaps even as likely as the one that eventuated - although such a recognition is a useful corrective to our propensity to see the present world as overdetermined. Rather, it is to encourage thought about the nature, importance and consequences of some features of this world by removing or changing others with which they interact.

Entrenched structures, processes and countries cannot readily be change or done away with by minimal rewrite counterfactuals. To do this, we need to go back years or decades to a time when these structures, processes or countries were merely one of many possible outcomes, and the political, economic, social or intellectual currents that gave rise to them were in a state of flux. Surgical changes in the fabric of reality in times like these can shift the balance of forces in ways that lead to long-term consequences greatly at variance with the outcomes that we know came to pass. Our goal here is not to prevent globalization, but rather to change the context in which it occurs, and with it, its consequences for security. We believe that this can most effectively be done by one counterfactual: a world without World War I.

Prior to 1914, the developed world had achieved a degree of globalization that was not equaled until the last quarter of the twentieth century. A greater percentage of national wealth was invested abroad, and goods, investments, technology and people moved across borders with only the most minor restrictions.[48] World War I and the events that flowed from it stopped the globalization clock for almost three decades, and then allowed it to tick only slowly for the next two. The Great War and ensuing upheavals prompted the universal introduction of passports, strict limits on immigration, national controls on the development and the export of sensitive technologies and the politicization of trade and investment. It led to revolution in Russia, and following the success of the Bolsheviks, the withdrawal of the Soviet Union from the world economy, along with efforts to isolate its citizens

---

[48] Labor is still less mobile than it was in the last century. Passports were then unnecessary and people moved freely across national borders in search of work, with no restraints. Immigration was generally easier, especially to North America, than it is today. Trade is only now becoming as free as it was in the 1860s. Even after the recession of 1875 began in Europe, 95 per cent of Germany's imports were free of duty. Trade was then as significant a component of the domestic economy as it is today. In the United States, for example, exports were 7 per cent of GNP in 1899; in 1999, they were 8 per cent. Capital movements as a proportion of economic output are only now reaching the levels reached in the 1880s. In the nineteenth century, the dominant currency was not state controlled, but rather credit created by private commercial banks. The gold standard severely restricted national fiscal and monetary policy. In this century, states captured control through the creation of central banks and - after 1973 - via floating national currencies that enhanced state control over monetary and fiscal policy. It has been just in the last three decades that levels of economic globalization have begun to approximate those reached last century.

from intellectual and cultural developments in the capitalist world. Nationalism everywhere received a new lease on life, and it was not really until the end of the Cold War in the early 1990s that Russia, Eastern Europe and China rejoined the world economy. In 2002, the free flow of ideas is still resisted by authoritarian regimes that rightly fear the consequences of open communications. Barriers to the free movement of peoples not only still exist everywhere, they are becoming more formidable as states everywhere seek to protect themselves from an influx of economic and political refugees. One of the few positive developments is the mobility available with the European Community to citizens of that Community. This has been achieved at the price of legislation and policing designed to make the Community less porous to outsiders.

How do we rewrite so much history? We have argued else where, that any number of small changes could have avoided the double assassinations at Sarajevo, and with it World War I. Those assassinations were not merely a pretext for a war, but one of its principal causes.[49] With a few more years of peace, some of the most important underlying conditions pushing the continent toward war (e.g., fear of encirclement in Austria and Germany, commitment to offensive military doctrines, widespread perceptions of the inevitability of war) could have been made moot by subsequent events or evolved in ways that made leaders less rather than more risk prone.[50]

In this optimistic scenario, Europe avoids a First World War and enjoys decades of sustained economic growth. Eastern Europe, not held back by two world wars and communism, enjoys the benefits of development sooner rather than later. Russia still undergoes a revolution, loses most of its empire and is governed by a quasi-authoritarian but avowedly capitalist regime. Like the countries of the Pacific rim in the late twentieth century, Russia and some of its successor states gradually develop more stable and democratic regimes, helped by economic prosperity and the emergence of a large, educated middle class and export-oriented business elite. Austria-Hungary survives, but in response to pressure from dissident nationalities and a Germany concerned about unrest along its southern border, adopts a looser, federal structure despite Magyar opposition. Later in the century,

---

[49] Lebow, Contingency, Catalysts and International System Change, develops this argument in detail.

[50] For details of this argument, see Richard Ned Lebow, "Franz Ferdinand Found Alive: World War I Unnecessary," forthcoming in Tetlock, Parker and Lebow, *Unmaking the West*.

European powers confront demands for independence in Africa and Asia. France in Algeria aside, decolonization works itself out in relatively peaceful ways, and in the absence of a Cold War and ideological competition, most newly independent countries maintain reasonably amicable relations with their former metropoles. Europe remains the political and economic center of the world but confronts stiff competition from the United States and Japan. In response, the continent evolves various forms of supranational cooperation and organization, a development facilitated by nearly universal knowledge of German by the region's political, business and intellectual elites.

For many people, especially non-Americans, globalization is synonymous with Americanization. The United States is, after all, the world's largest economy, and is twice the size of its nearest competitor, Japan. The only country to achieve such economic dominance was the United States at the end of World War II, when most other industrial economies where in a shambles. It is also the world's greatest military power, spending more every year on its armed forces than the next 15-20 most powerful nations combined. And even this comparison is misleading, because it does not take into account the great and growing lead of the United States in all areas of military technology (Brooks and Wohlforth forthcoming). But in the scenario drawn up above, the United States is at best *primus inter pares,* and certainly less economically powerful than the European Community. Americans who do not learn foreign languages in school, and American companies who refuse to switch to the metric system are seriously disadvantaged. Pan American is the dominant national carrier, and mindful of its competition, offers "X" rated movies and free cigarettes on all international flights.

Globalization in this scenario would express itself differently. The world would be both more cosmopolitan and more hierarchical. In the absence of World War I, the international society that transcended nation states and linked together, initially composed of aristocrats and clergy, and later encompassing scientific, medical, business and professional elites, would have endured and have been greatly strengthened. Over time, these networks would have reached out to include non-Europeans, beginning with those from the colonies. This process would have been far from tension free, as aristocrats everywhere would have struggled to maintain a social-political hierarchy with themselves at the apex. The resulting conflict, already underway in Victorian Europe, would have played out differently from country to country, with social mixing and upward mobility being more pronounced in western than central and eastern Europe. The same process might have gone on in colonies and independent power centers like China and Japan, perhaps encouraging the formation of trans-national alliances among competing groups and classes within societies. Such a development would further have strengthened the role of international society, and might have helped to diminish the importance of national differences.

Nationalism, especially in Eastern Europe, would still have represented a serious challenge to order. This conflict was already severe in Austria-Hungary, where, before 1914, it already pitted Germans against Czechs and Slavs against Hungarians. The latter conflict would have been even more acute after Franz Ferdinand introduced universal suffrage in 1917. The furthest reaches of the Balkans, and some of the former territories of the Russian Empire, might also have been engulfed by ethnic turmoil, but it is possible that the great powers would have collaborated, as they did more recently in former Yugoslavia, to keep the violence - and the refugees - as far as possible from their homelands. The biggest challenge of all would have been Poland, especially if Russian-Poland managed to establish itself as an independent country in the aftermath of a Russian Revolution. But it is possible that Russian Poland would have been reabsorbed, or that some political solution, involving independence or autonomy, would have been worked out. And if not, there is no reason why ethnic turmoil in eastern Europe would have led to war, as Berlin, Vienna and St. Petersburg would all have had a common interest in keeping the lid on the problem. With any of these outcomes, the overall peace of Europe - the odd Greek-Turkish or other Balkan imbroglio aside -- would have been preserved. The most serious conflicts of the century would have been *within* countries, not between them. In this connection, we should remember that international socialism would still be alive and well, and another one of the networks than constituted European - and trans-European society.

Without the First World War, there would have been no World War II - there would have been no revanchist Germany to start it. With or without the Great Depression - and without World War I, it is also less likely -- Western economies would have experienced steady growth, and globalization would have accelerated, not stalled. This judgment needs to be qualified in a several ways. Japan was also a developed economy in 1914, and in the succeeding decades became a powerful economic and political force in the Far East. With peace in Europe, Japanese foreign policy, of necessity, would have been more constrained. Even if Japanese domestic politics were as tumultuous, it seems much less likely in the absence of World War I that the military would have had the dominant position it did, or that Japan would have occupied Manchuria and then become involved in a wider war with China in the 1930s. A more restrained - and economically more powerful - Japan would have been the principal economic engine for the industrialization of north Asia, just as Germany would have been in Eastern Europe.

Globalization in this scenario is not perceived as Americanization, because the United States is merely one of its sources. Nor, because of the role of Japan, is globalization always seen as Westernization. Culture and economics would not be linked together nearly as much as they are in our world. Opponents of globalization - and there still would have been many - might not interpret it as another form of Western domination, and if they did, would not have focused their wrath almost entirely on Washington.

Decolonization would still have been a disruptive process, but it would have unfolded differently. Historians are in general agreement that both world wars hastened decolonization for a variety of reasons. The initial defeat of the Western powers by Japan destroyed the aura of Western invincibility, the allied war effort required training of regular and guerrilla forces which in some cases spearheaded postwar anti-colonial revolts, American interest after 1945 in decolonization for both economic and strategic reasons, British weakness and French internal divisions all contributed to the independence of almost all the territories under Dutch, Belgian, British and French flags. The remnants of the Portuguese and Spanish empires were not dismantled until the collapse of right-wing dictatorships in the 1980s. The French and the Portuguese fought costly, and ultimately, unsuccessful wars, to maintain control of key colonies, and the United States was drawn into one of these conflicts because of its perceived implications for the Cold War.

Without either World War, the United States would not have become a hegemon, there would have been no Cold War, with the additional pressures it generated for decolonization, and no Soviet Union to offer moral, political and material support to anti-imperialist liberation fronts. Nor would there have been a League of Nations, United Nations, or any kind of comprehensive world organization that would have provided a powerful political forum for the voices of anti-colonialism. Decolonization, to the extent it occurred, would have been a more gradual process. The one exception is Ireland, where Home Rule was only postponed because of war in 1914. Threats of civil war - by northern Protestants and dissident officers - were more bluff than substance. If civil war had been averted at the outset, there is good reason to believe that the "Irish Question," however it ultimately worked itself out, would have done so largely through parliamentary and peaceful political processes.

Other colonial situations are more difficult to call. There was great reluctance in Britain - by no means limited to the Conservatives - to give up India, oil rich holdings in the Middle East, and Egypt with the Suez Canal, the lifeline to the east. In the end, it was only American pressure that compelled a withdrawal from Palestine and Suez, and financial constraints that put an end to British rule in Southeast Asia. Without memories of a civil war in Ireland, the British might have been more uncompromising in other colonies, and without either World War, may well have had the resources to do so. With delayed decolonization of the British Empire, there would have been even less pressure on France to withdraw from north and sub-Saharan Africa and Indochina. Germany, of course, would also have still have had colonies in Africa and the Pacific. All the colonial empires might have survived the twentieth century, or much of it, although many would have undergone some kind of internal restructuring. Undoubtedly, this would have gone the furthest in Britain, where dominion status might have been extended to India at some point, and gradually, to other non-settler colonies. If socialism was alive and well on the continent, and perhaps in and out of power in Holland and Germany, and influential in France, there would have been internal pressures to improve the living conditions of "native peoples" and give them more political rights. Local political pressures combined with parliamentary representation and socialist support ultimately would have created strong pressures for change.

It is hard to image a fully peaceful transition to independence, and more difficult to imagine post-independence peace among conflicting communal groups. But there are two important qualifiers to consider. It is possible that there would have been no Israel, and that many former colonies would have been in a better position to face the challenge of independence. The Zionist movement drew strength from anti-Semitism in Europe, which had quasi-official support in imperial Russia. With a revolution and turmoil in Russia, anti-Semitism would have been worse in the short-term, but might have been ameliorated over time. Anti-Jewish prejudice was alive and well in Western Europe, but would have been much less pronounced in an extended era of peace and prosperity. Without World War I, the Balfour Declaration is unthinkable, and so too are Hitler and the Holocaust. European Jewry would have continued to make significant contributions to the economic, cultural and scientific life of Europe - and this chapter would have been written in French. Undoubtedly, there would have been continuing Jewish emigration to

Palestine, but it might not have been enough to constitute the core of a separate state. Nor in the absence of rapid postwar decolonization, would there have been the same incentive for non-European Jews to seek a haven in Israel. A smaller, less powerful Israel might nevertheless still have emerged, and some degree of Jewish-Arab conflict was perhaps inevitable in an atmosphere of conflict nationalisms.

Many colonies were unprepared to face the political, economic and administrative burdens of independence. There is a large literature that attributes the failure of state building and development in many former colonies, especially in Africa, to colonialism and its legacy. But it is also true - and especially in Africa - that colonialism created infrastructures without which most of these states would have been worse off. One possibility to consider is that delayed independence, with decades of pressure on European governments beforehand to provide more benefits to colonial populations, would have left many of these territories in a much better position to negotiate the shoals of independence.

Our alternative world is a much nicer one in many ways, and we have deliberately gone down some of the more attractive paths that open up in the absence of World War I, or something like it. We fully acknowledge that other, less pleasant possibilities also need to be considered. After all, we do not want to be in the untenable position of making the case for contingency when it comes to a European war, and then becoming determinist in exploring its consequences. A Russian revolution might still have brought a nasty regime to power that coped with domestic challenges by means of an aggressive foreign policy. This could have led to a war in Eastern Europe. Add to this recipe a Germany that fails to make a peaceful transition to a parliamentary democracy - a very real possibility - and for good measure throw in an Austria-Hungary consumed by ethnic hatred and violence, and a very different Europe emerges from our counterfactual blender. We have chosen the better outcome, not because we think it necessarily more likely, but because it offers us the sharpest contrast with the present in the sense that it does away with, or at least prevents a confluence, of the most important conditions that give our globalization such a threatening dimension.

Think of the Middle East, for example. With no Israel - Jews represent one more community among many in the Ottoman Empire or its successor states. It is also possible that Jews and Arabs would have cooperated against the Turks, and that Jewish investment and aid from Europe to the Yishuv [the Jewish settlement in Palestine] would have had wider benefits for the Arab population and helped to sustain what had been by then over a thousand years of generally good Jewish-Muslim relations. Without Israel, the Soviet Union and the Cold War, there are no Arab-Israeli wars. Local state building is hard to estimate, for it would depend on what happened to the Ottoman Empire. But with less war and more foreign investment from a prosperous Europe, the prospects of development improve. In these circumstances, globalization would have been regarded in a different light.

Let us return to our world, and the diverse political consequences of industrialization and globalization. If we track economic growth on one axis, and political tensions on another, industrialization within countries, and globalization across them, the resulting pattern resembles an inverted "U." Tension increases as growth accelerates because traditional livelihoods and hierarchies are threatened or marginalized. In democratic societies - rare at this stage of development - such conflicts have a better chance of being negotiated more or less peacefully. In authoritarian states, growth and change can be prevented or slowed by leaders (pre-Tokagawa Japan); permitted, or actively encouraged, with new elites being co-opted by older ones (Great Britain), or kept at an arm's length and out of political power (imperial Germany), postponing a political reckoning. Tensions decline when economic growth has reached the point where the living standards of a sizeable percentage of the society have been raised. Failure to manage the transition to new economies - leading to stalled growth or economic decline -- or a political failure to spread the wealth, invite revolution or insurgency.

The countries of Western Europe, North America, the antipodes, and some of the Pacific Rim, have all weathered this process. In the course of it, they suffered varying degrees of civil unrest, repression and war. Neither World War I nor World War II were unconnected with the destabilizing domestic consequences of rapid economic growth. But this turmoil is largely in the past. In the first decade of the twenty-first century, most of these countries have become, or are in the process of becoming, mature, post-industrial democracies. A number of other countries (e.g., Thailand, Poland, Chile) have the potential to move in this direction.

Political unrest will be most pronounced in countries where the transition to a modern economy has not been managed well. We see serious problems in states where growth has stalled or its rewards have been restricted to an elite or have differentially benefited one communal or ethnic group at the expense of another. But economics are only one dimension of the problem. Equally serious unrest develops in response to corrupt regimes (where a small elite reaps most of the economic rewards), and where conflict between traditional and modern elites remains unresolved. Saudi Arabia and China represent opposite faces of this problem. The Saudi regime has faced consistent opposition from traditional religious leaders and other groups opposed to modernity. The authorities have tried to buy them off, and in the process, have increasingly become their hostages. In China, a modernizing elite came to power in 1949, and succeeded in rapidly transforming their country. Fifty years later, the communist party has become an ingrown and corrupt political class that must rely on repression and violence to hold on to the reins of power at the village as well as national levels of authority.

Failure to negotiate the transition to modernity can have important international implications. Quite recently, Saudi Arabia has been something of a safe haven for well-funded groups, motivated by religious zeal, who have carried out disruptive violence abroad. Sixteen of the terrorists who carried out the September 11 attacks against the United States were Saudi citizens, and Al-Queda, the organization behind the attacks, was originally Saudi based and supported by Saudi money. In China, regime insecurity has encouraged leaders to play the nationalist card, and this has complicated relations with neighbors and the United States - especially when some of these states have behaved in equally irresponsible ways.

In our alternative world, the pace of life is slower, American is not a hegemon, decolonization came later and globalization earlier. Some degree of conflict and turmoil was inevitable as outside economic penetration and internal economic development has differential effects on the groups that make up societies. They also create new classes, or empower existing ones at the expense of others. Some conflict with Western countries was also likely, but not necessarily in the Middle East. Most importantly, failed state building, anti-colonialism and globalization do not overlap, and do not give rise to a "them and us" mentality among Muslims. The World Trade Center is not standing, but only because it was never built.

## Conclusions

The most frequently asked question about globalization concerns its inevitability. Can it be stopped, slowed down, or somehow transformed into something less destructive of local values, economies and the diverse life-styles they enable? We ask readers to consider the proposition that we already live in an alternative world designed to answer this question. Short of a meteor impact or nuclear war that destroyed the industrial world, or even snuffed out mammalian life on the planet, World War I fits the bill for a reasonable scenario designed to halt globalization by weakening its industrial heartland, reinvigorating nationalism and creating new divisions that led to a second, and even more destructive war. But globalization was not so easily sidetracked. It came back with a vengeance in the last decades of the twentieth century, and while it has not achieved the levels of mobility in investment, trade, technology, people and ideas that it might have in the absence of two world wars, it is making great strides. Barring some unforeseen catastrophe, it is possible that the globalization curves of the real and counterfactual worlds will cross sometime in the next few decades.

Scholars who engage in counterfactual analysis test the contingency of outcomes by inventing "second order" counterfactuals. These are developments that might follow from the initial counterfactual and return developments to the path they were on and bring about something close to the outcome the initial counterfactual sought to prevent. Suppose for the sake of the argument that our alternative world was the real world and that we constructed something like the world in which we actually live as a counterfactual thought experiment to prevent or slow down globalization. We see that even with two World Wars, a Cold War, and all the disruption they cause, that globalization nevertheless accelerates again in the latter part of the twentieth century. In effect, second order counterfactuals return developments to something like their initial course. To the extent that dramatic efforts to "untrack" the course of events are defeated by second order counterfactuals, the outcome can be considered extremely probable.

A second controversy concerns the overlap between Americanization and globalization. Are blue jeans, double arches, Starbucks and summer blockbuster movies manifestations of one or both of these processes? Is there a significant component of globalization that is not Americanization? We do not need to conduct a counterfactual thought experiment to answer these questions. The spread of American culture and products is one component - albeit a large one - of globalization. But America itself is an object of globalization. Even the most casual discussions with American businessmen, from executives in large corporations to owners of local business, reveal concerns for the way their operations and domestic markets have been affected by globalization. One often hears the same complaints voiced by their European and Asian counterparts. Our counterfactual thought experiment was nevertheless relevant for what it revealed about the relative dominance of the United States. Globalization may have been all but inevitable, but Americanization was not. Without the two World Wars, the United States would have been an economic powerhouse, but the gap between it and the rest of the world would not have been so great. For a start, the economies and finances of Europe would not have been devastated by two world wars, and that of Japan by one. Nor would the United States have benefited from the extraordinary influx of talent and entrepreneurship fleeing Russia and Eastern Europe after World War I, and Germany and central Europe in the 1930s. Without World War II, there would have been no G.I. Bill, perhaps the single most important contributor to the sustained postwar American economic boom. A Europe rooted in more traditional lifestyles and values, never occupied by American forces, and not semi-fluent in English, would also have been a less receptive market for American products and culture.

And finally, the security problematique would have looked very different. Even in the Pollyanna world we describe there is conflict, but it is less intense, more diffuse and more local. Conflicts do not combine and become reinforcing the way they do in our world. In less benign alternative worlds, some of these happen. But there is no "clash of civilizations." Even in our world, such a clash is largely in the minds of people; it is the frame of reference many Americans, Europeans, Middle Easterners and Europeans around the world increasingly bring to international politics. We cannot wish an alternative world into being. But we can become more sophisticated in our thinking, and by doing so, help reduce some of the most threatening aspects of the world in which we must continue to live.

## The Politics of the Invisible College: International Governance and the Politics of Expertise[51]

David Kennedy

### Humanitarians and Progressives Evaluate Global Governance

Progressive and humanitarian lawyers, like many left oriented intellectuals, have a hard time thinking pragmatically about the fact that international policy making now affects most every domain in which the contemporary welfare state is active. Our various enthusiasms and suspicions about international governance often reflect only loose prejudices and vague preferences about things local and things global. But global policy making has become too important not to be evaluated more rigorously. Although there remain activities barely touched by international policy initiatives and the density of international regulation varies in different places and policy sectors, there is no question that we have come to live under a new form of "governance," at once more international and more technical. The globalization of policy making may be the most significant change in the structure, site and substance of political culture since the consolidation of the nation state as an arena of popular political contestation a century or more ago.

We might begin an evaluation by working through a list of recent policy initiatives undertaken outside, among and between governments, tallying those aimed to make the world a more humane and progressive place. We would find an extremely wide range of initiatives and it would be easy to conclude that in one or another way most every item holds out some humanitarian promise: agriculture, arms control, banking, commercial law, criminal law, economic development, energy policy, environmental protection, health and safety, human rights, immigration and refugee affairs, insurance, intellectual property, labor, monetary policy, tax policy, trade and commercial policy, transport policy. Many people who are progressive, humanist, liberal, compassionate, in all the best senses of these terms, have let it go at that - perhaps bolstered by a general commitment to internationalism, cosmo-politanism, to thinking about things holistically, solving

---

[51] This chapter was first published as an article in the *European Human Rights Law Review*.

problems together for our whole planet. And indeed, many international policy making initiatives have sprung from humanitarian motives and had progressive results.

An international lawyer, thinking myself progressive, I am drawn to the humanist promises of international policy making. But I would like to develop our ability to assess global governance more pragmatically. Unfortunately, the most common arguments in favor of international policy making are the least helpful. Like the idea that internationalization is technically or historically inevitable. Or the idea that some social and economic problems simply *are* global phenomena which therefore require international policy solutions. By many measures social and economic life today is no less global than a century ago. Modernization is also a story of specialization, fragmentation and the rise of local identities. "The" environment or "the" market can be equally well contemplated, and regulated, as local phenomenon. Even problems which seem global may sometimes be addressed locally. International finance might well be regulated most successfully in a few global cities, just as global warming might best be addressed by local initiatives to curtail the most aggressive polluters. Addressing such matters with international policy initiatives can be a way of disengaging them from policy oversight altogether. Moreover, local policies often have broad global effects, while many global initiatives concern only narrow localities. In short, debating whether things are "getting more international" will not much help us understand the pros and cons of international policy making. However inevitable the internationalization of policy making seemed, if we concluded it was a bad idea, there might be much we could do as progressive and humanitarian people to slow its course.

In a sense, of course, international policy making should simply be evaluated like policy making anywhere, through careful assessment for particular policy initiatives of the costs and benefits, likely risks, outcomes, distributional consequences for various groups, and so forth. International policy making is prone to the same difficulties as policy making elsewhere - underestimating costs, overestimating benefits, over or under estimating the effects of rule changes, overlooking secondary costs, foreshortening time horizons, hyperbole in discussing the pros and cons of proposals, underestimating the plasticity of rules and institutions to appropriation and reinterpretation, and so forth. In this sense, there is not much that can or should be said about international policy making *in general*. All too often, good hearted people substitute general enthusiasm or resistance for difficult assessments of particular policy initiatives. Yet, the general conversation is also an important one. People often shape policy initiatives to advance or retard the globalization of governance, and the level of international policy making reflects the status of forces between friends and foes of internationalization. More significantly, the international policy making machinery may itself skew political outcomes at the wholesale level.

Progressive assessments of global governance run the gamut from enthusiasm to hostility. The enthusiasts focus on the most humanitarian elements of international policy – human rights, humanitarian law, environmental protection, arms control – and are swayed by a general sense that internationalization is inevitable and probably for the better – offering, on the whole, a more modern, technically expert, rational and civilized way of organizing the world than an irrational division into nation states. At the same time, those hostile to global governance, among them people who have mobilized on the streets in places like Seattle, Prague, Quebec, and Davos, as well as in Chiapas, Indonesia, India, or Brazil, criticize international policy making as biased against progressive and humanitarian policy. They are often swayed by a general fear that internationalization will roll back more politically promising local cultural, political and economic arrangements.

I come at this debate with ambivalence. I share with the progressive left a worry that we have overlooked or underestimated serious objections to international policy making. At the same time, much progressive skepticism about global governance leaves me cold. Progressive critics of global governance seem preoccupied with the constitutional structure in which policy is made and with the possibility that international policy makers and institutions are subject to capture by ideology, interest, or professional error. Although both are important, to me, constitutional inadequacies and capture seem far less significant parts of what ails the international policy process. Both misread the internal consciousness and vocabulary of the policy professions - overestimating their clarity or determinacy and underestimating their ubiquity and power.

Progressive critics share with international policy makers the perplexing sense that overt political efforts to influence matters in faraway places are not normally legitimate - that international governance, if necessary, should be exceptional, temporary, should require a special justification, and, when undertaken, should seek to leave local conditions, culture and politics as undisturbed as possible. And that international policy makers should therefore exercise power only as advisors, experts, knowledge professionals, representatives of a politics located someplace else. This wildly underestimates the role of international governance - of rules, standards, institutions, collective decisions and expert management - in the allocations of power or wealth in the world "before" the interventions of international policy making. By accepting the apolitical posture of policy making expertise, progressives forego the opportunity to assert our agenda forcefully at the international level.

But progressive enthusiasts about global governance don't get it right either. They overestimate the ability of international policy makers to affect outcomes as detached and exceptional interveners and underestimate the biases and blindnesses built into trying. They overlook the dark side of policy making expertise, often carried away by the idea that one or another *form* of policy intervention will quasi-automatically turn out to be progressive - intervention to defend human rights, intervention by non-governmental organizations from other places, intervention by experts who come only to share knowledge or technology, intervention in the form of "humanitarian assistance" and "aid," and so on. They forget that all too often saying "I'm from the United Nations and I've come to help you" will not sound promising at all.

Moreover, progressives — whether critics or enthusiasts — seem ambivalent about what they would have global governance accomplish. At times, of course, they advocate global policies which would distribute wealth, status, and power in ways they deem progressive — from those who profit by the generation of greenhouse gasses to those injured by global warming. But when speaking of "globalization" as a whole, progressives often seem to imagine that if the constitutional structure for global policy making is satisfactory — transparent, evenhanded, checked and balanced — and policy makers are not captured by outside interests or ideologies, the outcomes will be in some sense neutral or benign. Good for everybody — as if the distributional effects of policy making were aberrant. In this, progressives aspire to inoculation against the egg-breaking that accompanies all governance and rulership, for there simply is no policy — and no forbearance from policy — which does not distribute. In this, international governance *is* an exercise of power.

But it is also the work of experts and the product of expertise. Critics and enthusiasts underestimate the significance of the policy making professions — international lawyers, economists, political scientists — in global governance. Global governance is largely their creation and their ongoing practice. The background ideas common to the professional vocabularies of these people affect everyone who becomes involved in the international policy making process. In a real sense, we are all speaking policy prose — and yet we do not have intellectual tools or habits to grasp the politics or the centrality of what remains an expertise. And the political limits imposed by this vernacular affect even those who rail against globalization and its policy professionals from the streets.

Too many progressive voices have judged global governance without understanding the vernacular in which it takes place. Focusing on constitutional deficiencies or institutional capture avoids getting inside the mind of the policy maker - he is determined either by the structure within which he works or by external interests and ideas which have captured his allegiance. The odd thing is how many participants at the very center of the policy process also leave their professional vocabulary unexamined, content to treat the politics of their expertise as somehow external to themselves.

My suspicion is that as progressives come to understand the hidden-in-plain-view politics of this shared vocabulary, we will shed some of our customary enthusiasm — and suspicion — about global governance. Progressives, whether deep inside the international policy machinery or protesting far outside, have been both insufficiently critical of international policy making *and* insufficiently vigorous in asserting our political will on the international stage. By overestimating the political importance of constitutional structures and overlooking the biases of expertise, humanitarian and progressive intellectuals have reinforced policy makers' own claims to be structurally exceptional and technically a-political. One result is an unwarranted hesitance by humanitarian and progressive intellectuals to assert our political agendas on the international stage. We need a deeper sense of what can go wrong when international policy makers govern and a broader feeling of empowerment to pursue progressive objectives internationally. My hope is that as progressives come to appreciate the structural limitations and biases of international policy making expertise from the inside, perhaps we will shed our hesitance to see ourselves as participants in rulership.

In this essay, I first consider three common ways of evaluating global policy making which locate the politics of global governance outside the policy vocabulary — in the constitutional structure of global governance, in the tools used to implement global policy, or in forces which have, in one or another way, captured the policy making machinery. Although these can be helpful, they also contribute to our sense of distance from the decisions and responsibilities of political assertion. To counteract these tendencies, I propose that we replace constitutionalism with a focus on distribution, that we stop blaming the tools and focus on those who use them, and that we supplement our attention to capture with inquiry into the politics of our shared policy vocabulary itself. In the second half of the essay, I bring together five ideas about the politics of our policy making vocabularies.

## The Politics of Global Governance is Everywhere But in Its Vernacular

### *Constitutional fetishism: blaming the structure*

Debate about the desirability of global governance gets off the track when it worries too much about the constitutional structure of global governance. Progressives focus far too much on questions like: what is the right mix of centralization and decentralization in an ideal global governance system and how close do we come? How does the institutional apparatus for making international policy compare to the public law structures we are familiar with in industrial democracies, or about which we fantasize in fashionable theories about "justice" or "democracy"? Is there sufficient judicial review? Representation? Transparency? Notice and opportunity to be heard? A functioning separation of powers among three branches of government? Checks and balances? And above all, should we (internationalists, hegemons, leading powers) *intervene* or not?

These can be important questions, to be sure. For many people, constitutional structure will matter regardless of the policies which are made or the outcomes which result. But it seems odd to prefer one governmental level or structure over another without at least an intuitive sense for the specific policies and distributional outcomes which will result. Although policy outputs can differ when issues are addressed in different institutional structures, a focus on constitutional questions can lead us to mis-estimate the political outcomes of policy making. It also encourages us to view international policy making as *exceptional*, overlooking opportunities to contest the international rules, institutions, shared professional sensibilities and practices which structure the background situation onto which we imagine policy making its exceptional intervention.

People often have intuitions about distribution in mind when they say that some types of issues *can only* be handled internationally. What the speaker often means to suggest is that some *types* of solution, some *desirable* governmental interventions, some *worthy* distributions of power, resources or wealth, will, as a matter of fact, only be possible at the international level. Perhaps only the international community has the financial resources to bail out the central bank of a medium sized nation - the alternative to international policy making is the policy of allowing bank failure. Perhaps only the international community has the collective will to impose sanctions on a particular regime in an effective way - the alternative to international policy making is more freedom of action for "rogue" regimes, or for this particular regime. There is, in other words, behind the idea that "the environment" calls for international policy making, an idea about *what policy* is called for, and behind that an idea about the distributional outcomes progressives should prefer. A policy of unrestrained local environmental exploitation, for example, could be pursued perfectly adequately without resort to overt international policy making.

Or take the progressive insistence that we need an international labor policy. In a sense, of course, we already have one. The arrangement of rules, prohibitions, permissions, enforcements and so forth - about sovereignty, about trade, about contracting and ownership and labor association - effects a policy of differing levels of wage protection, raising some wages and lowering others. The historic use of the International Labor Organization (ILO) to "regulate" international labor conditions reflects a policy of authorizing local labor conditions and the political and legal arrangements which support them intact except as they can be affected by sporadic technical assistance and the enunciation of universal norms in widely ratified, if not always implemented, treaties. This policy arrangement makes relatively little use of "fair trade" laws and institutions to assess labor conditions. What proponents of the need for an *international* labor policy mean is a *particular kind* of policy - more aggressive top down regulation aimed to achieve different distributional results - forcing higher wages for some workers through stricter enforcement of at least formally universal norms, at some cost to other workers, consumers or investors.

When humanitarians and progressives consider whether to prefer locating international labor policy in the International Labor Organization or the World Trade Organization (WTO), it would be tempting to focus on the quite different constitutional structures these two institutions bring to the task - different memberships, powers, implementation authorities, and so forth. We might conclude that the WTO is constitutionally "stronger" and therefore more likely to be an "effective" enforcer of labor rights. This sort of analysis can be helpful — but the ILO and the WTO are not simply two different constitutional mechanisms for doing the same thing, different institutions for implementing public norms about the treatment of employees which we know as "international labor policy." The policy made in each institution will be a function of distinct professional cultures which think about what labor policy *is* in different terms. For example, systematic and aggressive use of the national and international trade law regime to challenge low wage regimes as trade subsidies or dumping practices might raise some wages (perhaps lowering others) without public law regulation or standard setting of any overt type.

Constitutional questions can sometimes raise distribution issues, to be sure. We might ask whether it is progressive to pursue labor policy through an institution (like the WTO, but unlike the ILO) in which labor has no constitutionally guaranteed voice. Different memberships, powers, organs, all may have an across the board distributive impact. But these constitutional differences are likely to be swamped by different political climates, different disciplinary vocabularies, institutional histories, contexts of engagement for other purposes, and so forth. As progressives, we would have been better off starting with some sense for the particular outcomes we prefer - whose wages increased or stabilized, whose working conditions transformed, at what costs to whom — and then focusing on the institutional mechanisms most likely to achieve this outcome. Although this sounds commonsensical enough, and is the practice of many sophisticated practitioners and strategists, it is surprising how often humanitarian and progressive voices focus instead on one or another institutional form or level as an unstated and largely unexamined proxy for their preferred outcomes.

Of course, placing distributional issues front and center may also bring to light conflicts among progressive and humanitarian voices - exactly whose ox should we gore, exactly where should we concentrate our resources? But when distributional issues remain in the background it is easy to get carried away by belief in the consistency of constitutional form, and in the importance of constitutional factors in generating results. The most classic example is probably the "race to the bottom" - the assumption that globalization of policy making will lead, through regulatory competition among national units in the absence of a strong centralized policy making capacity, to ever "lower" levels of environmental or health or labor or safety protection. Although this has an intuitive appeal, the empirical story is far more mixed. Sometimes there is a race to the top, sometimes other factors swamp the effects of "regulatory competition," it is difficult to figure out what are "high" and "low" standards where regulatory objectives themselves compete, and so on. More significantly, the idea of what public policy making "is" at the national and international level may well be different - a loss of public law regulatory capacity might well be made up, from a progressive standpoint, by other forms of political intervention and contestation in the international regime. And of course, in terms of outcomes, we might well prefer an ineffective international machinery to an effective national one where the policies implemented generate less progressive outcomes than the existing framework of background norms and practices.

Progressives should develop the habit of recasting our arguments in distributional terms - exactly what sorts of policies, benefiting whom, are "too hard" to implement nationally? When we say international policy making will be more "rational" or less "political," whose interests in what contexts are we thinking will be taken more and less into account? Which sorts of policy outcomes will be more or less likely if taken up by international policy making machinery? What is the distribution wrought by the default policy now in place against which more "international" or "national" policy making seems preferable? It may be easier to build coalitions around feel good constitutional generalizations - globalization is terrible or international policy making is inevitable or both — but doing so will retard, not advance, our understanding of the politics of global governance.

*Blaming the hammer: the politics of institutional and doctrinal tools*

Progressive evaluations of international governance go awry when they focus on the institutional and doctrinal tools used for policy making, rather than on the professional expertise and routine practices through which international policy making is undertaken. Of course, sometimes the available policy tools at the international, as opposed to the national level can affect the distributional outcomes of policy. To take a familiar example, it is easy to see that using international treaties to make rules will often have different outcomes from using a series of national statutes. It is notoriously difficult to enforce a treaty rule against or within the jurisdiction of a signatory state which is not committed to the treaty's enforcement, just as it is difficult to formulate rules which cut sharply into the prerogatives of other governmental entities through the consensual machinery of treaty making. Indeed, a strong national statute in a leading economy can have more international overspill than a treaty drawn in general terms. Treaties are often vague or embody loose compromises and may set back the regulatory agenda by licensing weak national regimes. Contemplating these facts as progressives, it is tempting to conclude that we should simply prefer the use of national regulatory machinery whenever practically possible, relying on treaty making only where the problem escapes national jurisdiction for one or another reason.

So long as we can be confident that progressive policy making means passing strong "progressive" rules for enforcement by public authorities in a context which would otherwise be less progressive, there is much to this conventional assessment of the treaty making tool. But the situation is not nearly that clear-cut. National regimes can protect local interests at significant cost to a general regulatory objective. A weak or differentially effective public law rule may prove more progressive where public authorities are not themselves pro-gressive or where background rules and institutions have more progressive potential. Vague treaties enforced by progressive judges may be much better than strong statutes passed by conservative legislatures. In the rush to generate the strongest possible public rules, opportunities to contest background norms and practices may be overlooked. Where public law norms license anti-progressive practices, this effect may be stronger for statutes than treaties.

Most importantly, the progressiveness of treaties will depend upon what is put in them and how their provisions are accepted by living people managing policy machinery. Much will depend upon the use made of policy tools by the professionals who wield them, and by what they have been trained to think plausible and proper. We are familiar with extremely weak treaties being very favorably received by local elites - and the reverse. Focusing on the tools themselves both turns our attention from their distributional consequences to their constitutional authority, and encourages us to act as if policy tools had a kind of inherent virility or potency, as well as a politics of their own. This idea obscures the effects of professional knowledge and practice about their uses, as well as the responsibility of real people for their consequences.

In a broader sense, focus on policy making "tools" assumes too readily that we know what "international governance" is. But global governance is not simply the sum of public law analogs developed by international policy makers to replicate the functions of national governments. The international "system" is an activity of people — of lawyers, economists, political scientists, bureaucrats, civil servants, street protesters, entrepreneurs, media moguls and businessmen in thousands of locations who share a commitment to international policy making. These people might work for the great international governmental bureaucracies, but they are equally likely to be found in national governments, in private enterprises, in non-governmental organizations, in the media, in universities or in the streets. Wherever they are located, these people propose, accept, expect, hope for, resist, yield to and interpret the internationalization of social and economic policy, and their shared consciousness is more important in setting the terms and extent of global governance than the formal powers or presence of the international policy making machinery. Consequently, international policy making is the collective practice and consciousness of a people. Not the people of a nation, but the people (from central bank presidents to street protesters) of the diffuse cosmopolitan and international space. Theirs is the "consciousness of an establishment," and the politics of global governance will be their collective politics.

Many, but by no means all, of these people are professionals who learned the policy making vernacular in their training to become economists, lawyers, political scientists, journalists and so forth. Their professional vocabularies give us a window into this more general establishment consciousness, both because they are influential, and because they articulate overtly what is common sense in the broader society of cosmopolitan people who influence international policy making. We might therefore begin our evaluation of the politics of international governance by evaluating the politics of these policy making disciplines.

This may seem odd at first, and not only because we are used to thinking of these disciplines as domains of relatively neutral "expertise." At the national level, we think of policy making as the servant to a political class implementing a political program, an ideological agenda, perhaps a democratic mandate. We think of policy makers – and they think of themselves – as bound, in their acts and in their imagination, by the delegated powers of their institutions. But to the extent international governance is the act of a diffuse establishment *above* or *outside* national political contestation, it floats free of these familiar conceptual restraints. Although savvy policy professionals rarely present themselves as naive voices of a neutral science, they think of themselves as participants in something altogether less parochial or ideological than "politics." They often feel they have left the bad old (national) politics of rent seeking, subjectivity, corruption, national and ethnic parochialism behind to build a shiny new and objective politics of cosmopolitan expertise. The term "policy" suggests the tendency to think in terms of "best practices," practical necessity, efficiency, rather than political positions or distributional outcomes. People have this in mind when they complain that European Union officials seem less to be implementing the left, right or center political program of a government than advancing their own authority in the name of the abstract ideological goal of "building Europe." International policy makers speak far more about the "best" policy or practice than about winners and losers, and about the work of the "international community" than about the prerogatives of this or that institution.

Of course, the politics of the professions is not only a function of their expertise, and it would be useful to know a great deal more than we do, sociologically and historically, about this cosmopolitan policy class. The professions encompass a broad range of political commitments and people who pride themselves on the flexibility and eclecticism of their expertise. International policy making elites pursue all sorts of projects using, stretching, ignoring, free-riding on their professional vocabularies, credentials, expertise and institutions. Sometimes these are projects of deep commitment or aversion, often, though not always, to the stated objectives of various policy initiatives - reduce global poverty, increase the efficiency of global capital markets - only some of which will, of course, be progressive or humanitarian. But also projects of affiliation and disaffiliation - associating themselves with those in power, with those out of power, with the hip, the helpful, the wise or the savvy. And, of course, projects of power and submission, willing themselves to rulership, to service, to marginality or centrality. As they pursue these quotidian professional practices, working within or against the possibilities of their professional vernacular, policy initiatives of one sort or another emerge.

When progressives focus on the politics of policy professionals, they can be disarmed by the fact that most international policy makers share a humanitarian and progressive sentiment. These are largely good people, humanist, rational, practical, cosmopolitan, liberal in sentiment. Theirs is an enlightenment project, a liberal project in the widest sense, embracing liberalisms of the right, the center, and the left, carrying with it all the problems and promises of the liberal philosophical tradition. It can be difficult to see much more of their politics than this. These are people who seek to govern, not in their own name, but as representatives of knowledge, necessity, reason. They imagine themselves governing from outside government, figuring themselves as knowledge, speaking to everyone else as power. These are people hesitant to act directly or openly on their progressive and humanitarian sentiment, people to whom the thought "personally I'd like nothing better, but unfortunately..." comes very easily.

They understand their entitlements to flow from their expertise, sharpened and certified by disciplinary training and validation, and their reference group is first and foremost collegial. They share the idea that the object of their expertise pre-exists their disciplinary formation - "the law" is out there, they study it, interpret it, reform it, apply it. "The economy" is out there - they study it, describe it, formulate its rules of action, manage it. Moreover, these professionals wear their expertise lightly. The best international policy makers are eclectic - used to flexibility, interdisciplinarity, alive to the experience of skepticism, to the failures of knowledge. We might say the best economist knows how little is known about the economy, the best lawyer how fluid and undecided the corpus of law — know that the work of the professions is less the application of expertise than a modest practice of eclectic social or institutional management.

Although it may seem obvious that the terms of the policy discussion may limit the policies which are made, these are extremely subtle and ambivalent vocabularies. It is not at all clear that the policy making vocabulary has a politics, except as practiced or applied. Like anyone, policy professionals bring a range of professional deformations to the task, the limits of their training, their imagination, their understanding of the terrain upon which they work, their sense of the sorts of solutions which will and will not work. But these may, and sometimes are, compensated for by the presence of other professional disciplines and other voices.

It can be difficult to get a good grip on the politics of the cosmopolitan policy making establishment, even by focusing on the vocabulary of the dominant policy making professions. Progressives who have tried to isolate the politics of the international policy establishment have taken two paths. Some take the vague flexibility and apolitical posture of the professional vocabularies themselves at face value, and focus rather on the possibility that the entire discussion has in one or another way been hijacked. Others, more skeptical about the notion of political capture have tried to isolate elements in the policy making vernacular itself, background understandings and shared assumptions, which might, in one or another context, turn out to skew the politics of global governance in an anti-progressive direction.

*Body snatchers: the politics of capture*

> a. The institutions and professions of global governance have been politically captured.

The most familiar claims about the distributional biases of international policy making are made in the language of political capture. International policy making will favor some policies and exclude others, and distribute resources from some groups to others, because the policy making machinery has been captured by political forces committed to these results. Capture seems bad both when specific politics dear to the speaker are made less possible, and when policy making departs from an abstractly desirable political range. There are three quite different ideas out there about how international policy making could be politically captured.

In the first vision, the global policy making machinery has (perhaps secretly) come under the influence of some group or set of economic interests. Whatever is said by international policy makers, and whatever the actual structure of decision making at the international level, the shots are really called by someone else – by capital, by industry, by the first world, by the United States, by the Trilateral Commission, and so forth. Those hostile to policy making by the European Union speak this way when they suggest that when policies are made in Brussels, decisions are *really* taken in Paris or Berlin. It is also familiar in claims that the world trading system serves the interests of "global capital" or has been taken over by the agents of multinational corporations.

A second idea is that the actual participants in international policy making are themselves ideologically or politically committed partisans of one or another faction rather than pragmatic and objective assessors of the costs and benefits of alternative policy options. International policy makers might be more conservative or socialist or liberal than policy makers elsewhere, or the range of political commitments among international policy makers might be narrower than the abstract range of possible political positions. These political commitments will either lead policy makers to distort their professional analyses or exploit opportunities left open for discretion within their professional analyses to promote their political agenda. We hear this idea in British debates about European policy making which suggest that Eurocrats are less liberal and more socialist in sentiment than policy makers in London. In the broader international context, the claim is more often the reverse:

international policy makers are liberals with a libertarian or mercantilist rather than a socialist bent.

A third vision of political capture stresses structural dimensions of the international policy making machinery which lead some interests to be under or over represented - in comparison either with an imaginary "justly" representative order, or with actual policy making machinery at the national or local level. To the extent we imagine policy makers to be themselves representative, rather than the implementers of political objectives set by other representative groups, some groups or interests may be under-represented. If we think of policy makers as more neutral experts, some interest groups may face structural impediments — through their own organizational structure or their distance from international machinery — in articulating their claims so as to be heard by international policy makers. The key here is participation, voice, presence, and the transparency of the international policy machinery. Claims of this sort are common - from both the third world and the first, from states as well as non-state actors and groups. Concerns of this type lie behind accusations that international policy making suffers from a "democracy deficit," whether in the European Union, the United Nations or the International Monetary Fund. Or that the machinery for trade governance favors the dominant interests within large diverse economies, favors producers over consumers, or proliferates machinery for defending and compromising the claims of first world interest groups while offering nothing compatible to interest groups in Third World locations.

There is no question that political capture of policy making in each of these three senses is possible, does happen, and should be a matter of concern to those whose interests or objectives are consequently not attended to. My own sense, however is that political capture claims have been exaggerated when it comes to assessing international policy making as a whole. The attention given these claims, moreover, has crowded out investigation of other sources of bias in international policy making which may well turn out to be more significant.

International policy making is simply too complex and multifaceted to be easily characterized as captured by one or another political tendency — it is no accident that people have charged international policy making with prejudices in all sorts of directions. People associated with international policy making themselves turn out to be diverse in their personal political affiliations. Far more are vaguely progressive than would be compatible with strong claims to conservative or neo-liberal capture – and far more are centrist liberals than would be compatible with claims of socialist or right-wing capture.

But my skepticism about political capture claims has another source. It is notoriously difficult to link particular policy alternatives with particular political interests in any determinative way – and far more difficult to do so for the array of policies implemented at the international level. What *is*, precisely, in *the* interests of capital or labor, of the first world or the third? The consequences of particular policy initiatives are extremely difficult to predict. These interests are themselves aggregates of various competing groups with divergent interests. Often their interests overlap. Once one begins to formulate an answer, one is in the slippery realm of international policy making itself, attuned to perverse effects, reverse interpretations, unexpected costs and benefits. To make policy is, after all, to distribute - too often claims of "capture" are simply ways of disagreeing with the policies which have been made.

Claims about a lack of representation have, at first blush, more plausibility. And yet if we think of the international policy making apparatus as a broad cultural process rather than a narrow institutional structure, it is hard to identify interests or groups whose claims have not, one way or another, been articulated on the international plane. For more than a century, reformers have insisted on, and generally received, ever more open patterns of participation and transparency. The outsiders have been repeatedly let in, and the feeling that international policy making is both biased and cut off from the possibilities of popular engagement remains. Of course, one could always conclude that as excluded voices are let into the room, the "real" decision making has moved elsewhere, and this certainly does happen. But it may also be that the outcome bias did not spring primarily from a lack of participation in the first place, or that the modes of marginal expression are themselves biased or self-limiting. Although thinking of international policy making as the activity of an establishment consciousness would seem to make claims of ideological capture easier to sustain, the consciousness of the policy establishment is extremely fluid. It would be more accurate to describe it as post-ideological, post-political, eclectic or flexible, than as politically captured.

I am left suspecting that the problem is not primarily one of transparency or participation or ideological closure. What is needed is not openness or "transparency" as that term is understood by even the most aggressive proposals to render intergovernmental institutions transparent - documents published sooner, meetings broadcast on the web, non-governmental representatives allowed access as observers. If there is a problem of "participation" or voice in international governance, it seems a far more profound one - an almost complete absence of politics, in the sense of collective contestation among groups over the allocation of power, wealth, services, or status. Legal structures for governance abound and an extremely wide array of people now participate in global governance. But an overt and conscious global political process is altogether absent, replaced by conversations and struggles within a limited policy vernacular. To evaluate the politics of the international policy making process, we need a far more nuanced conception of how professional expertise itself works, for assessing the biases of people who are eclectic in their commitments and committed to standing outside the terrain of commitment itself.

b. The policy making professions are subject to doctrinal, policy or methodological capture.

The claim here is that international policy making will distribute resources from some groups to others because the expertise of policy makers is itself biased to favor policies which in turn favor these groups. There are at least two common ideas about how this can happen. In the first, a policy making discipline will become gripped by a fashionable policy, theory or doctrine, and advocate it more forcefully and more often than good sense would dictate. The over-investment in this particular policy, theory or doctrine will then have unfortunate distributional consequences.

Of course international policy makers do succumb to fads. For years experts involved in development policy making at the international level were bullish about import substitution policies, fifteen years later export led growth was all the rage, five years after that experts seemed unanimous that neo-liberal polities of privatization and return to world prices were the only way to go. It would be entirely fair to say that the development policy profession was not able, in any of these periods, to embody the breadth of its own expertise. Broad public discussion about development largely ran parallel. Similarly, for years international policy makers approached situations of ethnic conflict offering minority rights and assimilation - and then switched to self-determination and population transfer - and then reversed again. This is the sort of thing people in the United Kingdom have in mind when they complain that policy making in Europe is captured by "corporatist" thinking, or when those in the third world charge the international financial institutions with a bias for neo-liberal free-market policies. International lawyers are constantly being accused of a professional overinvestment in the doctrine of "sovereignty" or in "the state."

In my experience, however, claims about doctrinal or theoretical capture often seem exaggerated. The policy choices against which the discipline is said to have closed its eyes turn out to be present in mainstream thinking. Policy alternatives which seem stark turn out to be more nuanced. The fluidity of the doctrinal or policy options themselves makes it notoriously difficult to tell exactly what the distributional consequences of different policy options will be. Routine professional practices of internecine conflict and criticism, although often sounding doctrinaire and sectarian, in fact leave the best professionals ambivalent and quite unlikely to lash themselves too long to any policy or doctrinal fad. It is no surprise that those accusing policy professionals of bias in this sense so rarely go on to articulate the outcome consequences they fear.

It is far too easy to conclude, for example, that since international policy makers are all advocating neo-liberal free market policies, they and the policy making system of which they are a part are biased in favor of, say, capital over labor, or the first world over the third. It turns out that within "free-market" ideas there lurks an exception for situations of "market failure" which can be interpreted in broad or narrow terms. Making out a case for bias would require saying quite a bit more about how policy makers resolve the various choices internal to this broad policy choice (how broadly or narrowly do they interpret "market failures") as well as a clear sense about what policies will in fact favor a group as diverse and general as "capital," or "the first world." A "free market" policy could turn out, if properly structured, to be more friendly to "workers" than its "socialist" alternative.

This sort of debate is more often about the rhetoric of international policy than the outcomes. Repeatedly, the expertise of the policy making professions returns to well worn argumentative alternatives - between import substitution and export led growth, between neo-classical and institutional economic ideas, between praise and condemnation of sovereignty. It is simply not true that experts in, say, the international financial institutions are committed to a neo-liberal policy panacea. There are those voices, to be sure, but they are not alone - in the institutions, or even in the expertise of individual professionals. As a result, efforts to locate professional bias in doctrinal or policy capture almost always seem to underestimate the range and flexibility of the professional expertise they seek to criticize.

A second vision of the biases in the expertise of international policy makers focuses on "methodological" or "theoretical" capture. In this conception, debate among policy professionals about things like "how much sovereignty is the right amount" or "what is the appropriate mix of import substitution protection and openness to free trade" assume, after a time, a predictable form. When this happens, schools of thought form within a discipline which tend to answer a range of similar questions the same way - always defaulting to more, rather than less, sovereignty, or more rather than less protectionism. It often comes to seem, at least to those involved, that the answers people in a school of thought give to specific policy questions are in some sense entailed by a "theory" about something quite general - what law is like, how economies work, what justice requires, and so forth. These theories (positivism, naturalism, neo-classicism, institutionalism, formalism, antiformalism) are then thought to have policy consequences.

Thus, if you "are" a formalist, we can reasonably predict that you will favor some doctrines over others, almost regardless of the policy context. You will favor rules over standards, doctrinal over institutional solutions, deference to sovereignty over the development of newfangled international authority structures. Moreover, once you "become" a formalist, you advocate some policies and not others because of what you believe *law* to be like. If disciplines are composed of people representing the full range of theories or methods or schools of thought, debate between different schools should ensure an appropriate doctrinal selection. But this turns out not to be the case. Professional disciplines do get captured at times by theories or methods, and this may bias their choice of doctrinal or policy options. Even in disciplines with vigorous methodological debate, doctrinal choices more often reflect the status of forces among theoretical combatants — the strength of theoretical sects - than pragmatic assessments of the appropriate solution to specific practical problems.

So, for example, it was long argued that international lawyers during the first half of the twentieth century were almost exclusively "positivist" and "formalist." As a result, so the story went, they tended to default to rules rather than standards, to treaties rather than custom, to sovereign and state based solutions rather than more open-ended or flexible institutional arrangements. And this, it was said, favored the first world over the third, and favored entrenched interests over newly emerging powers. To reform international law to take the needs of the decolonizing world into account, international lawyers would need to abandon their formalism in favor of more "process" or "policy" or "functional" approaches, would need to replace their attachment to sovereignty with something altogether more "transnational" and pragmatic. In similar fashion, it is often argued today that too many international policy makers, particularly lawyers with North American educational backgrounds, are antiformalist, and hence advocate policies which highlight opportunities for discretion and flexibility - a flexibility which, in turn, favors the hegemon.

There is no question that policy making professions in particular places can get mired in one or another theory and find themselves working with a dramatically reduced set of doctrinal and policy tools when confronting problems. I think American policy makers have something like this in mind when they complain that the international policy making machinery is too formalist, or too "European" it its attitudes about law, or what national policy makers mean when they suggest that the European Central Bank has been captured by economists who overestimate the threat of inflation and underestimate the threats of recession, or what third world policy makers mean when they charge that international financial institutions have been captured by neo-liberal supply-siders. Still, charges of methodological or theoretical capture, like claims of political, doctrinal or policy capture, underestimate ambivalences and exceptions within each contending school of thought which open the window for more diverse policy commitments. And if it is extremely difficult to trace the connection between a general theory or school of thought and a particular doctrine or policy in determinate ways, it is even more difficult to link these theories to outcome biases.

The argumentative materials which constitute the school of thought are generally simply too thin and porous, the contest between formal and antiformal positions too vigorous, the aggregation of interests and their link to policy formulations too tenuous, to be confident that methodological or theoretical capture could bias something as broad as international policy making in an interesting way. Of course it could turn out that people who are "formalists" or "antiformalists" are *also* captured by a political commitment of one or another sort, and that surely also happens. But it would seem more appropriate to see this as a case of political, rather than methodological capture. Contemporary international policy disciplines are self-consciously agnostic about political commitment and ideological alignment — agnostic about the doctrines, theories and schools of thought which divide their own disciplines. Sometimes it seems incontestable that normative flexibility will favor the hegemon, while formal rights will protect the weak, but sometimes the opposite will seem equally true. Figuring out which will be true when is what policy making is all about. To suggest that antiformalism a priori expresses hegemony is less to uncover methodological capture than to be methodologically captured.

c. Capture by disciplinary specialization and the false panacea of interdisciplinarity.

There remains a suspicion that policy making "experts" will nevertheless approach policy questions too narrowly. Unlike the common man, or, for that matter politicians, whose minds are expanded by campaigning about the polity, experts have had their thinking narrowed by professional specialization. The claim here is not that they have been captured by a political enthusiasm, nor that they are failing to engage the full range of positions and schools of thought made available by their discipline, but that their discipline as a whole is simply too narrow in ways which bias outcomes. To the extent broader public debate about global policy making occurs in these professional languages, it too will be too narrow. It is easy to think of examples - lawyers are too litigious and try to solve things with rules, economists only worry about what's efficient, businessmen worry only about the short term bottom line, military officers always want more hardware and are too prone (or not prone enough) to use it. Nobody seems professionally responsible for ethics or values, everyone over-discounts the future or too sharply privileges the past. This sort of bias does affect international policy making. Economists and political scientists and lawyers do focus on different sides of a problem and come up with different solutions. When violence breaks out, it makes a difference whether one sends lawyers, doctors, soldiers, priests, therapists or aid specialists to respond. In thinking about the pros and cons of international policy making, it would be useful to have a better sense for the particular biases of the various professionals who are likely to be involved.

If we focus only on international lawyers, with whom I am more familiar, much will depend on the person's specialty - human rights lawyers, public international lawyers, international economic lawyers, comparative lawyers all see different things, worry about different things, bring a different stock of solutions, reach out to different non-legal disciplines for assistance. International lawyers do seem to see a world of states, worry about how law can be possible among sovereigns, focus on avoiding the trauma of war, reach out to political science for inspiration, seek to strengthen global governance. International economic lawyers, by contrast, seem to see a world of would be buyers and sellers, worry about how the risks to trade can be contained, focus on avoiding economic depression, reach out to economics for inspiration, and seek to strengthen free trade. There is no doubt these disciplines think about an issue like international labor policy very differently. For an international lawyer, the problem will be a lack of governance capacity, a need for norms and institutions to ensure compliance with them. International labor policy will mean a network of international legal rules and standards and enforcement machinery. For an international economic lawyer, the problem will be the transformation of different national conceptions of normal labor practices into arguments for restricting trade. Producing against the background of a different national legal regime can seem like an "unfair" trade advantage. International labor policy will mean a process for adjusting, diffusing, coordinating such claims in ways which will not unduly impede trade flows. The policies which result from thinking about labor in these different ways may well differ dramatically. It may well be that progressive skepticism about international policy making might be grounded in the fact that too many economists or lawyers or political scientists, or whatever, are involved.

In my experience, however, many efforts to identify and address this sort of deformation run into trouble. As with political or methodological capture, it is terribly difficult to link disciplinary focal points to outcomes in any convincing way. Just because international economic lawyers focus on trade flows, even have a project of increasing trade, does not mean that they will, for example, be inhospitable to strengthening the international minimum wage, raising health and safety standards or promoting conditions more conducive to labor organization. As far as I have been able to see, there is nothing in the tools of their trade which would dispose them in that direction. Neither is it clear that the trade lawyers' efforts to develop an interface among different background national legal regimes is biased towards homogenization - let alone unity at a high, low or medium level of protection. Facilitating trade is, after all, about facilitating exploitation of comparative advantage - differences in the background conditions of production. Again, to think about professional specializations this narrowly is to be oneself captured by them.

The international economic lawyers we now *have* might, as a matter of fact, have been politically or methodologically captured, but that would be something altogether different. Similarly, just because international lawyers focus on states and seek to build a regime of law among them does not make them hostage to formalist conceptions of sovereignty —it places them in a professional vocabulary preoccupied with relations between formal and informal conceptions of law and sovereignty. In any event, it is not at all clear what the policy outcome bias of insistence on formal sovereignty would be. A more formal sovereignty, for example, might strengthen either high or low wage economies in defending their labor regimes, or might be the basis for a strengthened intergovernmental cooperative regime.

Moreover, although the terms and preoccupations of various policy making disciplines do differ, efforts to understand their relative weaknesses or blind spots are prone to underestimate the internal flexibility of each discipline. Are military professionals too prone, or not prone enough, to use force? It turns out that economists have a vocabulary for internalizing factors which non-economists tend to think of as matters of "value" rather than matters of "efficiency, " just as lawyers have a vocabulary for criticizing and limiting reliance on rules or litigation, broadening exceptions, promoting alternative dispute resolution, structuring administrative discretion and understanding the role of political life in constituting the rule of law. In a similar way, political scientists have a vocabulary for speaking about the influence of rules on the structure and operation of regimes, even if they often preface their stories about multilevel games and predictive stability with denunciations of "idealistic" lawyers who think politics can be tamed by rules or ethics.

As a result, it is easy to overestimate the differences between the preoccupations of the disciplines, and to underappreciate both their internal ambivalence and the contestability of what seem their central attachments. Indeed, mastery of any of these contemporary policy disciplines means mastery of precisely the arguments which turn against or reverse lay understandings about disciplinary conventions. The stock experience of first year law students, confronting the unexpected fluidity of rules, stability of standards and interdisciplinary nature of legal expertise, is repeated in the training of professional students from other disciplines. Indeed, it tends only to be people *outside* each of these disciplines who share most avidly the professional deformations and narrowings customarily associated with them. The flexibility, agnosticism and interdisciplinary enthusiasm of each discipline makes it difficult to pin bias in the policy making machinery as a whole to the over-representation of one or another professional specialization.

It is all too common in thinking about the limits of disciplinary imagination to imagine that interdisciplinary cooperation will provide a satisfactory remedy. There is no question that interdisciplinary work can often expand the imagination - if economists think too much about efficiency, the presence of priests and ethicists may well help to reset the balance. But faith in interdisciplinarity is often misplaced. The presence of priests and ethicists may well keep the economist from realizing the full potential of his own professional vocabulary - may encourage disciplines to live up to their stereotypes. More importantly, in thinking about international policy making as a whole, it may be that the most important sources of possible bias in the machinery are shared by the disciplines which come into association. As a result, their association may strengthen a common perception which is more crucial in limiting the policy imagination than the supposed limitations of each disciplines particular expertise.

There is no doubt that progressive and humanitarian people should worry about a capture of international policy making by anti-progressive ideas, interests, theories. When we sit outside the policy making process and look at it from afar, we should ask whether policy professions which claim political neutrality or disengagement have in fact been harnessed to anti-progressive objectives. But we should reject the idea that professional knowledge can or should be politically dispassionate. And we should not ourselves remain outside the fray. International governance distributes, makes some outcomes more likely and some less. Where the results are progressive, we should applaud, and where they are not, we should contest them. Doing so places us *in* the policy process, governing, ruling, no longer standing outside lamenting its "capture."

## The Politics of Global Governance and the Expertise of Policy Professionals

As participants in global governance, we must come to grips with the politics of the policy making vernacular, with our underlying consciousness, style or sensibility. We are still far from understanding the ways in which a shared policy vocabulary shapes the outcomes of the policy process - there is much work to do to understand the politics of professional knowledge and its relationship to the broader policy vernacular. In some ways, this underlying vocabulary is not different from the combinations of arguments, theories and methods which are on the surface of the discipline and are sometimes thought to "capture" its imagination. Just as a given debate or professional discipline can be captured by "positivism," so presumably could the broader policy making vernacular.

But this seems unlikely. Once they become conscious and are given names, specific schools of thought, doctrines or methods, tend to be contested – to be opposed by other schools and approaches. One almost always misses something with a claim of capture – somewhere in the discussion will be the opposing idea, the other school, sometimes even deep within the dominant strand itself. By underlying vernacular, I have in mind assumptions and conceptual boundaries which are more widely shared, which encompass both sides of these more common debates, and which are often less visible, perhaps less conscious, than adherence to a school of thought or enthusiasm for a dominant policy idea. Still, the boundary is a porous one. Aspects of the underlying vernacular can be contested and pop up as a school of thought or a policy fad, just as it can happen that a school of thought so dominates the consciousness of the policy making establishment that it recedes from view into the underlying vernacular. To make aspects of this underlying vernacular visible that we might assess their politics, I propose to ask rather simple questions about the preoccupations of policy makers of whatever school or tendency – how do they see their world, how do they understand their history, what do they see as the techniques and tools available to them, how do they define problems and solutions, how do they understand the possibilities and limits of their own roles?

### *How do they see "global governance?" Under and overestimating the special dimensions of policy making in the international context*

International policy makers tend to mis-apprehend the peculiarities of policy making at the international level, either over- or underestimating the unity and distinctness of the international system. Doing so can distort judgment about the likely consequences and effectiveness of international policy initiatives, often undercutting the plausibility of claims for their humanitarian potential. This quite common deformation is also a surprising one. The peculiar dilemmas of international governance are, of course, precisely the focal points of the international policy professional's special expertise, and are widely discussed in the theoretical literature of international law, politics, and economics. International "governance" is more process than institution, depends on law more than force, erects norms on the basis of horizontal consent rather than vertical authority, lacks common fiscal or monetary authority, stretches over numerous heterogeneous cultural and political contexts, relies upon decentralized enforcement machinery, the "mobilization of shame" rather than police, etc. The political culture within which international policy making takes place is structured by the voices and distributional clashes of national identities organized into state and governmental entities rather than by the clashes of class, ideology, religion or other interests organized as party, governmental, corporate, individual or social entities more characteristic of national political life. Each functional branch of the international governance machinery is far more diffuse than its national analog and is enmeshed in various local and national institutions. The international "judiciary" is not a uniform system hierarchically organized around the "World Court," but an ad hoc and shifting set of cooperative and deferential practices among numerous national, local and international adjudicative bodies. Similarly the "administrative" branch, where the importance of nominally "international" administrative bodies varies considerably in different places and the implementation structures of private institutions or national and local governments is key.

The claim is that the international policy professional knows all this – and forgets all this. After inventing international governmental organs as formal or functional imitations of national parliaments, executives, judiciaries, they then make policy in them as if their Potemkin government would operate like the domestic institutions on which they were modeled. As a consequence they overestimate their own effectiveness. They treat the adoption of a norm as the implementation of a policy, mistake the judgments of the World Court for the decisions of a judiciary embedded in a dense and functioning legal culture, mistake treaties and the resolutions of international organizations for statutes, anticipating their implementation, and so forth. They underestimate the diversity of political, legal and social contexts within which their policy initiatives will need to be realized. The policy solutions proposed by international policy makers often have a one size fits all quality which imagines that what works in one place will work in another. The idea here is not only that they fail to respect local cultures, but that they, paradoxically, underestimate the specificity of the culture of international governance itself.

When policy makers underestimate the uniqueness of the international policy making , they can easily overestimate the humanitarian potential of their initiatives. This happens when they applaud the extradition proceedings for Pinochet in the United Kingdom and the effort to try him in Spain as if there existed an cross-cultural criminal and humanitarian legal fabric which could be strengthened or affirmed by such a *sui generis* gesture. Or propose concluding a treaty to outlaw landmines as if consent to their elimination could have been procured absent recognition of their military uselessness, and as if their outlawry would translate into their elimination. Or promote an international criminal court for war crimes, as if the political and military contexts in which war crimes were likely to occur, and the forces which would be brought to bear in prosecution, were somehow analogous to the social forces surrounding other criminal behavior. Or when they promote the adoption of human rights norms and codes, without noticing how often doing so substitutes for developing the cultural and political machinery necessary to promote the human dignity they are meant to guarantee.

In each of these cases, the argument is not simply that the initiative will be less successful than hoped, or will not succeed until a more complete international government is in place, but that these seemingly progressive and humanitarian initiatives will either make the problems worse or have unintended bad effects. So, a trial about Pinochet in the United Kingdom or Spain, far from being the first step towards a working international criminal law to defend human rights, establishes a random and unpredictable international prosecutorial machinery which undermines the most basic rights of prospective defendants. Or, outlawing land mines and other marginal military techniques, rather than beating the first sword into a ploughshare, reinforces the legitimacy of more violence than it prevents.

It is quite common for international humanitarians to overestimate the integration of the international governance machinery, to fantasize administrative and judicial components subsidiary to its legislature, or think of a distinct commercial sector subject to regulation by public lawmaking. Because international policy makers so often downplay the importance of their own expertise and overestimate the importance of constitutional structures as sites for policy making, they overlook differences in the sensibilities and professional vocabularies of the various disciplines involved in global governance, and overestimate the clarity with which humanitarian policy initiatives composed in one vocabulary and location will be translated into another. The result has been a repeated effort in one after another discipline to catch too many different fish with the same hook – for international lawyers, for example, the hook of broad normative texts attached to institutional mechanisms for accumulating technical expertise and reporting on violations. Consequently, when progressive international lawyers think of international economic institutions as alternative sites for public law making, they underestimate the difficulty of translating progressive regulatory initiatives into the quite different argot of trade professionals and often miss the opportunity to enlist the professional vocabulary of trade or commercial policy makers in their progressive projects.

Overestimating the unity and specificity of international policy making can also mean taking too seriously the notion that the international system is a world outside culture and politics, a neutral world of expertise, a universal world of sovereign equality, a normative world of respect for sovereign autonomy or the benignly cooperative world invoked by the phrase "international community." International policy makers too often take the fantasy world of characters they have imagined into existence at face value, treating governments as stand-ins for their people, treating the "international community" as something other than a media reference to a particular group of elites, or treating international "civil society" as if it were an embedded part of global cultural and political life, rather than a reference to the hodge-podge of advocacy institutions which have managed to gain access to international institutional machinery.

The result has been policy makers who imagine themselves innocent of political commitment or identity, and policy initiatives which present themselves as best practices detached from knowledge of, or responsibility for, distributional choices. It has meant policy made in a relative political vacuum - policies for "development" or "transition" suitable for all time and places because hatched in the a-political and universal hothouse of international expertise and policy makers, including the most humanitarian and progressive, who underestimate their engagement with and responsibility for the policies they make.

I think people have this at least partly in mind when they criticize the European Union policy making machinery for a deficit of democracy or a lack of transparency - the deeper problem is the tendency of European Commission policy makers to imagine themselves outside politics altogether, to experience politics as always somewhere else (last month in the Council, next month in the Parliament, and so forth), to think of politics as a *fact* pressuring for a response, or as a temptation (more dangerous even than corruption), rather than as an aspect of their own work, and to find their own detachment from it a virtue rather than either a vice or a delusion. But it is also true of progressives enthusiastically planning international missions to stabilize this or that trouble spot, or respond one or another humanitarian catastrophe –

living in an international professional cocoon of their own imagination they will often be blind to the consequences of their policies as translated into other contexts. The effort to intervene in places like Kosovo or East Timor or Palestine to "keep the peace" or "rebuild the society" or "strengthen the state" or provide "humanitarian assistance" *without* effecting the background distribution of power and wealth betrays this bizarre belief in the possibility of an international governance which does not govern.

Thinking themselves situated in an imaginary international community, international policy makers are particularly prone to under - or over - estimate the differences between different geographical, political or cultural policy contexts. This often means over or underestimating differences between the first and third worlds. When international policy makers take the first world as the "normal" background condition for policy making and overlook the distinctiveness of the developing world, we get policies which look uniform, but can have dramatically skewed results. Guarantees of religious freedom which generate religious pluralism in the first world and contribute to the increasing hegemony of modern proselytizing religions in the third, or trade regimes which leave complex social welfare systems intact in the first world, but force the third world to live in the bracing deregulatory wind of the trade regime unmediated by national or regional regulatory interventions. At the same time, the association of the international community with civilization, enlightenment or liberal virtue can lead policy makers to overestimate the difference between the first and third worlds - "orientalizing" the developing world. This can eliminate opportunities for alliance among people in the first and third worlds who share interests, while encouraging domestic political cultures in the developing world to organize themselves around opposition between domestic "tradition" and foreign "modernisation" despite the obvious presence of a third world in the first or a first world in the third.

### *How do policy makers see their world? Spatial mistakes and geographical misconceptions*

As we can begin to see, international policy makers operate with a map of the world in their heads which affects the types of proposals they make, the outcomes they both expect and bring about. Each profession involved in international policy making, of course, has a map of its own: the one foregrounding central banks and currency flows, the other troop movements and supply lines, yet another trade flows and productivity measurement. It makes sense to ask about the limitations these maps impose on humanitarian policy making. But there is also a set of ideas about space common to a broad range of people involved in global governance.

On this map, "the international community" is a large and real place. As we might expect, the map is also marked by the exaggerated size of well known political and historical hotspots, and quite often by the foreshortened perspective available high in the United Nations headquarters building, or from the space one inhabits flying among conferences, summits, or the meetings of commissions, councils and expert working groups. From this perspective, the sites of prior international engagement and disengagement loom large - Paschendale, Somme, Munich, Bretton Woods, or, closer to our day, Vietnam, Somalia, Cambodia, Bosnia, Congo, Iraq, Rwanda and so forth. Each offers an opportunity for a range of more and less plausible analogies - humanitarian engagement will work, will fail. Each stands for a "lesson," has added or subtracted from the humanitarian policy maker's toolkit of possible solutions. More importantly, these places, in all their divergent reality, lead policy makers to exaggerate the uniformity of international policy making — their ability, whatever the differences on the ground, to know what a "sanctions regimes" or a "currency bailout" entails and to compare their success here and there. The map encourages policy makers to think of their techniques as having shape, potential, potency abstracted from the context of their application, and precisely to overlook the specificity of context. In a way, navigating on the map becomes a substitute for navigating in the world.

This conceptual map can encourage would-be humanitarians to underestimate the constitutive effect of their own policy work on the world they confront. Take "rogue states" - when global policy makers use the term, they know to what and whom they refer. These places seem similar — their modes of their engagement in the world seem shared, and it seems sensible to work out policy ideas which would work across a range of rogues. And yet, how does a rogue learn his trade, his position, his possibilities? Why do rogue regimes converge in tactic and technique? When we evaluate the humanitarian potential of measures addressed to pre-existing difficulties of this type, we are likely to underestimate the co-responsibility of international governance for the world it governs. The same type of argument could be made of "rebel groups," "ethnic minorities," "insurgents," "belligerents," "indigenous peoples," "failed states" and so forth - these are roles in the world, to be sure, but they are also policy categories, and it easy to forget that the world is also looking at the policy makers, mapping their own possibilities and strategies.

Thinking about the world the international policy maker sees suggests other built in limits on the possibilities for humanitarian policy making. For example, the professional vocabularies of policy makers all map political and economic entities in different colors. Often the political entities figure larger than the economic, and are thought to either pre-exist or to follow the movement of economic forces. Political identities are often associated with places, regions, terrains, while economic entities float more freely, somehow off the map, or outside the space of policy altogether. Where institutions are shown at all, they are public institutions - there is a tiny mark for the Federal Reserve and the World Bank, but nothing for General Motors or Shell. Rhode Island might be shown, Luxembourg certainly would be, but Ted Turner, whose private land holdings in the United States alone are larger than Rhode Island and Delaware put together, would not appear. The world's spaces are divided up into political and legal jurisdictions, which don't overlap - and all of which are at least nominally "countries." Turner is said to own land *in* this and that country - but it is hard to think the sentence "the Mexican authorities govern activities *in* this and that corporation."

People have criticized this professional map in many ways. The most familiar criticism - that this arranges the political world into formally separate public spaces - is in some ways the least helpful. It returns us to the claim that the policy making machinery has been methodologically captured, again by formalism. The overly "formal" map gives governments more authority than they can responsibly exercise while limiting artificially what the international policy maker can accomplish. It is often argued that national governments have retained the authority to disable international policy making, but have not retained the capacity to resolve problems on their own. There is something to this charge. Some humanitarian policy proposals do overestimate the stability of political boundaries, just as some underestimate the boundedness of economic life. Policy makers often fail to inhabit the full range of their professional vocabulary, and sometimes give exaggerated deference to the formal boundaries of state power. But international policy making has never had a purely formal or territorial conception of political authority. From the first, the policy professions have worked with two mental maps - an ideal map of perfect sovereigns holding complete bundles of rights over clear territories, and a map riddled with exceptions, shared jurisdictions, non-sovereign right holders, disputed areas, internationalized territories, half-sovereigns, and so forth. Indeed, many of these deviations are the work of international policy itself. To evaluate the humanitarian potential of global governance as a whole, we need to understand the political consequences of a professional practice of *two* minds about the centrality of hard political boundaries.

As we go beneath this familiar argument about capture to the underlying consciousness shared by both sides of the formal/antiformal boundaries debate, we will notice that however stable or flexible the boundaries, the shared mental map might discourages engagement with things which happen *below the line of sovereignty.* When international policy makers wash their hands of the violence and injustice which attended the creation of states and accompanies their ongoing exercise of authority, progressive and humanitarian voices should be concerned. In a similar way, progressives have criticized the international policy makers for relegating international policy to the space *outside and between* all these political/legal jurisdictions. To Antarctica. Outer space. The seabed. To the issues posed by jurisdictional conflicts and the recognition of immunities. To the space in which a refugee can be found after leaving his country of origin and before settling in his new country of settlement. The space of things which cross boundaries, like smoke or fish. The space of transport. The result are progressive policies which address only those elements of a problem which cross or exceed national borders.

Consequently, international environmental policy has an odd shape – it covers the oceans, but with decreasing density as one moves closer to shore or on board a ship, it covers outer space, it covers those aspects of pollution flows which cross boundaries, it applies more densely to smoke than to sewage. Of course, with clever and expansive interpretation, international policy makers *could* stretch the reach of their engagement until very little escaped their purview. International policy makers know *how* to blur the boundaries which restrict their ambit, but their default conception is, from this point of view, unnecessarily self-limiting. The gradation and segmentation of authority leads international policy making to have a widely differential impact, and can reinforce the authority of precisely the boundaries it might be thought committed to undermine.

Regardless of how the boundaries of sovereignty constrain the ambit of international policy making, they also reinforce a limited conception of what international governance itself can be. Whether flexible or firm, the rights which international policy makers unbundle and apportion are the ideal rights of an ideal state with an ideal territory. Other conceptions of the points for policy engagement - private rights the most salient — are not part of the picture. This makes it more plausible to treat economic "forces" as naturally global, and political opportunities as naturally channeled through the jurisdictional capillaries of government. Whether or not the international policy maker is too respectful of sovereign rights, sovereign rights is what international policy making is, and can be, about. The arrangement of the world's political spaces into national and international domains, the distinction between an international space of governance and a local or national space of its application and enforcement can dramatically constrict the humanitarian potential for international policy making. Governance on this map is a public matter of exceptional intervention from "above," an oscillation between respecting and re-allocating public rights, policy the extension of a public regulatory order *into* or *onto* a pre-existing natural private order.

The policy makers' map is the map of potential public intervenors, of a space *above* sovereignty, a space in which sovereigns *conceptually* mingle, communicate, have "disputes." Things that happen in the international policy space are disembodied, the a-cultural and apolitical interactions of representatives and experts. For something to get into this space - to be "taken up on the international plane" - it must be a *grave* matter, a *serious* breach, cause *material* damage, result in *irrevocable* harm, *shock* the conscience - or meet any of numerous other substantive tests for reversing the presumption that things below the line of sovereignty are not within the purview of the international policy maker. Sovereigns can do as they like at home - for their actions to be respected *on the international plane* they must meet certain standards. Of the things which cross borders and of the exercises of sovereign power which annoy other sovereigns, international policy gives its overt attention only to the most serious and grievous. Its influence on the background conditions in which more and less grievous problems develop is off the screen.

Although we might well think "the environment" simply *is* a global phenomenon when we argue for international environmental policy making in the environmental field - when we then *do* international policy making, the environment has become something else altogether. There is the terrain of physical activity, private activity, economic activity, of snail darters, financiers and property owners. Above that are public rights to intervene, regulate, distort, reorganize. These are mostly, usually, normally, allocated to national sovereigns and their sub-entities. The question for international policy makers is when this presumption should be reversed. International environmental issues occur, and international policy making begins, when the activities of fish and air and capital — whose primary existence is below the line of a formal sovereignty - somehow escape those boundaries, cross them, when one or another sovereign has become annoyed at a *particularly grievous* environmental act of another. In this sense, international policy making is about the tips of icebergs, while ignoring the influence of international governance on what lies beneath the waterline.

This way of thinking also focuses international policy making on the boundaries of its own exercise - on the relationship between sovereign discretion and the rearrangements required by international public policy. The line between the global and the local is harnessed to the task of holding back - and then engaging — the domains of politics, culture, economy, society, from the distanced height of reason. And the progressive readjustments in the line - raising issues to the international plane, descending to manage local disputes, re-allocating sovereign rights over territory to other entities - are themselves exercises, indeed the primary exercises, of policy.

One consequence is that international policy makers become invested in their proposals as signs for the possibility of international policy making itself. At stake in every policy making effort is the much larger promise that international policy making is possible at all. As a result, individual policy making exercises are easily overwhelmed by the needs and ambitions of the policy making apparatus itself. We find humanitarian and progressive voices arguing that trying Pinochet in Britain might well be bad for Chile, for reconciliation, for justice, for the victims and the defendants — but it was great for the emergence of an international criminal law of individual responsibility. As progressives, we have overinvested in the status of "international" sites and situations, and under-invested in people and problems which have not risen onto the international plane. We have allowed allegiance to a cosmopolitan promise of *future* humanitarian governance to distract us from the political work necessary for humanitarian government today.

*What do policy makers think they are doing? Intervening.*

Humanitarian and progressive participants in global governance think of international policy making as intervention by the international community on or into a local world which is, until the moment of intervention, animated by forces endogenous to it. They share with other international policy makers the idea that there is no international policy where international policy makers have not acted, and a preoccupation with debate about *whether or not* to intervene. Intervention requires justification and authorization, requires that someone make an exception. This familiar liberal idea about public policy making has a particular resonance in the international context, where policy makers think of themselves spatially as *outside* the vertical authority of any sovereign. Although many international policy regimes have been self-consciously designed as modes of non-intervention or neutrality for either the international community or its members, the idea that the terrain is already covered by a layer of responsible sovereigns makes it easy for the international policy maker to sustain the idea that not making an exception to intervene is letting someone else take responsibility.

The idea that one should not intervene without good reason and good authority erects a conceptual hurdle in front of their every initiative. What standing do they have? In what sense is the situation exceptional enough to warrant their engagement? By whose leave do they/we act? International policy makers, including the most humanitarian, find it all too easy to take responsibility for engagements, but not for disengagements. They find it easier to take responsibility for successes than for failures - which can always seem to have been the result of forces on the ground, of resistance to intervention by people outside the international community.

And they find it easier to imagine that intervention can itself be accomplished without disturbing local conditions, without taking responsibility for local political and economic conditions, without compromising the posture of neutrality, of remaining external to the allocation of stakes so central to the project of governing. That one can also intervene without intervening - freezing the situation, inserting oneself between "the" parties, that one can govern on an interim basis, preparing the way for a future political reconstitution, impose policies as passive assistance in a natural process of "structural adjustment."

The autonomy and disengagement of the most caring international intervenor is embraced by tradition and defended by numerous rules and institutional practices. Think of the Red Cross inspector going in and out of prisons, the peacekeeper wearing a United Nations helmet, the agricultural or health advisor on the ground in a rural village. We imagine these people wandering about the scenes of local catastrophe in a kind of parallel universe. There and not there, in the world, but not of it.

The hesitance to "intervene" is not evenly distributed. It is stronger when the "intervention" will have a clearer impact on background norms and institutions – when it will, for example, affect private property rights rather than public regulatory claims, when the situation can be figured as part of the naturally occurring market rather than the natural domain of state authority, or as part of the naturally occurring local culture, rather than as a technical aspect of a global problem. These conceptual boundaries – between the local and the global, between private and public law, between the economy and the state, between culture and the technical, act like spatial boundaries, cabining and channeling policy making. Regardless of the nature of the problem, it will be easier to make policy through public law than private law, when framed as a political rather than an economic matter, or as a technical rather than a cultural matter. In each case, it will be understood to be less aggressive an "intervention," and will require a lower threshold of justification and authority to act.

Innumerable progressive and humanitarian policy initiatives have crashed on the rocks of this hesitation to engage in "cultural imperialism." The hesitation to intervene when it would seem to implicate "culture" is troubling not only because it ignores the effects of international governance on the arrangements of power or wealth within the "cultural," but also because the cultural frame is itself so much a construct of the vocabulary which uses it as a reason to avoid engagement. From a progressive point of view, this is particularly unfortunate because it turns out that the vague and malleable term "culture" often seems to be invoked where issues of concern to the left are at stake – in matters which implicate local solidarities and communal forms, individual health and welfare, traditional beliefs, and the status of marginal members of society or disadvantaged groups, including women. A willingness to intervene to achieve economic development or political peace, but not to affect "culture" often introduces an anti-progressive bias into international policy making.

We can see this easily by thinking about a national market based economic regulatory scheme aimed to bring about "development." This can often be supported by international institutions without seeming like an intervention at all – the scheme is a national one, its policies are passive enablers for the decisions of market actors, property rights are left alone. To blame the international institutions for the results would be unfair – they are designed by local elites to whose call the international institutions have merely responded, and the agent of their implementation is the "force" of "the market." The threshold level of justification and authority necessary for international policy making here is very low – commercial and economic policies, nationally developed, market inspired. Of course this sort of scheme can have dramatic effects on the fabric of social life, moving people from rural to urban settings, transforming educational opportunities, making workers of peasants, changing the distribution of religious belief, the authority of traditional communal leaders, changing the opportunities for young people, for women, and so forth. The collection of such changes we know as "modernization" is what we mean by development, and is the objective of all sorts of economic policy making, both nationally and internationally.

But now let us imagine an international policy initiative which would bring about directly what these economic reforms have brought about indirectly - transferring ownership of assets to and among private parties, restructuring local production, transforming the social and educational opportunities available for rural and urban workers, for women, secularizing the economy, destroying traditional cultural sites of resistance to economic modernization - suddenly the hurdle of justification and authorization jumps up. Lots of people oppose the intervention, including many progressives and humanitarians. Those who favored it begin to lose confidence. Imagine further that an international institution or foreign NGO responded to requests by local feminists with a policy initiative to reduce the incidence of a traditional practice like clitorodectomy in the countryside. The bar is much higher - now we are in the core of culture, religion, the family, personal autonomy. Even the most progressive internationalist gets uncomfortable. Gets uncomfortable even if it turns out the original national market-based development policy will have a far more profound effect on the actual level of female genital mutilation in the countryside - may even eliminate country life altogether.

It is no wonder good hearted internationalists have a hard time evaluating global governance initiatives in pragmatic terms, or remaining focused on distributional consequences. Their policy making vernacular shifts their attention to a set of conceptual worries - what is culture and what is economy, what is local and what is global, what is public and what is private? Above all, when will we be said to have "intervened?" And what then was our exceptional justification and authority? By what *right* did we go so far? International policy makers focus on who makes policy rather than the policy they will make, and on the appropriate form for policy rather than the resulting outcomes of policy-making. Discussions about what policy to make are transformed into discussions about how much and whether to intervene, with conceptual boundaries between public and private operating as vague proxies for outcomes.

*What do policy makers see as movable and immovable in their world? What is the background terrain for policy making, and what is open to policy initiatives and professional intervention?*

Policy makers typically focus their attention on the *intervention*, on the justifications , authorizations and modalities for action, and think of their interventions as open to their manipulation. Legal policy makers, for example, are often quick to think of ways to rearrange and rebundle legal entitlements, treating the entire domain of law as an artificial and plastic one. The *terrain* upon which policy makers see themselves intervening, by contrast, seems more natural, a pre-existing domain less amenable to manipulation. For legal policy makers, it is normal to think of politics or economics as natural processes to which they can only react. This idea of a passive background and an active foreground leads policy makers to underestimate both the degree of agency in the context to accept or resist policy projects and their own ongoing influence in the background terrain.

Of course difference professional disciplines may see different things as background and foreground. For political scientists or economists, "the law" may be background - and it is common that they would treat its provisions in an overly rigid fashion, underestimating the plasticity of the law as experienced from the inside, as well as its ongoing engagement with both politics and economics. Ideas about foreground and background will often be part of arguments about the deficiencies of specialization. It turns out, as we have seen, that things often look more rigid from the outside.

It may turn out, however, that an entire policy vernacular may share a set of underlying ideas about what is foreground and what background. The political consequences will hinge, of course, on what is, in fact, understood to be open to active intervention and what seems to belong to the naturally passive terrain. For the international humanitarian, it is common to think of international policy making as a domain of reason, civilization, pragmatism, modernity, expertise, arriving on a terrain of passion, backwardness, tradition. It is easy to see how this might rub people living in that terrain the wrong way, stiffening opposition. Identifying the local as "traditional," when it may well have been some amalgam of serendipity and the effect of prior interventions, can reinforce the authority of what the international policy maker has come to change. It can also encourage international policy makers to overestimate the novelty of their initiatives, and miss opportunities for weaving their efforts into the existing local context. This took on a dramatic dimension when international policy makers turned their attention to restructuring the economies of post-socialist societies, undervaluing existing economic and social relations and the opportunities for their engagement in the project of restructuring.

But the policy vernacular can also become limited by the process of continually separating foreground from background, and remaining committed to the idea that policy is about the foreground, regardless of what precisely figures where. Consider humanitarian efforts to restrict the international use of force. If we were to catalog the norms and institutions which affect the incidence of military violence, which structure the incentives and possibilities for using military force and protect those who do from scrutiny, many would be cultural, private, local, religious and economic institutions, norms and practices. A full catalog of the "law about war," would include private law rules about producing, selling and transporting arms, norms and institutional structures facilitating logistical supply, norms affecting incentives to become soldiers, and many more. Many of these would be international - or would have been affected by international policy making — just as many would be national. International norms, like national norms, would often justify and legitimate the use of force.

Humanitarian policy making attention will focus on only some of these norms - often, but not necessarily, those which are international and public, rather than national or private. It is not surprising that humanitarians will associate their own efforts with this class of norms, and associate the production of force with all the rest. As humanitarians become ever more focused on those norms they think of as foreground, they may become fixated on those which are the least significant in generating military violence, even as they underestimate the extent to which their favorite tools have anti-humanitarian potentials and uses.

This phenomenon is quite general. Across a range of initiatives and policy sectors, policy makers underestimate the plasticity and policy potential of what they take to be the "background" and overestimate the benevolence and instrumental effectiveness of what they take to be the foreground of policy. Politics can be background to law, passion to reason, the economy to the state, private to public law — and also the other way around. In each case, policy makers underestimate the contestable and their own complicity in what they see as background.

Assumptions about foreground and background can bias even scrupulously evenhanded policy making. To the extent some economies rely on public and others on private law norms to achieve distributive aims, an apparently universal international arbitration regime which treats public and private norms differently - as part of a malleable foreground and an undisturbed background - will have different effects in different places even if its procedural structure and substantive morns are completely neutral. An international mediation effort which treats "states" as pre-existing political entities and other international "entities" or "institutions" as malleable or artificial constructions of law or policy may well come to a conflict with every good intention of remaining evenhanded, but be unable to avoid a bias in favor, say, of the Israeli "state," and against the Palestinian "entity."

The idea that politics pre-exists an artificial legal intervention also encourages international policy makers to think of their own policy work as weak, against the powerful forces of nature unleashed through the political activities of others. Although it seems natural to think of Macedonia or Mexico as more "real" than the UNHCR, it is unclear why we should. And doing so can dramatically affect the range of policy engagements which seem legitimate.

It can also make it seem as if one can never get enough international law - but that one always already has an excess of international politics. As progressives, we should be concerned about precisely the reverse problem. There is no shortage of international governance mechanisms and regimes, but almost no attention, by international policy makers or anyone else, to constructing a conscious global politics and shared political culture.

*How do they understand history? Progress narratives as programs and international policy making as a humanitarian religion*

Policy makers also share ideas about time and history which channel and limit their work. Unsurprisingly, moments of international policy making success and failure figure prominently in their shared historical narrative. This is a grand story of the slow and unsteady progress of law against power, policy against politics, reason against ideology, international against national, order against chaos in international affairs over three hundred and fifty years. In this story, international governance is itself a mark of civilization's progress: law brought to politics, civilization brought to primitive societies, reason brought to passion, the universal brought to the particular. International policy making has always or aspired to be the same thing: a humanitarian, rational and civilized alternative to the messy worlds of national politics. Over time global governance has had advances and set-backs. There have been sharp breaks in the story — the two world wars of the last century, the global depression of the 1930s, various moments of economic or political nationalism, during which only a few have carried the torch for the cosmopolitan promise of international governance. And there have been great moments of institutional and normative renewal. When you add it all up, there has been a great deal of progress - the world today is more international and more governed — but there remains a long way to go.

That this story is largely a myth, retold in different ways in each of the professional disciplines associated with international governance, is not surprising. This sort of mythologizing is common - policy makers turning their own achievements into the stuff of legend. But it can be more than that. Progress narratives of this sort can become policy programs, both by solidifying a professional consensus about what has worked and by defining what counts as progress for the international governance system as a whole. This can redirect policy makers from solving problems to completing the work of a mythological history, orienting or shaping their efforts to build the international system.

These progress myths affect the spatial maps policy makers have in their heads, identifying the in and the out, the up-to-date and the old fashioned. The idea that post-socialist or third world societies are "behind" and need to "catch up" before it is sensible to think of them as full participants in the international arrangements common to wealthy industrial societies affects the pace and substance of much international policy making. International policy makers find it natural to think of these societies being shocked by the market in ways which would be unthinkable within the industrialized West. We need only compare the idea that Portugal or Greece needed to be jump-started on democracy by immediate entry into the European Communities with the treatment accorded Eastern European applicants who need to "catch up" before membership can be contemplated to see the effects of progress narratives of this type. Within international policy making, something similar distinguishes the legitimacy and weight of voices articulating their objectives in different terms.

Those who speak the language of antiformalism, transnationalism, functionalism, civil society, are understood to speak the language of international community - while those who insist upon their sovereign entitlements, while often respected, are understood to be more primitive players. This can turn out to have an anti-progressive effect, if marginal countries like Iraq more often express themselves in terms more formal than those used to defend the prerogatives of the great powers or the international community itself. We need only think of Saddam Hussein, insisting on his sovereignty, his autonomy, on a narrow and formal reading of the Security Council's various resolutions. Or of the Third World recent conferences on the environment or women or intellectual property, insisting on their sovereignty, their autonomy, their rights. Although the savvy policy maker would recognize these as completely plausible moves in the vernacular, they are also marked as discrediting. To be for international law is to go beyond forms, as we have gone beyond politics. To be humanitarian or progressive is to be for the progress of international law, without focusing on the distributional outcomes of professional ideas of this type. Whether form favors or disfavors the weak in a given case becomes less important to policy makers than the sense that formal claims constitute and mark the marginal as outdated.

These historical stories solidify the sense that something called an "international community" exists, even if in a spatially disembodied way. Indeed, the "international community" seems to exist more firmly in time than in space. Through time it can be said to have acted, to have "agreed" to some things and foregone agreement on others. The international community is the thing which has repeatedly aspired to respond to war with law and reason, which has built an ever more solid normative fabric, an ever more elaborated list of precedents for intervention, an ever larger toolkit for policy making, whose constituents were in the forefront of the battle for human rights and so forth. Such progress narratives reinforce the collective identity of participants in global governance – we are those who have stood against politics, against religion, in favor of peace and humanitarianism, and not those who fail to share our secular, cosmopolitan, and pragmatic history. Ours is not the history of a culture or a people or a place, but of an idea, an abstraction, a commitment, an orientation.

But more importantly, these stories establish a tradition of progress against which individual doctrinal innovations can be judged. The common myth of a more formal past of state sovereignty out of which an international community developed by rendering itself more fluid and active in rearranging sovereign rights becomes itself a sign for progress. To be fluid and antiformal is to be part of a governance capacity more attuned not only to doing things globally, but to doing progressive things globally. This makes it easy for policy makers to mix up their progressive or humanitarian ambitions for society with their commitment to the progress of what they understand to be their own humanitarian professions.

It is surprising how many international policy arguments read as arguments for international policy, how often more global governance becomes a substitute for addressing particular conflicts and social problems. International policy makers should certainly care about human rights or alleviating the AIDS crisis or reducing the violence of warfare --- but when one reforms the human rights machinery to be less formal, or purges the World Health Organization of its attachment to sovereign forms, or relativizes the law of war to erase its formal commitments to a distinction between war and peace, neutral and belligerent, there is progress --- a progress more important, more general, more historically enduring and reliable, than the quotidian matter of actually helping any particular person avoid AIDS or landmines or torture.

International policy making sees itself, the conditions of its deployment and the likely results of its engagement, as in some sense automatically humanitarian. The idea that international policy making is already and automatically part of the solution rather than the problem has numerous sources - the tendency to think of policy choices in constitutional (centralized/decentralized) rather than substantive terms, the association of international policy making with the triumph of an enlightened civilization over a primitive politics, the tendency to overlook background conditions or treat them as exclusively responsible for difficulties or setbacks - all this gives international policy making the feeling of being a religion rather than a governance practice. The incidence of international policy making has become itself an object of humanist devotion, a sort of fetish for those committed to humanitarian objectives. It seems a progressive or humanitarian thing for policies to be made internationally, regardless of what those policies are.

This sort of prejudice can blind international policy makers to the regressive consequences of their own activities. If you speak of international environmental law, you typically speak of the effort to throw a few environmentally protective norms over the despoliation practices of individuals and governments. And yet, if you asked for a catalog of all the international norms which affect the international incidence of environmental damage, the list would include many which encouraged despoliation - perhaps more than the number encouraging protection. International law and policy offer the environmental despoiler, like the war criminal or the human rights abuser, a great deal of comfort and protection - and yet the effort to address these "problems" through international policy making has an automatic humanitarian feel.

In fact, even when the particular projects misfire, and solution to the practical problems remains out of reach, so long as the field remains oriented towards "governing," particular failures of government become simply warnings to do more, to intensify one's efforts to build the system as a whole. International policy makers, in this sense, live in an interminable procedural or constitutional present, polishing their tools, embroidering their technique, strengthening itself, that it might one day tackle particular substantive problems. It would perhaps be more accurate to say that solutions to particular problems emerge as a by-product of this system building agenda, as an almost accidental consequence of professional practices of self-effacement, marginalization and a need not to know that one is governing.

## Progressives and International Policy Making

One makes international policy to distribute. Humanitarian and progressive policy making, when it works, results in more humanitarian or progressive distributions of resources, status, authority, wealth. We should evaluate policy making by its likely consequences, and we should evaluate global governance by its outcomes. Too often, progressives hesitate to do so. They share with other policy makers an allergy to the mantle of rulership. Like other policy makers, progressives have cultivated a posture of disengaged modesty about the exercise of governmental authority, protected by a policy making vernacular which stresses the exceptional and technical nature of their "interventions."

The policy making vernacular gives policy makers many substitutes for a clear-eyed look at the consequences of their action. They can find comfort in the forms of engagement, in the structures and signs of international policy making itself. When progressives and humanitarians evaluate global governance, they tend either to accept its humanitarian motives at face value, or suspect that the machinery has been captured by unfriendly forces. What remains difficult is either an overt politics which acknowledges its will to rule or an acknowledgment of the underlying politics of the policy making vocabulary used to imagine, propose, engage, accept and implement international policy initiatives.

We see this reticence to acknowledge the exercise of power in an allergy to colonialism. Despite the similarities between the efforts of international policy makers to extend their influence over places like Kosovo or East Timor and those of colonial powers of the last two centuries, we struggle to understand these interventions in a different way. Any different way will do: as willed, consented to, in the interest of the governed, respectful of local cultures and powers, mirror to sovereign desire, interventions which do not alter local arrangements, which are temporary, which facilitate integration into a larger world, mere technical assistance, structural adjustment, humanitarian aid, peace keeping, a thin blue line. But colonialism spoke about itself similarly in its time - the intervenor who would not intervene, the civilizer, consented to, invited, cautiously respectful. International policy making is a government without responsibility, without the face of engagement, without a name it could dare to speak, even to itself.

Progressives who worry about the limits and politics of the constitution for global governance and about the political capture of the policy making professions have helped us to break free of this mold. Institutional structure can matter, and the policy professions often do narrow the range of political possibility by becoming caught in one or another ideology or policy fad. This can limit policy making the way languages which are word rich or word poor may shape their literature. But this sort of limit turns out to be less significant than it would at first appear. Word poor languages come up with all sorts of ways to express things, just as word rich languages can become expressively stalled.

I have suggested questions we might ask to get beyond worry about constitutions and capture – what do the policy makers see, where do they think they are in the world, how do they understand progress, what do they think is their work, how do they experience their own role? These aspects of the policy making vocabulary are more difficult to identify, their consequences often more difficult to assess. The policy making vernacular is more widely shared, but also less conscious and more difficult to see, its politics in particular cases harder to understand.

As a participant in global governance who shares both the impulse for more enlightened social and economic policy and the intuition that this will mean policy at the international level, I am dismayed by the difficulty humanitarian internationalists have had understanding the limits and the politics of their expertise. The objections I have brought together here are intended to highlight dimensions of international policy making which are often overlooked. But because they go so directly to the sensibility and spirit with which so much international policy making is undertaken, it is hard to imagine the international policy maker taking them to heart. They call for a completely different sort of mental map, a different understanding of the tools and vocabularies with which international policy makers engage the world, a rereading of the progressive historical myths which provide so many of the default ideas proposed in the name of international policy reform, an altered consciousness about the will to power and false modesty of policy making, an embrace of policy making as the exercise of power, not as advice or description or service – policy making as decision, rather than analysis, in the present rather than in the indefinite future. Perhaps all we can do at this point is try to unthink those habits of mind which prevent international policy makers from confronting the political consequences of their vernacular. We might practice mental exercises or heuristics to help us unravel the effects of the establishment consciousness about policy making.

One practice of mental resistance would be this: set aside the impulse to think about international policy making in constitutional terms. Simply set aside questions about the level at which policy should be made, pursue an aggressively Zen-like agnosticism about *whether or not to intervene*, about the appropriate mix of *centralization and decentralization*, and about the form policy should take in general. Ask not whether we prefer *formal or antiformal* legal structures, *substantive or procedural* legal rules, or how much *discretion* is optimal. Ask how we wish to transform the distribution of power, status and authority in society, and speak about winners and losers, about gains and losses.

Another useful heuristic: abandon faith in the automatically progressive and humanitarian character of international policy making itself. Reject the idea that international law and governance are a worthy end in themselves, and embrace the dark side, the ambivalence, the historical involvement of our own professional tools in constituting the problems we now seek to solve. This would mean foregrounding the role of international policy making in the constitution of national power – the powers and political cultures against which it sets itself as a weak reformer. It would mean acknowledging the range of background norms of international and national law which legitimate and defend the projects and distributions we understand as obstacles to humanism. And it would mean accepting the pathology of our own professional vernacular.

Finally, root out the idea that international policy making is weak, partial, fragile, and in need of our fealty. Stop thinking our goal is to advance or retard the cause of international governance, of policy making itself. Abandon the image of policy making as advising, wishing, foreshadowing, describing, rather than governing, ruling, exercising authority. Rather than marginal players throwing a frail network of norms and institutions over an unruly world or intervening exceptionally on a pre-existing terrain, we should see ourselves as participants in that world, with our own culture, power and authority, pursuing projects with consequences for ourselves and others.

This will mean conflict and disagreement about outcomes, also on the left. But only if we give up the posture of speaking to power from the domain of knowledge, *without* giving up our role as experts who speak the policy making vernacular, will we become active participants in an engaged global politics. It should be our task to build a mode of politics, and a mode of governance, which takes responsibility for itself as a ruler, allocating and deciding in a world for which our policy vocabulary offers no sure guidance, and in which our progressive and humanitarian commitments have been opened to contestation and conflict. The posture of progressive policy makers after the fall of expertise and commitment into doubt should not be modesty, but affirmation and decision.

NORTH
EAST
SOUTH
WEST

## The Instrumentalization of the State by Transnational Corporations: The Case of Public Services

Matthias Finger

### Introduction

The State has always been an ambiguous construct: from the hope and promise of the poor in the form of generalized democracy, freedom from oppression, equity and justice to military destruction, colonization, and ruthless conquest, the State spans all variations from the best to the worst. Its ambiguity constitutes in fact its very nature. Literature abounds as to what the State exactly is, and the appreciation of the State depends to a large extent on the perspective one adopts: right and left share the belief in a profoundly good State, albeit of different dimensions, whereas anarchists have been skeptical since its very inception. Until the recent globalizations, believers in the State have always prevailed. But now, it has become possible and legitimate to look at the Nation-State from a more critical perspective. This is the perspective of its instrumentalization.

Indeed, while the State was controversial as a sovereign actor, its dangers might become even more obvious once it becomes instrumentalized by supra-national powers. As a matter of fact, so goes my argumentation, the State might well be more dangerous as an instrument of TNCs than it is an autonomous actor. Furthermore, the more organized the State is, the more dangerous it will become in its instrumentalization. On the contrary, a bureaucratic and inefficient State might also be inefficient in the hands of TNCs. The question thus is whether the State can resist its own instrumentalization or which strategies it can adopt to avoid it. Some authors have written about the State and its instrumentalization from a political or even from an ideological perspective. They have shown, for example, that States are subservient to neo-liberal ideologies or otherwise adopt policies favorable to TNCs (e.g., Coméliau 2002). In this chapter, however, we want to look at the State and its instrumentalization from an institutional and an organizational perspective. We examine how the State reacts as a set of organizations and as an institution in the age of globalization, and how TNCs precisely take advantage of this very situation.

This chapter is structured in the following way: in a first section, I will briefly recall the history of the Nation-State and its ambiguous nature, which is, as I will argue, its very essence. In other words, the State is a militaristic construct to begin with, originally created to defend itself against outside enemies, yet managing to convince its inhabitants that this is in their main interest as well (e.g., the argument of the citizen-soldier). In this chapter, I will also outline the main stages of State development, namely via the process of industrialization up to today's age of globalization.

The second section will then address the issue of globalization. Of course, the first signs of threats to the State appear as far back as the 1970s (e.g., financial crisis, cultural crisis), but it is since the 1990s that the State is coming under increasingly severe pressures. In this section, I will furthermore describe the State as an organization and as an institution, showing how it has to evolve also in these dimensions (e.g., organizational ands institutional transformations) if it wants to survive. Finally, I will outline here several adaptation strategies of the State and assess their likelihood.

The third section addresses a parallel evolution, namely the rise of TNCs. This is a new phenomenon, which has taken place over the past 20 years only. After a general introduction on TNC evolution, I will look at a particular group of TNCs, i.e., the ones that make their money with the public sector and with providing public services. Their growth perfectly mirrors the transformation of the State as an institution and as a set of organizations. In a short historical overview, I will show how the State has given birth to the very TNCs that now are instrumentalizing it.

The fourth section will then examine the exact mechanisms by which the State is currently being instrumentalized by the TNCs. Again, I will focus mainly on so-called "public services TNCs", as they are the most perfect illustration of this process. I will not only identify the various strategies TNCs use to instrumentalize the State, but I will moreover illustrate these strategies with examples from the water sector, where public services TNCs have been most prominent so far.

The fifth section will attempt to generalize from the example of public services TNCs to TNCs' strategies more generally. I will argue that not only public services TNCs currently are and increasingly will instrumentalize the State and at the same time I will highlight how the State itself is selling out to TNCs as it fights for its own survival in the age of globalization. Furthermore, I will examine the possibilities as well as the likelihood to resist such instrumentalization, and what forms such resistance would take. Finally, I will assess current State reform efforts against this overall tendency towards the State's instrumentalization: will such reforms make such instrumentalization more or less likely?

## History of the Nation-State

Instrumentalization is not something the Nation-State was worried about during its inception phase. Rather, the main worry of the Nation-State was security and sovereignty, i.e., the ability to control its borders and what happened within it. This ambition to control - more precisely to command and control - shaped the very nature of the State, and, we argue, will be of interest to its instrumentalizers. In this first section, I would therefore like to crystallize the very nature of the Nation-State and identify more precisely what, in its very nature, makes the State interesting for instrumentalizers. In a second step, I will highlight the main steps of the development of the Nation-State, leading up to the public services it provides which are of particular interest to us in this article. Finally, I will highlight my particular look at the Nation-State as an institution and as a set of organizations, i.e., the look which theoretically underpins my instrumentalization argument.

### *The epistemological nature of the Nation-State*

The Nation-State is of military origin (e.g., Clarke 1971, Giddens 1985, McNeill 1982). As such, its main concern is - and has remained ever since - its sovereignty and control over its territory, which of course also implies the control over the peoples within its territory. The originality of the Nation-State, as opposed to all previous forms of territorial control is the fact that the peoples are included and so-to-speak themselves "involved" in their own control. This is done by so-called democracy theory, whereby each individual is given a vote by which it can, theoretically, participate in the management of its own yet collective destiny. Not astonishingly, the inhabitants of any given national territory are now simultaneously citizens *and* soldiers. They are from now on interested in shaping their national destiny, as they are, at the same time, interested in defending the territory and future they are shaping (Meinecke 1957; Scott 1998).

Indeed, as Max Weber has convincingly argued, the competitive advantage of the State over all other forms of domination is its legitimacy, i.e. the legitimate nature of domination. People will accept such domination, he argues, because of the democratic nature of the

State. In our view, which admittedly is inspired by anarchism, it is domination nevertheless. Therefore, and even though such domination may be legitimate and codified by law and administrative procedures, the fact of the matter is that the State is an authoritarian construct of military origin. As such, it is able to coerce its inhabitants, albeit in the name of some larger democratic principles. This is its very competitive advantage over any other form of coercion (Weber 1922).

This epistemological nature of the State makes it particularly interesting for whoever would like to use it for its own purposes. In fact, what makes the State an interesting instrument for potential instrumentalizers is (1) the fact that it is structured around control of whatever happens within, and (2) that the peoples are tied to their own control (e.g., democracy) through all kind of "participatory mechanisms". As we will argue, the fact that the State is the currently the only known and available legitimate form of domination, makes it particularly relevant for TNCs who would like to have it their own way, without however having the legitimacy to do so.

*The evolution of the Nation-State's main functions*

Besides its above epistemological nature, the Nation-State of course also has an organizational and an institutional nature. As such, we may recall that the Nation-State is, above all, a European product, which, thanks to colonization, has been exported to the rest of the world. Furthermore, the State is also a pre-industrial construct, which gradually had to learn to adjust to substantial changes in its environment, in particular to the process of industrialization (e.g., McNeill 1963; Nef 1954).

More precisely, the Nation-State in its modern form emerges in the context of the French Revolution in response to popular pressure. From then on, individuals want to play an active role as citizens in shaping their destiny, thus the new institutional arrangements guaranteeing their active participation in decision-making. However, at that time, the State's main functions still mainly pertain to issues of external and internal security.

These functions are substantially enlarged as the industrial revolution progresses, thus creating new challenges for the Nation-State. Indeed, the process of industrialization created all kinds of serious problems for its citizens, namely inequalities, poverty, uprooting, and many others more. It was therefore logical that the State, which after all was supposed to defend the interests of its citizens, stepped in and sought to repair the worst effects of industrialization. Thus emerged a new social function of the State, along with all kinds of social programs. During the 1960s and 1970s, similar challenges emerged for the Nation-State, which took the form of environmental destruction. Again, the State stepped in as a repair actor, thus seeking to offset the worst environmental effects of industrialization.

It is towards the end of the 19th century and again within the context of the industrial revolution, that the State acquired yet another function, namely the function of service provider or producer. Indeed, industrial development needed an active and powerful promoter, given the fact that capital accumulation was too small so far. More precisely, the dynamics unleashed by industrialization required a strong promoter, especially in the area of infrastructure technologies, where investment and risk bearing was, and still today is, particularly needed. In other words, the State stepped in and became a "development agency" active in the communications (telecommunications, postal services), energy (electricity production and distribution), and transport (railways, roads) sectors.

In short, over time, the State has accumulated three different functions, namely (1) defense, security, and law and order, (2) repair, and (3) production. In parallel, the resources needed and used by the State in order to fulfill these functions have grown accordingly. In other words, from being a defense entity, the State has now gradually become a development agency whose future is entirely intertwined with the economic development. The prosperity of the State as an institution and as a set of organizations and the one of the national economy can no longer be separated. In other words, and in addition to its epistemological nature as a legitimate source of power, one must now also think of the State as a development agency. As such, the destiny of the State is inseparably tied to continued economic growth and expansion. And this is precisely what makes the State vulnerable to pressure, as it puts its own survival as an institution and as a set of organizations above serving the people.

*The Nation-State as institution and as a set of organizations*

This evolution in the State's main functions has, of course, not taken place without significant changes and developments in the State's main organizational entities, most of which have simply expanded. This can be said of the national administration, of the judicial apparatus, but also of regional and local government. More precisely, these administrative entities pertain to the State's different functions, which means that the defense organizations have become a State in the State, that the health and social security organizations have become equally powerful, not to mention that the various public enterprises have generally behaved quite autonomously.

Conceptually, all these different organizations are supposed to be part of the same State, but organizational dynamics makes it obvious that the coherence of the State is at jeopardy parallel to its growth as an organization. This is, in fact, a simple matter of organizational sociology (e.g., Clegg 1989; Crozier 1987). As the State grows, it diversifies functionally. Different organizational entities develop different goals, which are no longer necessarily coherent or compatible, a typical phenomenon of goal enlargement and goal displacement. Once under pressure, these different organizational entities will fight for their own survival. Quite logically, then, recent public sector reform efforts have become a means to help these organizational entities to survive, rather than a means to streamline the State (e.g., Pollitt 1990).

Paradoxically, and despite its growth as an organization, not much change has occurred in the institutional nature of the State. Indeed, the institutional mechanisms have roughly stayed the same since the State's pre-industrial origins: for example, the respective powers of the citizens, of the political parties, of the parliament, and of the government have roughly stayed the same, while only the administration has significantly increased its powers. But, because the administration has simultaneously become fragmented, its increase in power has not had any significant effects on the overall power balance. During the late 1960s and the 1970s, the institutional structure of the State was challenged by social movements, but finally the State managed to absorb this opposition and channel it into strengthening itself, in part by allowing for new political parties. In short, until the early 1990s, when globalization started to have its first effects, the State had increased its functions, had substantially grown as an organization, but had hardly changed from an institutional point of view. This all is going to change with "globalization".

## Globalizations and the Nation-State

Globalization has multiple dimensions, which constitute as many challenges for the Nation-State. Indeed, my argument is that the State as a profoundly pre-industrial institution has managed to adapt to the industrial revolution, has thrived during the Cold War, and will also adjust to globalization. Nevertheless, globalization is, in my view, the biggest challenge so far, requiring some substantial changes (from the Nation-State). In this section, I will first crystallize the main aspects of globalization, derive from there the main threats to the State, and then identify the main four challenges, including the challenge of its instrumentalization. Finally, I will indicate how the State is trying to react to these challenges.

*The different dimensions of globalization*

Globalization has numerous dimensions, not all of which have emerged simultaneously. Nevertheless, all dimensions lead to the same conclusion, namely to the fact that everything is currently being globalized or potentially globalizable, except the Nation-State (e.g., Eatwell 1998; Goldblatt, Held, McGrew, and Perraton 1997). Let me briefly recall these main dimensions of globalization by listing them in the order of their historical emergence, i.e., technological, financial, ecological, economic, and cultural globalizations.

Technological development is totally intertwined with globalization, as technology is potentially universal in nature. Indeed, building on scientific progress, which, by its very nature, is universal, technology has quite logically global aspirations. If this is true of technology in general, technological globalization has particularly been boosted by the new information and communication technologies (NTICs), which have emerged since the late 1970s. NTICs, by their very nature, are expanding much more rapidly around the globe as they are less material based and can be spread thanks to telecommunications networks, satellites, and other wireless devices. It is also these NTICs that significantly accelerate financial and economic globalizations. In short, technology and especially NTICs are global in nature and in turn accelerate globalization. Needless to say that such technological developments, as well as their consequences, are now more or less beyond State control.

Financial globalization is the combined result of the NTICs and the liberalization of financial markets. Indeed, financial deregulation, in particular the abolition of exchange rate controls, as well as the creation of increasingly global financial markets has fostered the free flow of capital. Consequently, money is seeking the highest yield no matter where this can be achieved on the planet. Financial globalization, along with emerging stock markets, has ever since come to put significant pressures on corporations pushing them also towards globalization. As a result, stock markets have come under pressure, as well leading them to merge. Therefore, and maybe with the exception of the United States, the dynamics of global finance are today beyond national control.

Starting in the 1980s, one can observe yet another type of globalization, namely the globalization of ecological problems. Such globalization, which can be seen as a direct consequence of the pursuit of industrial development, takes the form of global ecological problems such as climate change, natural resources depletion, ozone destruction, and many others more. Consequently, these global ecological problems call for global solutions, which generally go far beyond the capacities of the Nation-State. Though ecological globalization is different from the other globalizations, it nevertheless significantly contributes to the problems of the Nation-State. Indeed, the Nation-State is increasingly overwhelmed by global ecological problems it can no longer control or mitigate by itself. It thus must seek new governance mechanisms, which generally involve the private sector and civil society and often take place above the national level.

Economic globalization of both production and consumption is the next step in this process of globalization. Indeed, as a result of technological and financial globalizations, combined with cheap oil – i.e., cheap transport means – production is delocalizing, while consumption of standardized products is spreading globally (see below cultural globalization). This process is accelerated by all kinds of new managerial methods made possible thanks to the new technologies, especially in the area of logistics, just-in-time management and production, e-business, and the like. Moreover, economic globalization is, of course, also being boosted thanks to trade liberalization, especially since the end of the Cold War. As a result, Nation-States are less and less capable to control industrial production and consumption, and become more and more subject to global forces governing the movement of goods and services. Economic globalization is furthermore underpinning the growth of transnational corporations, as we will see in the next section.

It is in this context that one has to mention cultural globalization, which is probably the main force underlying the globalization of consumption. Indeed, technological developments in terms of communications, as well as globalization of transport and tourism, have lead to a considerably spreading "global culture". Such a global culture is generally characterized by the spread of individualism, Western values, and homogenization. The challenge for the Nation-State here is the fragmentation of its societies, whereby parts of society increasingly function according to some global values and culture, while other parts continue to operate in traditional ways, if they do not flatly react to global Western culture by reverting to fundamentalism and localism.

### The Main Threat to the Nation-State: or How to Bridge the Local and the Global

All these globalizations mean that the State is being bypassed parallel to the emergence of a new global cultural, economic, financial, technological, and ecological reality. This new global reality is indeed a significant threat for any Nation-State (e.g., Buelens 1999; Cerny 1990; Foster and Plowden 1996; Holton 1998; van Creveld 1999). To recall, the specificity of the Nation-State is its rootedness in territory, i.e., the legitimacy it draws from the people inhabiting its territory. This is, as said above, the direct result of the epistemological nature of the State, or in other words the price that had to be paid for making dominance acceptable. In the age of globalizations, this rootedness is now rapidly turning into a handicap. As a matter of fact, this very rootedness prevents the State from becoming mobile, whereas everything else - i.e., capital, technology, production, and even peoples - is increasingly mobile.

However, I think that globalization only describes one part of the picture. In order to understand the picture one has to analyze the very dynamics of globalization. In my view, these dynamics can be described as an ever wider gap between the global and the local, in the midst of which the State now finds itself. The following graphic illustrates the threat to the territorially-based Nation-State:

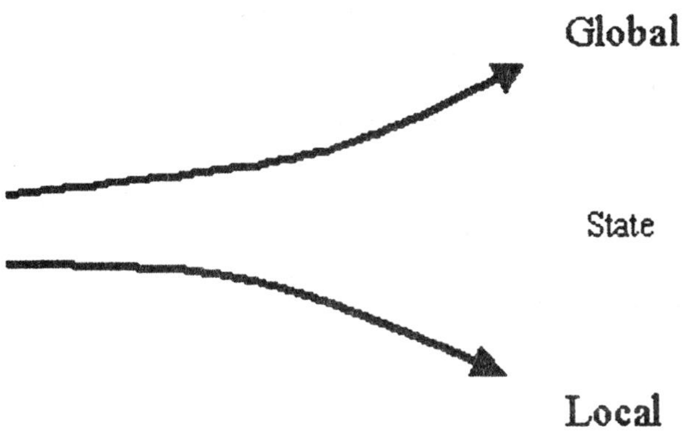

In other words, the State increasingly finds itself in a growing tension between the local and the global. This tension is best characterized by the fact that everything lucrative and mobile has a tendency to globalize, whereas everything non-lucrative and non-mobile has a tendency to localize. This is, in my view, a tension of epistemological proportions, as it is the tension between the financial means the State needs in order to thrive on the one hand and the legitimacy needed in order to exert legitimate power on the other. If money is increasingly linked to a global circuit, yet legitimacy is derived from peoples who ultimately all live locally, the challenge for the State is to bridge these two. Or in other words, how can the State generate legitimacy from its citizens without having the money to offer them services? This is the question of State credibility.

*The four main challenges*

More concretely, this fundamental threat translates into four main challenges I want to discuss here, the main one of which is instrumentalization. The other three are a financial challenge, the challenge of legitimacy, and the challenge of competition.

Let me start with the financial challenge: this challenge directly results from the fact that everything that is potentially lucrative has a tendency to globalize, while everything that is non lucrative has a tendency to localize. In order to buy the loyalty of its citizens, the State however must address local problems, at least the problems the peoples face who live on its territory. Addressing these problems requires money. This money cannot be taxed locally, as the financially most lucrative activities and peoples are also the most mobile. Taxing must moreover be seen in the context of global competition among Nation-States, where a too heavy tax burden will reduce a State's competitiveness. Still, I do think that the financial challenge is the least serious one for a Nation-State, as the State will learn or has already learned to find ways and means to procure the financial resources, for example by means of taxes no citizen can escape (e.g., VAT) or licenses companies need to acquire in order to operate on a given territory. Also, States will, to a certain extent, agree to collaborate in such financial matters given the fact that their financial survival is at stake. Of course, State reform is also a means by which the State seeks to continue to do the same with less. State reform thus is a direct consequence of the financial pressures due to globalization.

The second challenge, i.e., the challenge of legitimacy is in my view much more serious. Indeed, if problems increasingly require global solutions while being faced locally, the challenge for the State is to find the legitimacy necessary to impose global solutions on local citizens. This is even more difficult, given the fact that the State has little money to buy loyalty. Therefore, the State must find other ways and means to generate loyalty, while at the same time imposing solutions in which the citizens have no means to participate. This is a particular challenge, to which the State will respond with all kinds of strategies for participation, namely participation not only in decision-making, but also in public management, and even policy evaluation.

The third challenge pertains to competition between the States. Indeed, in the age of globalization, Nation-States increasingly have to compete against each other in order to attract business, namely production, but also technology and finances for investment. This is a new situation for the State, which was used, so far, to conflict with other States, but not (economic) competition. This challenge is even bigger given the fact that often it is not the State as a whole that is competing, but sub-units of it, such as regions or even cities, thus further weakening the Nation-State. The State generally responds to this challenge by developing a new and fourth public policy area, i.e., besides security, repair, and production, the area of competitiveness.

The fourth and probably most serious challenge for the State in the age of globalization is the challenge of its instrumentalization. This is a challenge the State is not really aware of, given that it still considers it as a form of lobbying. But the fact of the matter is, that the State is now subject to all kinds of actors which are now clearly more powerful than itself, such as transnational corporations (TNCs), but also multilateral organizations, international organizations, global non-governmental organizations (NGOs), and others more. I will come back to such instrumentalization in the fourth section of this article.

### *How the State responds*

I have identified, so far, the four main challenges the State faces as a result of simultaneous globalization and localization, namely financial pressure, legitimacy problems, competition, and instrumentalization. Instrumentalization, I think, is by far the most serious challenge, but also the one which the State is least aware of and where it will, as I will argue below, most easily give in. But before doing that, let me quickly look at likely responses by the State to these challenges.

The response of the State to these different challenges must be divided into a substantive (policy), an organizational, and an institutional aspect. On a substantive level, I have shown how the State, over time has acquired three functions, namely security (law and order), repair, and production. It is easily understandable that the State will abandon the repair function, as this is the most costly one, as well as the production function, where the State is being lobbied for lucrative business. It will keep the law and order function, as this is the State's core business to be abandoned under no circumstances. Furthermore, as argued above, it will take on the new function or policy area of competitiveness.

On the organizational side, the State will seek to streamline its activities and the services it provides, eventually get rid of some, and privatize others. Generally, this is done along so-called New Public Management (NPM) lines, whereby the State is restructuring its operations. In doing so, there is a certain danger that each of the State's organizational (and operational) units pursues its own strategy, leading it often to be ready to sell out to the highest bidder in order to survive. This is, in my view, a particular danger when it comes to the instrumentalization of the State (Finger and Ruchat 1997).

On the institutional side, the State is slow to react, as any form of change inevitably affects the power relationships among the different actors involved in running public affairs, such as the parliament, the government, the political parties, the administrations. Generally, the State responds by offering power sharing to so far disenfranchised actors, for instance associations or corporations, as well as new governance mechanisms such as partnerships.

The following table illustrates the State's multiple strategies to adapt to the four challenges in its main three dimensions:

| | Financial challenges | Legitimacy challenges | Competition | Instrumen-talization |
|---|---|---|---|---|
| Substantive dimension | Let go repair functions, privatize production | Stress law and order policies | Competi-tiveness policies | Stress law and order, as well as competitiveness policies |
| Organiza-tional dimension | Privatization, partnerships, outsourcing, reengineering, NPM | Participatory management | Corpo-ratization | Public organizations in the service of the private sector |
| Institutional dimension | Coercion and control of citizens | Participatory policies, decentraliza-tion | New governance mechanisms | Regulation, partnerships, Governance |

In order to fully understand the dynamics of the instrumentalization of the State in the age of simultaneous globalization and localization, I now have to briefly turn to TNCs and their historical evolution, as their growth and power perfectly mirror the growing challenges before the State.

## The Rise of TNCs

In this section, I will briefly highlight the rise of transnational corporations in general and of so-called "public services TNCs" in particular. To recall, TNCs are basically a phenomenon of the 1980s. As such they follow the process of mainly economic globalization. In a first section, I will define TNCs and document their rise. In a second section, I will then look at the specific case of public services TNCs and show how their rise is closely tied to the recent transformation of the State.

### *TNCs and their growth*

The rise of TNCs is typically related to globalization (e.g. UNCTAD 2002). It is useful, here, to distinguish three different phases of TNCs' rise, namely the phases of internationalization, of multinationalization, and transnationalization. By internationalization, one must understand the process of growing trade among Nation-States, in particular the trade of raw materials and goods, but rarely of services. The relevant unit here is the Nation-State, which is concerned with imports, exports, balance of payment, trade deficits, and the like. Even though internationalization has taken place ever since colonialism started, it has nevertheless significantly accelerated after the Second World War. For corporations, this means being rooted in one country and mainly active in cross-border imports of raw materials and exports of valued added products.

As of the 1970s, but especially during the 1980s, corporations start to create subsidiaries in other countries, which are generally fully owned by the mother company. This is the process of multinationalization, whereby corporations start to actively invest in other countries. Natural resources are therefore increasingly processed locally, and goods are produced in a decentralized manner and in different locations. Nevertheless, the corporations still do have home countries, from where they operate, and home cultures, which they refer to. Often, governments do actively support "their" national corporations and which in turn lobby "their" home country government so that it supports them in their efforts to go abroad.

The next step, which one can observe since the 1980s and especially during the 1990s, is the transnationalization of TNCs. This is the phase where TNCs no longer have a home country to operate from, but have come to constitute a global network. Their look at the world is now a global one, which, as ABB (Asea Brown Boveri) says in one of its advertisements, is the *"art of being local everywhere"*. Global corporations no longer have any particular allegiance to a given country, and their stock is often owned by equally global investors. Consequently, also their look at governments changes: of course, they still lobby governments, but as they now place themselves above Nation-States, they are able to play governments against each other und therefore instrumentalize them much more efficiently than when they were still dependent on a physical location.

It is during this last phase of transnationalization that TNCs have most rapidly grown, and this to the point where many of them have a turnover that now exceeds national GDPs. In many cases, they have become more powerful than Nation-States. Such growing power of TNCs can be measured by their amount, by their turnover, by the growth in their intra-firm trade, by their foreign direct investments, as well as by cross-border mergers and acquisitions. All corresponding figures will highlight an exponential growth of TNCs since the late 1980s and a process, which has only accelerated since. The consequences of such TNC growth on the Nation-State still have to be fully appreciated, but the recent evolution of so-called public services TNCs offers an early illustration of what these implications might be.

*Public services TNCs and the changing State*

The public sector is not exempt from these trends of internationalization, multinationalization, and transnationalization, in particular when it comes to its operational aspects, i.e., the delivery of public services (Martin 1993). Indeed, in the process of globalization, many of these services traditionally provided by the State are now becoming subject to competition. This results either from liberalization policies or simply from market creation, as private corporations enter markets previously reserved to State operators. Simultaneously, and as the State modernizes its operational functions (see above), many formerly public operators start to behave like private ones, especially when being allowed to offer their (public) services abroad. In other words, it is above all, the operational functions of the State, that are being modernized as a result of the pressures above highlighted. This, in turn, opens up commercial opportunities for public enterprises on the one hand and allows for private competitors to enter the public sector on the other. Most typically, this is the case in all of the infrastructure sectors (e.g., telecommunications, postal services, transport, water, energy).

In developing countries, but increasingly also in industrialized countries, it is not just operations which is opened up for competition, but also financing: indeed, as the State comes under financial pressure, financing of such operations, especially in the infrastructure sectors, is increasingly provided by private institutions or by multilateral organizations (e.g., IMF, World Bank, regional development banks). In this case, the State takes on a new and unprecedented role, namely the one of "risk-bearer". In other words, infrastructure projects are generally only financed if the State is willing to ensure the risks that inevitably come with such projects.

So-called "public services TNCs" are the ones that take advantage of this transformation of the State in both operations and financing. However, I will focus here only on the operational and not on the financial part, as public services TNCs often do not provide financing themselves, but revert to multilateral institutions for doing so. As for operations, public services TNCs increasingly provide the services the State used to provide earlier on, generally through some public enterprise. Sometimes, public services TNCs even are former public enterprises having successfully globalized.

The unique niche of such public services TNCs is the interface between the State and the citizen who has evolved into a consumer. This evolution, in turn, was made possible by the changing behavior of the citizen vis-à-vis the State, which again cannot be separated from, especially, cultural globalization and the rise of consumerism. In other words, citizens increasingly consume public services in the same way that they consume private goods and services, even though, often, such services remain heavily subsidized. Consequently, the main difference between the public services TNCs and all other TNCs is the fact that their main "customer" is not the citizen-consumer, but the State. It is the State that often subsidizes these services and, in any case, shapes the regulatory framework for providing such services, and thus determines the levels of (monopoly) profits. Not astonishingly, as these public services TNCs come to operate on a global level and across the sectors, they increasingly see the State as a source of lucrative business.

Public services TNCs are thus a typical product of the 1980s and 1990s, i.e. the period when the State started to substantially modernize its operations and transform the delivery of its public services (e.g. outsourcing, privatization, partnerships). The origin or precursor of such public services TNCs are therefore mainly public enterprises, which have successfully transformed, i.e., emancipated themselves from the control of national politics and embraced global expansion strategies. Of course, the ones that are best placed to do so are the ones that were private to begin with, and thus only needed to take advantage of globalization and the changing State. This is typically the case of French water companies (e.g. Suez Lyonnaise des Eaux and Vivendi-Universal), which had significant experience with national politics, yet were not constrained by such national politics because of public ownership. Other successful public services TNCs are public enterprises, which are actively supported and promoted by their home country, i.e., so-called "national champions" such as Electricité de France (EDF), Deutsche Post, or Rheinisch Westfälische Elektrizitätswerke (RWE).

These and some other public services TNCs are today among the biggest corporations globally, and have grown ever since, mainly through acquiring other formerly State-owned enterprises in foreign countries. But their growth also builds on diversification. Indeed, while these public services TNCs generally start out in one particular sector –

typically water, electricity or postal service –, they have diversified to the point where they generally cover water, energy (electricity and gas), logistics, public transport, telecommunications, and broadcasting. But some of the biggest public services TNCs even span into the housing (facility management), construction, health, education, and even security sectors (e.g. prison management).

## The Instrumentalization of the State by TNCs

The combined globalization and transformation of the State has thus given rise to a new type of TNC, namely the one whose main customer is the State and which derives its main business from the State either by way of its financing or by way of the regulatory conditions under which it operates. From here on, it is easy to understand its strategies to instrumentalize the State so that it can operate under the most favorable conditions possible. However, I think that such instrumentalization is a strategy which ultimately all TNCs will come to pursue, given the ultimately quite lucrative nature of State business. At the moment, however, such strategies crystallize most clearly in the case of public services TNCs (e.g., Finger and Allouche 2002). This fourth section will therefore look at State instrumentalization by public services TNCs. I will start from the case of water TNCs to generalize from there to other public services TNCs. This can be justified by the fact that the major public services TNCs, in particular Vivendi and Suez, did start out in the water sector, and have, from there, spread out to all other public services. In conclusion, I will try to systematize their strategies vis-à-vis the State.

### *Water TNCs' strategies vis-à-vis the State*

When it comes to water TNCs, one must clearly distinguish between their strategies in the South and in the North. To recall, water TNCs originate in France, where they take advantage of the fact that they are among the rare, if not the only, corporations never to be nationalized by any French government. Indeed, in France, the dominant model in the water sector is so-called "gestion déléguée", i.e., delegated management. Concretely, this means that water infrastructures - water supply and sanitation - are owned by the municipalities, while operation is ensured by the corporations. The relationship between the operator (corporation) and the municipality can take different forms. Generally, one distinguishes between three different forms, namely management contracts (1-4 years), lease contracts (4-15) and concessions (10-35 years). These contracts basically differ in terms of the risk the corporation and the municipality incur. The longer the contract the more risk to the company, which it is willing to take if the political-economic environment is stable.

Building on this French situation, these water companies have now extended all over the world. Their reach ranges across the Third World, where the World Bank plays a significant role. Indeed, Third World countries lack money, and often the water infrastructures are in very bad shape. The trick is to get these countries to upgrade their infrastructure without incurring the risks involved in such investments. This is done means of World Bank or IMF loans given to national governments, but rarely to municipalities directly, and almost never to local water companies. With these credits, the country, the municipality or the water company upgrades the infrastructure. Generally, such upgrading is outsourced to a building company, which again is a subsidiary of one of the big water TNCs. To recall, such upgrading is generally done selectively, i.e. by choosing the potentially most lucrative municipalities. Once the infrastructures are rehabilitated, or sometimes even during the rehabilitation process, structural adjustment policies are being applied. Concretely, this means that the World Bank forces a given Third World country to privatize its public enterprise, to undertake public sector reform, to decentralize, and to municipalize. In the water sector, as said above, the TNCs are generally not interested in privatization, but in delegated management. They therefore generally like the World Bank to promote what they call municipalization, i.e. the shifting of ownership of water supply and sanitation infrastructures from national governments to local municipalities. Sometimes, even the debts are shifted to the municipalities as well. It is then the municipality that contracts directly with the TNC for service delivery. One can easily understand that such municipalization is in favor of the TNC, as the power relationship between these two is totally unequal. During this process, the TNC generally profits twice: first from the rehabilitation contract and secondly from the long-term delegated management contract. It is therefore not astonishing that water TNCs strongly lobby the World Bank to support the rehabilitation or construction of infrastructures. Proof of this is the fact that they have managed to convince the Bank that delegated management is the way to go in the water sector(s). Consequently, delegated management is no longer the model pushed only by the TNCs, but it is now proposed by the World

Bank, who has to rely on the water TNCs, in turn, to solve its problems (World Bank, 1997a+b).

In terms of empirical reality, it appears that many big cities of developing countries are now under some form of management contract with one of the big French TNCs. So far, among the world's biggest agglomerations (more than 11 million inhabitants) only Buenos Aires has a concession with a French operator in the water supply (Suez). But many other big cities already have private French operators, namely Santiago, Chile (Suez), La Paz (Suez), Bogotá (Suez), Casablanca (Suez), Amman (Suez), Abidjan (Bouygues), Kampala (Suez), Niamey (Vivendi).

Ultimately, however, TNCs are not after developing countries. Rather, they are after industrialized countries, where, however, their strategy is different, as the World Bank does not play any role. In Europe, at least, their main strategy is vis-à-vis the European Union, following a dual track, namely standards and tendering. On the standards side, water TNCs are lobbying for stronger environmental and sanitation standards, which they can meet and their competitors cannot. Such standards pertain to drinking water, as well as to sanitation, i.e., quality of water that can be rejected into the environment. Obviously, the costs of cleaning water are very high, requiring large investments. Simultaneously and separately, the water TNCs are lobbying for compulsory tendering, meaning that water supply and sanitation should be put up for tender on a regular basis throughout Europe. It is the combination of these two lobbying strategies, which ultimately leads to the competitive advantage of the water TNCs over municipal companies. Indeed, as standards get higher and the obligation to tender is enforced, municipalities often do not have the necessary cash to rehabilitate their infrastructures to the required standards, and therefore will be forced to adopt some form of delegated management.

In terms of empirical reality, one can observe in Europe that the French water TNCs have already entered several cities. They generally do so by creating new companies in joint ventures with established ones. In Spain, for example, Suez is with Aguas de Barcelona, Bouygues with Aguas de Valencia, and Vivendi with FCC. In Germany, Vivendi created with the City of Berlin what is now called Berlinwasser. In the UK, Suez works with Northumbrian, whereas RWE has just acquired Thames Water.

To recall, the strategy of the water TNCs in both the North and the South is to acquire delegated management contracts, often by buying into existing companies. Also, they generally diversify in order to be in a better position vis-à-vis the municipalities whom they can therefore offer comprehensive public services packages. As said above and quite typically, all the big water TNCs have by now diversified into multi-utilities offering water, energy, public transport, telecommunications, audiovisual services, facility management, and many other services more.

*"Multi-utilities"*

Delegated management appears to become increasingly a model for all public services, in particular the public services that require heavy infrastructures, and therefore need substantial (public) investments. Besides water supply and especially sanitation, this is particularly the case with respect to telecommunications, railways, roads, broadcasting (especially television), and energy, but also airports, schools, correction facilities, and public housing. Again, one must distinguish between two separate steps, namely the building and rehabilitation on the one hand, and delegated management on the other. Not astonishingly, it is easier to acquire delegated management contracts if one has been involved in the construction or the rehabilitation of the infrastructure to begin with.

Building and rehabilitation applies, so far, primarily to developing countries, but it is possible that this will increasingly also become applied in industrialized countries in the not so far future. Indeed, in the developing countries, TNCs not only build and rehabilitate water supply or sanitation systems, they also build dams, power lines, electricity distribution networks, toll roads, railway tracks, ports and airports. They can do so by taking advantage of World Bank or IMF loans contracted by national governments. In this matter of infrastructure financing, the World Bank has quite logically developed numerous models known as BOT (Build Operate Transfer), BOOT (Build Own Operate Transfer), BTO (Build Transfer Operate) and the like.

Once the infrastructures are built or rehabilitated, these TNCs then seek management contracts, lease contracts, or concessions. The interesting and most lucrative aspect of doing this is the fact that these contracts generally guarantee monopoly positions and that services can now be combined, thus still enhancing the monopoly position. In other words, a public service TNC can now offer to the municipality a variety of services, ranging from water to public transport, to energy, to facility management, and others more. In doing so, it can not only price its services creatively, but it also holds a monopoly position vis-à-vis municipality, the national government, or both.

*Instrumentalization of the State*

Based on the above developments, I would now like to systematize the different strategies used by these TNCs active in the public sector. I will identify five such strategies, all leading to the instrumentalization of the State for the purpose of business advantage. Indeed, based on the examples of these public services TNCs, the State appears to be (1) a source of financing, (2) a guarantor of regular revenues, (3) a risk bearer, (4) a guarantor of political and economic stability, and (5) an enforcement tool. Let me look at each of them more systematically.

- As seen above, the State is above all a *source of financing*. Indeed, the State either finances infrastructure projects directly, or takes credit from lending agencies in order to finance infrastructure development or rehabilitation. This is important for most public services TNCs, not only because they can make a profit from such infrastructure development and rehabilitation, but also because infrastructure works constitute a privileged entry point to then even more lucrative delegated management contracts.

- Secondly, the State is a *guarantor of regular revenues*. Indeed, by granting management contracts, lease contracts and especially by granting concessions, the State allows the public services TNCs to collect fees from their customers, and simultaneously guarantees that these fees will be flowing for a certain, generally quite long, period of time. In other words, the State grants public services TNCs a temporary monopoly. Of course, such monopolies are generally regulated by the State, but public services TNCs have often learned - building on their past history as public enterprises - how to shape such regulation to their advantage. Not to mention the fact that they generally renegotiate the contracts once they have been signed, thus taking States hostage. In most cases, such renegotiations result in higher monopoly profits.

- Thirdly, the State is a *risk bearer*. As said above, TNCs seek to avoid the risks that come with heavy infrastructures. These are mainly the risks of financing these infrastructures without being sure to recover the costs, but also the risks of owning them. In both cases, the State plays a crucial role, inasmuch as it is the State that takes the World Bank loans. Also, it is the State or a municipality that generally keeps ownership of the infrastructure. Should anything go wrong, the TNC can easily pull out, while the State remains tied to the infrastructures it can no longer run by itself.

- Fourthly, the State is a *guarantor of stability*. Such stability has two aspects: on the one hand, TNCs are interested in political and economic stability, and the State is there to provide exactly that. Only in a stable social and economic climate can the corporation plan ahead and is it willing to take risks. The more unstable the political, economic and social climate, the more the TNCs will calculate their risk premium and the more short-term it is willing to engage itself. On the other hand, one must also mention legal stability or security, namely the fact that ownership is respected and contracts are enforced. Here, TNCs actually have an interest in a strong State, capable of protecting private property and investments, and of enforcing contracts once negotiated. In other words, a strong law and order State focusing on security, along with a focus on competitiveness, is precisely in the interest of these TNCs.

- Finally, and as one can see in the case of the EU, the State is also a *vehicle to enforce norms and rules,* which have been defined at supranational levels. This, of course, also applies to (structural adjustment) conditions, which are imposed upon a State, but have to be enforced within the national borders. Indeed, strong environmental, sanitation or other standards, in the elaboration of which the public services TNCs have generally participated, are first adopted at a supranational level and then must be enforced by Nation-States. This same mechanism also applies to other supranational organizations, such as the World Bank, the IMF, but also the World Trade Organization, the International Organization for Standardization (ISO), and others more. In all these cases, it is interesting and efficient for TNCs to lobby global organizations and build on the agreements States have signed with these organizations to get lobbied standards and norms imposed nationally and locally.

## Conclusion: Towards an Instrumentalized State

If one wants to generalize from the above empirical observations in the water and more generally in all the infrastructure sectors, one can infer, in fact, three main strategies simultaneously applied by public services TNCs, namely a globalization strategy, a localization strategy, and the strategy to instrumentalize what remains of the State. I think that these strategies are more generally applicable to all TNCs. Let me examine each of these in more detail.

- The *globalization strategy* aims at shifting norm making from the national to the global or at least to the supra-national level, while in parallel advocating new governance mechanisms above the Nation-State. Indeed, by "governance" TNCs mean the fact that governments are no longer regulating business, but now sit at the same table along with business representatives who have equal rights. At times, civil society representatives are invited to participate in such governance arrangements as well, but, weak as they are, they are often lobbied by both States and TNCs to defend the latter's interests. As a result of such a globalization strategy, TNCs now have an increasingly important say in international rule and norm making, and, as I would argue, a disproportionate power, given the weakness of governments and the fragmentation of civil society. I have argued above that this is currently the case in the EU, but it is even more obvious in the case of international standards setting (e.g. ISO), where TNCs define standards which then have to be applied by each government.

- The *localization strategy*, on the other hand, aims at shifting decision making power about operations, ownership, management, and evaluation downwards, i.e., to the local levels. Often this goes hand in hand with arguments such as decentralization, municipalization, participation, and even democratization. In this respect, it is interesting to note that for the World Bank, for example, decentralization is synonymous with privatization. Consequently, local democracy is being idealized, and so is local ownership, along with all kinds of citizens' participations. Yet, localization for TNCs above all means the establishment of a favorable power relationship, whereby municipalities with little resources have to negotiate with TNCs whose resources are virtually unlimited.

- In between, *the State is so-to-speak hollowed out*: decision-making power is shifted upwards as well as sometimes downwards, while operations is generally pushed downwards. Ownership is sometimes privatized, but if TNCs are not interested in buying, it is generally also shifted downwards. What remains of the State at the national level is its law and order (or security) function, sometimes along with the function to promote national competitiveness. Indeed, the State - no longer capable of delivering services - can still provide security, including legal security, and this may be the only function TNCs are willing to accept. In this perspective, it is interesting to note that, as of 1997, the World Bank no longer calls for dismantling the State, but advocates *a "small, yet strong State"*, i.e., a State that will do precisely what TNCs want it to do: promote national competitiveness, guarantee economic and political stability, and enforce legal security. In this sense, the transformation of the Nation-State in the age of globalization perfectly coincides with the TNCs' plans for its instrumentalization.

# Globalization and Governance: The Role of the International Financial Institutions

Corneliu Dan Berari

Among the concepts brought to the forefront of the intellectual debates in international relations theory and international political economy by the recent preoccupation with "globalization," the concept of "governance" occupies a distinctive place. Whereas "globalization" has emerged as a useful concept to encapsulate into a single word the breath-taking transformations taking place in our time, the concept of "governance" has the role of signifying new types of politics created by globalization. The fundamental assumptions behind the concept of governance are that governments are no longer central to politics and that in the era of globalization, the exercise and legitimation of power can be uncoupled from national governments (Gamble 2000). In contrast to globalization, which for many is a challenging and even frightening phenomenon, governance appears as a reassuring concept which articulates the hope that the transformations wrought by globalization can be controlled and steered in a convenient direction. No wonder, therefore, that an important part of the huge literature of globalization deals precisely with the possibilities of governance in the contemporary world. The fundamental theoretical stake in this literature is thus to identify the political consequences of globalization and to conceptualize the alleged new types of politics made possible by globalization.

In the following pages, I will try to contribute to the contemporary research on globalization and governance through an examination of the roles played by the International Monetary Fund and the World Bank in the management of the world economy. In a certain sense, it is almost needless to argue why an investigation of the International Monetary Fund (IMF) and of its sister institution, the World Bank, is indispensable in any debate about the possibilities and limits of international economic governance in our time. There is first the widespread image of these organizations as main incarnations of what "globalization" is all about: the transfer of authority from national to supra-national institutions, the accumulation of power in the hands of "faceless international bureaucrats," the triumph of neo-liberal policies all over the world. As proven by the recurrent demonstrations against these organizations, to be anti-globalization and anti-IMF and anti-World Bank are practically the same things for many social activists fighting "globalization."

Moreover, this popular perception of the IMF and the World Bank is apparently supported by arguments put forward by respected academics. Indeed, if, as argued by scholars like Keinichi Ohmae (1990 and 1995), Robert Reich (1993), and Susan Strange (1995 and 1996), globalization leads to the eclipse of the state as a form of social organization, then it is logical to expect that the decline of the state will be counterbalanced by the increasing salience of the public international organizations in the international arena. Arguments in support of this thesis have been advanced by scholars like Jan Aart Scholte (2000a) and Bob Deacon (1997), who contend that a global public space has already emerged around public international organizations like the IMF and the World Bank. Apparently, a new structure of global governance is in the making; thus, besides states - which, as Hirst and Thompson (1995) claim, retain a pivotal role as mediators between global forces and local constituencies - international organizations are destined to become the main loci of authority and power in the emerging global economy.

Given the global controversy surrounding the IMF and the World Bank and the central importance attributed to these organizations in many analyses of the causes and the consequences of globalization, this paper sets out to assess the actual contribution of the Bretton Woods institutions to the management of the world economy. Thus, the main question I will address in this paper is whether the governance structures of the world economy at the beginning of the twenty-first century are characterized by a significant transfer of authority and power from states to public international organizations. To answer this question, I will focus my research on the main structural features of the international monetary and financial systems and discuss the IMF's and the World Bank's whereabouts in the complex architecture of these systems. The overarching goal of the paper is to present evidence that can be used to assess the validity of some of the claims advanced in the ongoing debate on globalization. Thus, depending on whether the answer to the question is positive or negative, we will have good reasons to admit or to reject the thesis that globalization has led to a decline of the state and to the emergence of new forms of non-state authority in the world economy.

Following the current practice in the literature on the IMF and the World Bank, I will designate these organizations as the international financial institutions (IFIs).

## The International Financial Institutions and the Governance Structures of the World Economy at the Beginning of the Twenty-First Century: An Assessment

The establishment of the International Monetary Fund and of the International Bank for Reconstruction and Development (later: the World Bank) at the Bretton Woods conference represented a qualitative leap in the evolution of the process of international organization. The Bretton Woods conference was, as Harold James (1996, p. 57) remarks in the latest official history of the IMF, "the first conference to establish a permanent international institutional and legal framework for ensuring cooperation between states, requiring commitments by states to limit their sovereignty for the sake of cooperation and to observe specified rules in economic intercourse." The Bretton Woods conference therefore created the first structure of international monetary governance in which international organizations played an important role alongside states.

The institutional framework for the international economic system established by the Bretton Woods agreements was characterized by comprehensiveness and clarity. The adjustable peg exchange rate regime was also a financial regime; in order to maintain the exchange parity, states were to control the flows of capitals across borders. The system also had clear provisos about the type of adjustment that was to be used by the participants. Despite the opposition mounted by Lord Keynes, the chief British negotiator, the point of view of the American delegation prevailed, and the burden of adjustment was to be borne exclusively by the deficit countries. Moreover, the Bretton Woods conference came close to the creation of an international regime for development through the creation of the International Bank for Reconstruction and Development (IBRD). The main reason for the creation of this institution was that both Keynes and White (the chief American negotiator) were convinced that the capital markets are inherently imperfect and that the operators in these markets tend to place disproportionate amounts of funds in short-term, speculative investments. Accordingly, the IBRD was established as an international public institution mandated to channel funds in war-torn and underdeveloped areas.

The central international organization of the Bretton Woods system was the International Monetary Fund. Primarily, the Fund has been an institution of international economic surveillance, in fact the first international organization with such a mandate.[52] In the Bretton Woods

[52] The mandate to exercise "firm surveillance" appears only since the Second Amendment to the Articles of Agreement. However, even though the word

system, the Fund's main role was to make sure that the policies pursued by individual members did not undermine the agreed upon exchange parity. In case a country experienced balance of payments difficulties, the Fund was to provide short-term finance in order to support an adjustment process compatible with the overarching goals of the system (e.g. maintenance of exchange rate stability, prevention of competitive exchange depreciation, balanced growth of international trade).[53]

As remarked by competent observers of the Bretton Woods system,[54] a main quality of this structure of international economic governance was that it struck a fair balance between the principle of national sovereignty and the imperatives of international cooperation. Thus, while allowing for a quite large amount of discretion in the pursuit of the national economic policies, the Bretton Woods agreements also established a clear-cut code of international economic interaction. The Bretton Woods system was also a state-centric formula of international economic governance. Even though an international organization (the IMF) played an important role in the management of the system, there was no question of a transfer of sovereign rights from states to this supra-national entity. The international obligations assumed by states under the Articles of Agreement of the IMF were meant to foster the capacity of individual states to pursue autonomous economic policies at the national level. This intention was fully realized. By and large, the "embedded liberalism" of the Bretton Woods system (Ruggie 1982) was an extremely successful formula of economic governance at both national and international levels.

I will not discuss here the actual evolution of the Bretton Woods system and the discrepancies between what was written in the Bretton Woods agreement and what happened in reality. It suffices to say that while in theory the Articles of Agreement of the IMF was an international treaty spelling out rights and obligations in the area of exchange rate policies, in practice the Bretton Woods system depended crucially on the willingness of the USA to comply with the rules of the game. In his excellent book on the history of international economic surveillance, Louis Pauly (1997, p. 136) pinpoints the essential conundrum of the Bretton Woods system:

---

"surveillance" did not appear in the original Bretton Woods agreements, since its inception the IMF has been engaged in activities of international economic surveillance. For a good discussion of this dimension of the IMF see Pauly (1997).

[53] For a complete list of the purposes of the IMF see the Articles of the Agreement of the International Monetary Fund, Article I.

[54] See, for instance, the analysis of the Bretton Woods system by Guitian (1992).

> The U.S. dollar and the dominant U.S. economy, underpinned the system that evolved when the Bretton Woods agreement was finally implemented. But it was vitally important to a generation of policymakers that a broadly accepted international treaty provide the foundation of the system. The system as a whole was said to rest, much as in the ancient Roman sense, on the rule of law. In fact, it continued to rest on power. Power was not banished, only tamed to some extent. In practical terms, the norms of the treaty were set against the continuing ability of states to manipulate the value of their currencies. Some had more ability than others.

No wonder, then, that the fate of the Bretton Woods system was sealed by the USA decision to pursue policies which were at variance with the norms and rules of this system.

However, if the Bretton Wood system has been gone for more than three decades, the Bretton Woods institutions (i.e., the IMF and the World Bank) are still with us, and they seem to be doing pretty well in the present world economy. The fundamental task now is to identify the governance structures of the present world economy and to assess the roles played by the IMF and the World Bank in these structures. Only in this way will it become possible to answer the original question of this paper, namely whether the governance structures of the present world economy are characterized by a transfer of power and authority from nation states to supra-national entities like the IFIs.

Since the IMF is an institution of international monetary cooperation, a short overview of the fundamental structures of the present international monetary system should provide us with a convenient starting point for answering this question. The task is thus to find out the most important outcomes of the historical move from specie money to paper money and from an international system of fixed but adjustable exchange rate to a situation in which each state has (re)gained the liberty to adopt exchange arrangements of its own choice.

The first and somewhat paradoxical outcome is that the Fund has been maintained as the "permanent institution which provides machinery for consultation and collaboration on international monetary problems," despite the fact that with the collapse of the adjustable peg exchange rate the main rationale for an international institution like the IMF disappeared. Beyond reasons of institutional inertia, the need to maintain a minimal amount of legitimacy in international monetary relations was the apparently decisive motive behind the decision to maintain the Fund and to mandate it to "exercise firm surveillance over the exchange rate policies of members." (Articles of Agreement of the IMF, Article IV, Section 3, Paragraph B). As in the time of the Bretton Woods system, the Articles of Agreement of the IMF are the foundational legal text of the present international monetary system.

Nevertheless, if from a legal point of view the differences between the Bretton Woods system and the present system might not look too significant, in practical terms the differences are enormous. Foremost, in contrast to both the Bretton Woods system and the gold standard, in the present monetary international system there are no generally accepted international rules or understandings about fundamental issues like exchange rates adjustments or liquidity creation. In these conditions, the present international system can be characterized as an international monetary non-system or, at least in the periods when central banks of the major economic powers intervene to restrict large exchange rate fluctuations, as a "reference range system" (Gilpin 2000, p. 124).

The non-existence of such rules has made the task of international economic coordination much more difficult than it was in the previous monetary systems, at least in theory. Compounded by the very sketchy rules governing the functioning of the international financial system, the absence of rules about adjustment and liquidity creation explains to an important extent the ad-hoc nature of the process of international economic coordination in the present world economy. Thus, for more than twenty years the most important efforts of macroeconomic coordination in the world economy have been undertaken on an ad-hoc basis in the summits of the leaders of the seven most industrialized states (Canada, France, Germany, Italy, Japan, United Kingdom, and USA). The G-7 summits[55] (to which Russia has been also admitted in the last few years) have proven to be an effective and a satisfactory formula of international economic governance, at least for countries participating in them. Essentially, this formula is a compromise between the principle of national economic sovereignty and the imperative of international economic cooperation; whereas each state can make free use of the economic autonomy (re)gained with the return to a system of flexible exchange rates, the G-7 meetings make possible (at least) that minimal level of inter-state policy coordination that is necessary for the functioning of the world economy. By and large, the G-7 formula is a state-centric formula of international economic governance that has striking similarities to the concert of the European powers in the nineteenth century.

---

[55] For an extensive analysis of the G-7 process see Putnam and Bayne (1987).

Given the unquestionable preeminence enjoyed by the G-7 states (either as individual or as collective actors) in the management of the world affairs, it is hardly possible to speak of an overall transfer of power from states to supra-state entities. No matter how profound the alleged transformations wrought by globalization can be, they have so far not affected the firm grips of the G-7 states over their economies and over the world economy as a whole. Just as was the case ten, twenty, or thirty years ago, at the beginning of the twenty-first century a few states are the most important loci of social power in the world; despite the endless talk of "governance without governments," there are no signs that the leaders of the seven most industrialized countries think of forsaking their powers in favor of global NGOs or international public organizations. The salience acquired in the last decades by several public and private forums in the process of consultation and consensus formation among the elites of the advanced capitalist states should not be seen as expressing a transfer of power from "national" to "supra-national levels." On the contrary, as demonstrated by two excellent analyses of this process (Gill 1990, van der Pijl 1998), it reflects the strengthening of the transnational linkages among the elites of the developed world.

How little sense it makes to speak of an overall transfer of power from national to supra-national institutions and of the emergence of "governance without government" is proven also by the minimal influence exercised by the IMF over the policies of the developed countries, the participation of the Managing Director of this institution in the G-7 summits notwithstanding. At most, given the extensive use of IMF data in the G-7 consultations, the IMF can be credited with an indirect influence over the decisions taken in this forum. However, by and large the IMF's influence does not go much beyond that of a consultant who is sometimes listened to but very rarely (if ever) obeyed.[56]

The insignificant influence exercised by the Fund over the policies of the G-7 governments or, for that matter, of policies of most developed countries, becomes explainable if we take into consideration the consequences of the financial revolution of the last two decades. As the liquidity available on the international capital markets has increased enormously, it has become much easier for states with good credit standing to finance ever growing levels of deficits. No wonder that in

[56] For a lucid analysis of the relationship between the IMF and the G-7 see the comments of the former managing director Jacques de Laroisiere in Boughton and Lateef (1995, p. 214-215)

these conditions the countries which could take this option have preferred to borrow from the international capital markets and to dispense altogether with the IMF (and with the conditionality attached to the Fund's loans). Since the British and the Italian adjustment programs in late 70s, no developed country has made use again of the Fund's resources.

The growing reliance on international capital markets could not but affect the policies of the developed countries with large deficits as well. These states not only had to abandon the classical Keynesian macroeconomic policies in a world economy characterized by financial laissez-faire, but they also had to dismantle much of the welfare edifice built after the Second World War in favor of market friendly policies, which they now had to pursue in order to placate their creditors. Moreover, besides the "daily plebiscite" exercised by markets, the policies of states are now also increasingly subjected (and shaped) by assessments made by private market authorities (Cutler, Haufler and Porter 1999). The current move toward more marketization and the markets' steady encroachment on states should nevertheless not obscure the fundamental fact that the move toward financial liberalization has been actively promoted by some states, and especially by the United States and the United Kingdom (Helleiner 1994).

What is extraordinary about the present international financial system is that, as Robert Gilpin (2001, p. 268) points out, "there is no mechanism to regulate international finance." The enormous growth of the financial markets has been greatly facilitated by the non-existence of an international financial regime in the period elapsed since the end of the Bretton Woods system. The ensuing financial laissez-faire has not only favored the explosive growth of international markets but has also made the international financial system extremely fragile. Competent observers like the international political economist Susan Strange (1986, 1998) and the successful speculator and philanthropist George Soros (1998, 2001) agree that the international financial system is the "Achilles heel" of contemporary capitalism and that the vagaries of international financial markets might undermine the long-run survivability of the global capitalist system in the absence of substantial reforms.

The fragility of the post-Bretton Woods financial system has been revealed by the recurrent financial crises of the last twenty years. In fact, except for the crisis-ridden 1920s and 1930s, the period since 1973 has been characterized by the highest frequency of financial crises known in history (Bordo, Eichengreen, Klienebiel, Martinez-Pereira 2001). One has to add also that most of these financial crises (e.g., the debt crisis in the

80s, the 1994 "tequila" crisis in Mexico, the Asian financial crises of 1996-1998, the 1998 financial meltdown in Russia) have affected the periphery of the global capitalist system.

It is in the context of these financial crises that the International Financial Institutions and especially the International Monetary Fund have proven to be indispensable for the management of the world economy. In a system lacking any formal rules of monetary and financial international cooperation, these institutions are apparently the best instruments available to cope with the inherent instability and fragility of the system. As managers of financial crises, the IFIs have fulfilled three main roles. First, at the peak of the crises, they played an instrumental role in the multilateral and bilateral efforts to mobilize the financial packages needed to overcome and confine these crises. Second, in the post-crisis environment, they supervised the implementation of programs of structural reforms aiming to do away with the domestic causes of the financial crises. Third, in anticipation of future crises, they have worked to strengthen the institutional foundations of the international financial system. This third function has become particularly salient during the last decade. In the aftermath of the crises in Mexico and South Asia, the IMF has set out to improve its data gathering and information dissemination capacities and to develop *codes of good practices on transparency in monetary and financial policies* which it has proposed for adoption to its member countries (IMF 1999, 2000). Covering a large spectrum of issues (e.g., data dissemination; fiscal, monetary and financial policy transparency; banking regulation and supervision; securities and insurance regulation; accounting, auditing, bankruptcy and corporate governance), these codes of good practices are intended to make the structures of the states implementing them more compatible with the systemic option for free capital mobility. If this package of reforms is adopted by a significant number of countries, then it is likely that something like the contours of a global financial regime will emerge at last.

It remains, nevertheless, an open question in what direction the ongoing efforts to build a more secure international financial architecture will progress in the first decade(s) of the twenty-first century. Will the new financial architecture result in more scope for markets and a diminished (and perhaps even abolished) IMF, as was demanded by the Meltzer commission and by the conservative critics of this institution? Or will these efforts lead to a stronger IMF, with expanded surveillance competencies and, perhaps, even with a mandate in the area of global credit creation (as was proposed, among others, by

John Williamson and George Soros)?[57] No matter what course will prevail eventually, it is certain that the future financial architecture is bound to reshape the distribution of power among states, markets, and international institutions.

So far, it is clear that the financial revolution of the last decades has had very uneven consequences and that states have been very differently affected by the re-emergence of global financial markets according to their position in the world economy (and, one can argue, according to their voting power in the IMF). For a small group of (developed) states, the growth of global finance has brought unequivocal benefits, as they have been able to borrow at relatively low costs and to postpone or smooth the adjustment of their economies. This is particularly true for the USA, the main promoter of the process of financial liberalization and the host country of the biggest financial corporations in the world. By taking advantage of the new opportunities opened by the global financial markets, the USA was able to finance unprecedented high levels of deficits during the last twenty years. As Soros (2001) has argued the big developed economies (and especially the USA) can still pursue counter-cyclical policies in order to counteract economic downturns or impeding financial crises. Very revealing in this respect are first, the counter-cyclical economic package implemented by the Bush government in the last part of the year 2001, and second, the capacity of the American Federal System in 1998 to prevent the global financial turmoil from spilling over into the USA economy after the collapse of the Long Term Capital Management Fund. In these conditions, in which a state can make use of the opportunities opened up by the global financial markets and, concomitantly, still has the capacity to steer these markets with the help of national institutions (such as the American Fed), it is hardly possible to argue that the ongoing financial liberalization has - to a similar extent - decreased the power of all states. On the contrary, this combination of relatively unproblematic access to global finance and availability of counter-cyclical adjustment policies might explain the relative good performance of the developed countries in the last twenty years, in contrast with the rather bleak performance of the developing world.[58]

This point will became clearer when we take into account the role played by the International Financial Institutions in the adjustment

---

[57] For a comprehensive overview of the most important proposals to reform the international financial system after the South-Asian crisis see Eichengreen (1999).

[58] For an interesting discussion of the growth problems of the developing world since 1980 see Easterly (2001).

process in the third and the (former) second world. Except for a rather small number of countries (most of them oil producers), almost all less developed countries[59] went through grave economic and financial crises at some moment in the last twenty years and, as a rule, they relied upon IMF and World Bank adjustment packages in order to cope with these crises. Many of these economic troubles originated in the huge debts accumulated in the 70s by less developed countries, when the surge of liquidity caused by the breakdown of the Bretton Woods system and by the second oil crisis enabled the then leaders of these countries to borrow heavily on the international capital markets. However, when the day of reckoning came and these countries were cut off from the international financial markets, either because of their own policy mistakes or simply because of changed "markets sentiments," the only solution left for them was to make use of the IMF stabilization programs. As is known, the core prescriptions of these programs concern the reduction of the aggregate demand and the opening of the crisis-hit economies to the international markets. The bet behind the IMF stabilization programs is that these programs, if correctly and consistently implemented, will achieve that improvement of the economic fundamentals (inflation, budget deficit, balance of payments, debt pro capita) which a country needs in order to have steady access to the international capital markets. The price is, however, a worsening of the economic crisis, at least in the short-run. No wonder then that since the IMF clients had to implement pro-cyclical adjustment programs, their economic evolution has been punctuated by the severe reductions of output caused by these programs.

Moreover, in a broader perspective, the price these less developed countries have to pay is a certain loss of their economic autonomy in favor of the IMF and the World Bank. This loss of autonomy is particularly evident in the cases of the highly indebted countries, whose only sources of external finance are the IMF and the World Bank loans. In such countries, the IMF and the World Bank have a de facto veto over the governmental patterns of expenditure and economic policies. The IMF holds substantial sway over even the economic policies of those less developed countries who have a relatively secure access to international capital markets. As "emerging markets," these countries are particularly vulnerable to changes in "markets' sentiments"; and the "markets' sentiments," in turn, are very sensitive to the IMF's assessment of the economic policies pursued by particular countries. According to the

[59] For the sake of brevity, I use the phrase "less developed countries" to cover all the countries from what used to be the second and the former third world.

IMF's seal of (dis)approval, a country can have access to or can be cut off from international capital markets. This position of "gate-keeper" to international financial markets has enabled the IMF to reshape the policies of many less developed countries and to convert them, at least partially, to a neo-liberal vision of development. More than the simple conditionality attached to its and (the World Bank's) loans, the authoritative position occupied by the IMF in the architecture of the international financial system accounts for the substantial influence exercised by this institution (usually in collaboration with the World Bank) over the policies and, to a certain extent, the politics of many less developed countries. In fact, the sway acquired by these international organizations over many of their member states at the periphery of global capitalism can be regarded as one of the indubitable historical novelties in the world economy of the early twenty-first century.

In conclusion, after this overview of the main structural features of the present international monetary and financial system, it is possible to advance some general propositions about the role of the international financial institutions in the governance structures of the present global capitalism. The main conclusion that can be drawn is that there are no grounds to speak either of an overarching unique structure of multilateral governance or of an overall transfer of power from states to supra-national institutions like the IMF, despite the promise of multilateral economic governance built into the Articles of Agreement of these institutions. At most, if we take as a reference point the IFIs' whereabouts in the complex architecture of early twenty-first global capitalism, we can speak of the existence of a two-tiered structure of international economic governance.

Thus, at the center of the global capitalist system we have the developed states, which coordinate their individual economic policies in forums like G-7 or the European Union. Among these states, the USA is more than the *primus inter pares*. With its dominance of the financial, knowledge, military and, to a certain extent, production structures of global capitalism (Strange, 1994a), the USA remains the unchallenged economic and political power of our time. The decisions (and non-decisions) taken by the USA are determinative for the overall dynamics of the world economy. Given the unchallenged preeminence enjoyed by the developed states both in the management of their own economies and in the management of the world economy as a whole, it is hardly possible to claim that in the developed world "globalization" (whatever this term might mean) brings an irreversible decline of state power. On the contrary, in the core area of the world economy, the states are still the main institution of economic governance; thus, the key public decisions with economic character are still firmly in the hands of state officials (even though many of them, like the chiefs of central banks, are not accountable to an electorate). At most, as in the case of the EU states, it is possible to speak of a phenomenon of sovereignty-pooling. Nevertheless, there are no reasons to claim that any developed state is sharing its economic sovereignty with international institutions such as the IMF or World Bank.

The picture is entirely different at the periphery of the capitalist system. At the periphery, many states have come to share an important part of their economic sovereignty with the IFIs. States are no longer the main loci of economic governance, rather the IMF and the World Bank are authoritative actors setting rules for the economic game and shaping the patterns of resource allocation in many less developed countries. On the whole, one can say that the IFIs play two distinctive but interrelated functions of economic governance in the peripheral area of the world economy.

First, there is what we could call "systemic governance," which refers to the IFIs' particular position in the complex structure of the global capitalist system. In the aftermath of the global move to financial laissez faire (and of the subsequent financial crises experienced by many less developed countries), the IFIs have become managers of maybe the most critical juncture in the architecture of the global capitalist system: the juncture between the global financial markets and the fragile less developed economies in the third and former second world. Therefore, one can say without exaggeration that the IFIs occupy a vital place in the governance structures of global capitalism.[60] As guardians of global capitalism and as gatekeepers of the less developed countries' access to international capital markets, the International Financial Institutions have been able to promote a pattern of adjustment at the periphery compatible with the ideal of an open and free international economy.

A second governance function of the IFIs results from their recent pursuit of fundamental institutional reforms in their client countries. After two decades of experimentation with the programs of structural adjustment, these institutions have started to promote substantial institutional reforms in many of the less developed countries. After the

---

[60] Let us recall in this context that from a critical perspective a major "accomplishment" of these institutions has been that they have so far succeeded in fending off and confining all major financial crises of the last twenty years to the periphery of the global capitalist system (even if at the price of the lost decades in the third and the former second world).

reform of the economic structures, a restructuring of the state institutions is apparently in the making in order to assure a firmer and more "productive" integration of the less developed countries in the open global economy of the twenty-first century. The policies and ideas summed up with the catchword "good governance" then reflect the further growth in the IFI's salience at the periphery of the global capitalist system.

The "good governance" agenda of the IFIs is one of the most fascinating and maybe far-reaching developments in the international political economy of our time, as it presupposes a further increase of the entanglement of the IFIs in the internal affairs of their member countries and suggests a further shift of power and authority from the less developed countries toward the IFIs. It is also particularly interesting due to its long-term implications for global economic governance and the respective role of the IFIs

## From "Structural Adjustment" to "Good Governance": the International Financial Institutions and the Long-Run Consequences of the Systemic Move to Financial Laissez-Faire

"Governance" was used for the first time as a major explanatory concept in a World Bank study about the growth problems of the African countries (World Bank 1989). The main claim advanced by this study, namely that at the core of Africa's development problems lay a "crisis of governance," was bound to have revolutionary implications. Thus, by using this concept, the World Bank was willing to admit openly for the first time in its history that a political component was a necessary part of the development process. This document opened a series of long lists of World Bank studies on governance that were to contribute to the major policy turn undergone by this institution in the second half of the 90s. Eventually, the concern for "governance" was to play a crucial role in the attempts to transcend the "Washington consensus," the intellectual paradigm to which the IFIs subscribed for the most part of the 80s and in the early 90s.

The policy prescriptions of the Washington consensus (fiscal discipline, deregulation, tax reform, positive but market-determined interest rates, competitive exchange rates, liberal trade policies, openness to foreign direct investment, privatization, public expenditure priorities in health and education, and property rights) (Williamson 1990) have been at the core of the IFIs' strategies to restructure the economies affected by the debt crisis and the transition economies in Eastern Europe and the former Soviet Union. The fundamental idea behind the Washington consensus was that the market is the most efficient institution for allocating resources; accordingly, the only solution in these economies was to push the state out of the way of private markets (Stiglitz 1998a). After more than a decade of reforms carried out along the lines of the Washington consensus in different corners of the world, from Estonia to Chile, it can be concluded that this reform strategy has registered only a limited success. The strategy has been successful to the extent to which a global financial meltdown has been avoided and the IFIs' clients have given up the failing state-centered strategies of development (to which most of them had adhered to different degrees in the post-war period) and have embraced market reforms. On the other hand, as is acknowledged even by scholars associated with the IFIs, the policy prescriptions of the Washington consensus (Burki and Perri 1998, Stiglitz 1998a and 1998b) have proven less capable of generating durable rates of economic growth consistent with the aims of poverty and inequality reduction. Moreover, despite the continuous popularity of the Washington consensus with the IFIs' decision-makers, by the mid-90s a series of troubling developments seriously called into question the wisdom of this approach. The discouraging experience with the IFIs' programs in several countries (and particularly on the African continent) showed that the "right institutions" and even the "right politics" are at least as important as "getting the prices right" and implementing the "right policies" for putting a country on a growth track. The partial failure of the transition to a market economy in several communist countries (and, foremost, the bungled transition in Russia) also underscored the importance of institutions in the process of economic reform. Finally, the financial crises of the 90s, starting with the Mexican crisis of 1994, showed that openness toward mobile international capital markets in the absence of appropriate domestic institutions can be disastrous for otherwise reasonably functioning market economies.

As an answer to these developments, the IFIs started to make the first steps beyond the "Washington consensus" and to speak of the importance of "good governance" and of the necessity of a "second generation of reforms" (Camdessus 1999). Even though it remains an open question whether the IFIs have really moved beyond the "Washington consensus," since the mid-1990s, the IMF and the World Bank have shown a growing concern for "institutions" and "good governance." This concern has been due not only to the transformations mentioned above, but also to the increasing popularity of the so-called "neo-institutional economics" among economists and social scientists. In these conditions, after the neo-liberal phase dominant in the 80s and early 90s, the IFIs have started to show the signs of a certain "institutional" turn in their policies and intellectual outlook since the mid-90s.

The World Bank has been at the forefront of this "institutional turn," a policy change substantially reinforced by James Wolfensohn's election as president of the World Bank in 1995. This institutional turn is recognizable also in the "comprehensive development framework" officially adopted by the World Bank in 1998. This new approach "suggests a long term holistic approach to development that recognizes the importance of macroeconomic fundamentals but gives equal weight to the institutional, structural, and social underpinnings of a robust market economy. It emphasizes strong partnerships among governments, donors, civil society, the private sector, and other development actors."[61] No wonder, then, that in the context of this institutional turn, the problem of governance has become so salient in the publications and programs of the Bank.

But what is "governance" in the Bank's perspective? Throughout the 90s, several World Bank publications (World Bank 1989, 1992, 1994, 1997a, 2000a) have tried to give a more precise (and, one can add, a less political) answer to this question. I shall present here the latest outcome of these conceptual efforts, the definition put forward in the World Bank studies "*Governance Matters*" (Kaufmann, Kray and Zoido-Labadon 1999) and *Aggregating Governance Indicators* (Kaufmann, Kray and Zoido-Labadon 2000b). According to Kaufmann, Kray and Zoido-Labadon (1999, p. 1), governance is to be understood "as the traditions and institutions by which authority in a country is exercised. These include (1) the process by which governments are selected, monitored, and replaced (2) the capacity of the government to effectively formulate and implement sound policies (3) the respect of the citizens for the institutions that govern economic and social interactions among them." Governance is, then, disaggregated into six clusters grouping more than 300 indicators: "*voice and accountability,*" "*political instability and violence,*" "*government effectiveness,*" "*regulatory burden,*" "*rule of law*" and "*graft.*" This study also claims to have found a strong causal relationship between the quality of governance and the quality of economic development: "we find that governance matters a great deal for economic outcomes. In particular, a one-standard deviation increase in

[61] "Background and Overview of the Comprehensive Development Framework" at http://www.worldbank.org/cdf/overview.htm

any of our governance indicators causes between a two-and-a-half and four-fold increase (decrease) in per capita incomes (infant mortality), and a 15 to 25 percent increase in literacy" (Kaufmann, Kray and Labadon 1999, p. 3).

What is striking about this definition of governance is that under a neutral and technical disguise, it shows without any trace of doubt that politics matter for development and that the institutional arrangements in a country are decisive for the prospects of growth. Consequently, to improve "governance" means nothing else but to carry out a program of extensive institutional reforms with unmistakable political overtones.

Following this new diagnosis of development, during the last couple of years the World Bank has started to invest massively in "good governance." The scope of the recent mutations in the activity of the World Bank is made manifest by the anti-corruption campaign launched by Wolfensohn as a core component of the package of programs aiming to improve the quality of governance in the Bank's member countries. According to Wolfensohn (2001), "six years ago, we in the Bank did not speak about corruption - it was seen as too political, and for many, an impossible challenge. Today we are working on anti-corruption and good governance programs in 95 countries, and are a leader in many aspects of this work." Alongside corruption, the World Bank's "governance" programs are tackling issues of crucial importance for the patterns of resource allocation in its member countries like the reform of administrative and civil services, reform of state finance, re-design of the patterns of public expenditure, decentralization of state activities, or the reform of the civil justice systems. In these conditions, if it is carried out fully, the "good governance" campaign of the World Bank will amount to a radical restructuring of the state at the periphery of the global capitalist system.

The IMF has joined the World Bank in this world-wide crusade for "good governance" and "sound institutions." As acknowledged by Horst Köhler (2000), the present Managing Director of the IMF, the IMF has "underestimated the importance of institutions building which needs time and requires crucially ownership by the societies affected" for many years. This neglect can be at least partially explained by the short-term focus of the IMF's programs (which, as a rule, deal with temporary balance of payments difficulties) and by the orthodox neo-liberal outlook shared by most of the top decision-makers at the IMF (in fact, to this day the IMF remains a stronghold of neo-liberalism). However, the IMF could no longer overlook the importance of "institutions" and "good governance" once the financial crises of the 90s showed how fateful the lack of solid and appropriate institutions can be for the countries trying to join the global financial markets. As a result of the lessons drawn from these crises (and from the huge scandal surrounding the alleged embezzlement of IMF money in Russia), the IMF clarified its own position toward issues of "good governance" (IMF 1997) and developed a wide range of codes of good financial and monetary practices that thereafter were proposed for implementation to all of its members. If implemented, these codes will lead to a substantial overhaul of the structures of economic governance from the IMF's member countries.

In conclusion, the reforms promoted by the World Bank and by the IMF converge toward what Robert Cox named the "internationalization of state." According to Cox (1987, p. 253), the "internationalization of state" is "the global process whereby national policies and practices have been adjusted to the exigencies of the world economy of international production." And, indeed, the main thrust of the IFIs' programs during the last twenty years has been to transform the economic and state structures of the peripheral countries in order to make them compatible with an international economy characterized by both trade and financial liberalization. Initially, after global financial markets came close to unleashing a global financial meltdown, the IFIs' main task was to manage the debt crisis and to keep the international financial system afloat. In order to achieve this goal, the IFIs have supervised the painful process of adjustment at the periphery and have made sure that this process took place according to the basic rules of the present world economy. However, while the programs of "structural adjustment" succeeded in opening the economies of many developed countries, it seems that the mainly economic reforms undertaken in the name of the "structural adjustment" were not sufficient to generate growth-cum-poverty reduction or to make the "emerging markets" safe for the outside investors. The next step identified as obligatory, therefore, was to complement these economic reforms with the institutional reforms necessary to modernize the state structures of the less developed countries and to make them capable of sustaining the burden of economic liberalization. In the end, the internationalization of the peripheral economies, then, was accompanied by a similar process of "internationalization of the state." As the local elites in many less developed countries are too weak, too divided, or too corrupt to implement the reforms demanded by the exigencies of global economic integration, the IFIs have themselves assumed the task of restructuring the less developed countries in order to make them compatible with a liberalized world economy. This internationalization of the state and the economy, then, has been the substance of the shift of authority from the state to IFIs in the second tier of global economic governance.

## The Long Term Future of Global Economic Governance under the IFIs

What are the long term implications of the IFIs acquisition of authoritative political capacity at the periphery and their pursuit of good governance? To answer this question, let us recall the fundamental fact emphasized long ago by Karl Polanyi (1957) in his analysis of the nineteenth-century capitalist civilization and recently "rediscovered" by institutional economics, namely that "market" is not a natural self-regulating natural mechanism (as always has been claimed by the market fundamentalists from yore and from now) but a social institution which needs a radical restructuring of the society as a whole in order to exist and to function. In the language of institutional economics, this idea is expressed in the argument about the necessity of market-supporting institutions such as property rights, institutions for economic stabilization, institutions for social insurance, and institutions of conflict management in order to work properly (Rodrik 1999). Polanyi's analysis of the institutional support of markets went further though. He showed that a market society is crucially and paradoxically dependent on three fundamental fictional commodities, labor, land and money. A market society (i.e., a society in which the allocation of resources takes place mainly through a market) can emerge only after these non-commodities are turned into "fictional commodities" and subjected to the logic of market mechanisms. At the same time, however, because of the special nature of these fictional commodities (which cannot be produced via market mechanisms), a market society can survive in the long run only if the marketization of labor, land, and money is limited and regulated; otherwise, the society as a whole will succumb to the "satanic mill" of the market.

The Polanyian analysis of markets can help us to understand the fundamental conundrum posed by current role of the IMF and World Bank in the architecture of global capitalism. The original *raison d'etre* of these institutions was, of course, to provide an embedding framework for the capitalist world economy of the post-war period. Specifically, by relying upon the institutional framework of the Bretton Woods system, the states could control the international flow of money and, subsequently, engage in the vast post-war project to put limits to the capitalist commodification of labor. The etatization of international money was a fundamental prerequisite for the social-democratic and welfare state arrangements of that time. Not surprisingly, these arrangements became impracticable once the re-emergence of global finance put an end to the Bretton Woods system and undermined the ability of the states to control and manage the flows of money.

If we adopt a Polanyian understanding of markets, however, we can conclude that the problems plaguing the emerging global market society do not stem only from the deficient way in which the global markets are (not) regulated today. Rather, it appears that a main problem with the present structures of international market regulation, besides the ad-hoc nature of the structures of economic governance of the present global capitalism, is the way in which they solve (or better said, do not solve) the problem of de-commodifying the fictional commodities of the global market society. In contrast to the Bretton Woods system, the present international regulatory frameworks do not constrain the actions of markets but instead promote the further commodification of land, labor, and money. This is particularly true for the IFIs, which throughout the post Bretton Woods period have pushed their clients to allow the market forces to play a larger role in their economies. Under slogans like "good governance" or "building institutions for markets," the IFIs' programs aim to achieve a full-fledged marketization of the less developed societies at the periphery of the global capitalist system.

The fundamental problem emerging, then, is that the long term success of this strategy is highly doubtful due to the inherent limits to the commodification of land, labor, and money. The looming environmental disaster and the mass protests against the neo-liberal policies promoted by the IFIs seem to indicate that we are already very close to these limits. In the end, even citizens of developed countries confronted with the social consequences of the privatization and commodification of moneys may start asking that most pressing question of our time: *who elected the bankers* (Pauly 1997)? The citizens of many less developed countries have already asked themselves: *who elected the IMF?*

## Conclusion

This paper investigated the structures of international economic governance from the perspective of the roles played by the International Monetary Fund and the World Bank in the management of the world economy. The initial puzzle behind this investigation was whether the process of globalization has brought about a new structure of international economic governance in which states have to share a significant part of their authority with international organizations like the IFIs, as some globalization theorists claim.

This investigation was focused primarily on the structural characteristics of the present monetary and financial systems. The main claim advanced in this paper is that the present world economy is characterized by a two-tiered structure of economic governance due to the absence of any general rules and norms to regulate the international financial and monetary systems. The first tier is composed of a small number of developed states which coordinate their economic policies in forums of international cooperation like the G-7 summits. In fact, the G-7 process can be regarded as the most important forum of international governance in the present world economy. Given the unquestionable preeminence enjoyed by the G-7 states (either as individual or as collective actors) in the management of world affairs, I argued that there are no grounds to speak of an overall transfer of power from states to supra-national entities like the IFIs. The ultimate decisions in matters of international economic governance are still taken by the G-7 under the leadership of the USA. With its structural domination of the world economy, the USA continues to be the unchallenged world economic power at the beginning of the twenty-first century.

In this paper, I also showed that the IMF and the World Bank have acquired an extraordinary influence over the policies of many countries at the periphery of the global capitalist system. With the IFIs' growing involvement in the affairs of the third and former second world, a new type of economic governance has emerged. The fundamental characteristic of this type of economic governance is the authoritative influence exercised by these international organizations over the policies of many less developed countries. The second tier of the structure of economic governance in the world economy, then, is constituted through the interaction between the IFIs and their client countries. As guardians of the international financial systems and promoters of the norms embraced by the core states in the world economy, the IFIs have been able to induce substantial changes in the economic policies and institutional structures of the less developed countries. On the whole, the IFIs have succeeded in promoting in the third and former second world a pattern of economic and institutional adjustment that is convergent with the exigencies of a world economy characterized by a liberal trade and finance regime.

Therefore, given the structural leverage exercised by the International Monetary Fund and the World Bank over many of their client countries, I argued that there are solid grounds to claim that a transfer of authority from nation states to the IFIs has already taken place at the periphery of the global capitalist system. However, it remains an open question whether the sway exercised by these international organizations over the policies of many less developed countries can be maintained in the long run in conditions in which the neo-liberal project is confronted all over the world with the inherent limits of the process of commodifying land, labor, and money.

B
A

# Global Culture and International Human Rights Norms: The Case of Female Genital Mutilation in Germany

Heike Brabandt

## Introduction[62]

Some scholars argue that globalization has led to an increasingly global culture and brought about a transnational "legal order" characterized by world-cultural principles and institutions that shape the actions of states and other subunits (Boli 2001, McNeely 1995, Meyer, Boli et al 1997, Strang 1990, Thomas 1993). Thus, globalization is supposed to foster the diffusion of international human rights norms, including women's rights. John Boli and George M. Thomas (1999) - who are among the most influential scholars of this strand of thought – argue firstly that empirical studies of nation-states find striking structural homology across countries in "education, women's rights, social security programs, environmental policy, and constitutional arrangements" (p. 14). Secondly, they consider International Non-Governmental Organizations (INGOs) as significant actors in achieving such a homology, as their primary concern is "enacting, codifying, modifying, and propagating world-cultural structures and principles" (p. 19). Most scholars focusing on the role of social movements in a globalized world also find Non-Governmental Organizations (NGOs), whose main scope of activity is in the national arena, significant in this respect. Both INGOs and NGOs are thought to play an important role in the implementation of international norms (Commission on Global Governance 1995, Keck and Sikkink 1998, Smith, Pagnucco, and Lopez 1998, Wapner 1997, Willetts 1996).

This contribution aims at critically assessing these two arguments in the area of women's human rights in Germany with a focus on the human rights violation Female Genital Mutilation (FGM). Firstly, I show that world-cultural principles are not necessarily assumed by states - not even by industrialized Western states like Germany that are expected to be among the "Western human rights protectors" and that strongly

62 This contribution is based on my M.A. thesis (Brabandt 1999). For their invaluable advice and most helpful comments on this contribution I am grateful to Rainer Baumann, Anna Collins, Doris A. Fuchs, Friedrich Kratochwil, Mary Meyer, Lisa Prügl, and Thomas Nielebock.

promote international women's human rights norms as world cultural principles in the arena of UN institutions and expect so-called Third World countries to adhere to these norms. I argue that the existence of international human rights norms may increase the leverage of actors working towards implementation of the norms and provide these actors with a "legitimized space" for their activism. Whether the norms are implemented, however, depends not only on the willingness of (I)NGOs and other actors to work for their implementation but ultimately on the costs the respective government attributes to their implementation.

Secondly, I argue that while pointing out that (I)NGOs may play a significant role in the process of the implementation of international norms, the literature has failed to examine this role in detail. Even in a globalized world, the state remains the locus of power with respect to the implementation of international human rights norms. While NGOs may disseminate information about norms on the individual level and aim at mobilizing the population to engage in activities on behalf of the norms' implementation, they cannot introduce bills in parliament, nor do they have any executive powers. In most cases, activities by the legislative and/or the executive branch are required in order to achieve the implementation of international human rights norms. As Margaret Keck and Kathryn Sikkink (1998, p. 204) have shown in their work, it is very unlikely that (I)NGOs would be able to manage to mobilize citizens to such an extent that governments would feel it necessary to react accordingly. Therefore, in order for NGOs to influence national politics, they need access to the state, that is, parliamentary factions, the respective government, and its ministries in order to disseminate information about the norms among those actors and in particular to lobby them[63] (Leatherman, Pagnucco, and Smith 1994, Smith, Pagnucco, and Chatfield 1997, Smith, Pagnucco, and Lopez 1998). For these reasons, studies on the role of NGOs in the implementation of international norms need particularly to investigate the interaction between NGOs on the one hand and actors of the political and executive establishment on the other. The chapter does so drawing among other things on interviews I conducted with representatives of both groups.

I borrow the term "norm" from social constructivism. Norms are defined as intersubjectively shared, value-based expectations providing, within a given social system, immediate orientation about appropriate behavior (Finnemore 1996, p. 22f). To identify the relevant norms, I

[63] The range of these activities is only applicable for NGOs working in democratic political systems. In authoritarian or totalitarian political systems, NGOs are far more restricted in their scope of activity (see Gränzer/Jetschke/Risse/Schmitz 1998).

investigated the pertinent international documents from June 1993 (World Human Rights Conference) until March 2002. For the process of the norms' implementation in Germany, I examined the period from November 1994 (when NGOs and members of parliament began to prepare for the Fourth World Women's Conference) until March 2002. No activities aiming at the norms' implementation were launched before that stage. I focused mainly on the period between 1994-1998 (the 13th sitting period of the German parliament, the Bundestag) since most activities were launched then.

In what follows, I first provide some background information on the field of women's human rights and identify the international norms telling states how to deal with the practice of FGM. Next, I discuss the prevailing pattern of the implementation of the norms in Germany. I then analyze the role of NGOs in the process of the norms' implementation focusing in particular on the interaction of NGOs with political actors and members of the executive. In the final section, I discuss the findings.

## Women's Rights as Human Rights: International Norms Telling States How to Deal with the Practice of FGM

In the 1980s, women's networks and activists all over the world started campaigning for the recognition of women's rights as human rights. The World Conference on Human Rights in Vienna (1993) acknowledged their claim. This was celebrated as a great success since it overcame the public-private dichotomy and the exclusion of the private sphere from human rights norms. The international community now recognizes practices that violate women's bodily integrity as human rights violations, in particular the practice of FGM. Women's human rights are now considered an integral part of international human rights norms and have been frequently reaffirmed (Schmidt-Häuer 1998). Before the recognition of women's rights as human rights in 1993, FGM had been accepted as a traditional practice on the basis of cultural relativist assumptions and as a matter of the private sphere in which the state had no wish to interfere.

Cases of FGM occur frequently among the immigrant population in Germany.[64] Therefore, there is a need for the implementation of the

---

[64] The chairwoman of the German Women Doctors' Association is convinced that no week passes in which some little girl somewhere is not being mutilated (Focus 13/1999, p. 40).

international human rights norms telling states how to deal with FGM. Before it was dealt with in UN-institutions and before international norms were developed, the practice had been considered a foreign custom in German politics and a private matter in which the state would not interfere. Even after FGM was recognized as a human rights violation, the German public still regarded it as an "African problem".[65] Not only German politicians but Western politicians in general have frequently expressed their outrage about the practice. They have tended to associate it with notions of somehow "less civilized societies" which are not able to stop the practice, and in the process have tended to "other" African countries.[66] Against this background, it is particularly intriguing to investigate whether the norms German politicians have fervently agreed upon on the international level are being implemented in their own country since this amounts to challenging their notion of Germany constituting a "civilized" society in contrast to "uncivilized savage" societies. Not surprisingly, German administrative bodies have closed their eyes to incidents of FGM occurring in Germany, as will be shown later.

In order to identify the international human rights norms on FGM, I examined the pertinent *international treaties* (for example, Convention on the Elimination of All Forms of Discrimination Against Women and the Convention on the Rights of the Child); *legal acts of the UN* (for example, Resolutions of the General Assembly[67], of the Human Rights Commission and its Sub-Commission); and the *final acts of UN World Conferences* (for example, the World Human Rights Conference [1993] and the Fourth World Women's Conference [1995]). Six norms appear frequently in all of these documents: States are urged (1) to explicitly prohibit the practice and make it a prosecutable offence; (2) to protect

---

[65] Although FGM occurs mostly in Africa, it is also practiced on the South-Arabian peninsula, as for example in the Oman, Yemen, Bahrain, and the United Arab Emirates. In addition, it is practiced among some ethnicities in Indonesia, India, Malaysia, and Sri Lanka as well as by some tribes of Aborigines in Australia. It is not - as widely held - an Islamic ritual. The *Koran* does not require it. Furthermore, it dates back to the Old Egyptians. Some Christian groups practice it, for instance in Kenya, as well as the Jewish *Falashas* in Ethiopia (Günttner 1995, p. 7, Glaubrecht 1995a, p. 22).

[66] France is a notable exception in this respect. It has not only publicly admitted that cases of FGM occur frequently within its jurisdiction but is also prosecuting such cases.

[67] In particular, the "Declaration on the Elimination of Violence Against Women (48/104) and the "Resolution on Traditional or Customary Practices Affecting the Health of Women and Girls" (52/99).

girls and women who fled their home countries in order to escape the practice, that is, to provide them with refugee status or political asylum; (3) to inform law enforcement officers, police personnel, and judicial, medical, and social workers, as well as those who deal with migration and refugee issues, of the causes and consequences of the practice and to avoid judicial and enforcement practices which might revictimize the victims; (4) to initiate campaigns informing the public about the practice and its causes and consequences, and to support NGOs' information campaigns on the practice; (5) to provide counseling services for girls/women concerned and for their next of kin; and (6) to support NGOs fighting the practice world-wide.

Not only the majority of UN member states, but in most cases even all member states agreed unanimously on the norms. In all cases, Germany was among the norms' supporters. In addition, the norms are very clear about which behavior is regarded appropriate and should shape Germany's action. Now, the intriguing question is what has happened to these international norms in German domestic politics.

## German Governments, Domestic Politics, World-Cultural Principles and FGM

Bills that aimed at implementing the international norms were introduced in the sitting period of the *Bundestag* from November 1994 to September 1998 (13th period). In October 1998, power changed from a governing coalition between the Christian Democratic Union/Christian Social Union (CDU/CSU) and the Free Democratic Party (F.D.P.)[68] to a governing coalition between the Social Democratic Party (SPD) and Bündnis 90/Die Grünen (the Green Party),[69] who have been in power since the 14th sitting period (1998-2002). While in opposition, the SPD and the Green Party had urged the government to implement the international norms telling states how to deal with FGM. They not only introduced bills with this aim in the sitting period from 1994-1998, but they also pestered the CDU/CSU - F.D.P. government with numerous "small questions" ("kleine Anfrage") and "great questions" ("große Anfrage"). Examining the nearly complete term of their office provides the oppor-

---

68 The CDU/CSU faction was the "big partner" in this coalition with 41.5% of votes and the F.D.P. the "small partner" with 6.9% of votes.

69 In this coalition, the SPD is the "big partner" with 40.9% of votes and the Green Party the "small partner" with 6.7% of votes.

tunity to determine whether they got down to action once in the position to do so.

From the incomplete state of the norms' implementation as of March 2002, a pattern can be discerned. The former (1994-1998) and the present government (1998-) undertook only those steps for the sake of the norms' implementation which (1) did not put high demands on their budget and (2) did not require long processes of decision-making. In addition, (3) measures expected to lead to a loss of political support were avoided as long as they were not linked with other issues that would lead to an even greater loss of support if not dealt with.

*(1) Norms were not implemented if their implementation was thought to be expensive.* The complete implementation of norm 3 would be costly. Informing specific professional groups on FGM and bringing in specifically trained female judges whenever a girl/woman refugee claims to have been in danger of being mutilated would be much more expensive than the *status quo*. In an interview with the author in April 1999, the new Federal Minister of Justice, Herta Däubler-Gmelin (SPD), confirmed that German police officers, public prosecutors, and judges have not been well informed on the topic. Some investigative journalists had discovered that neither the police nor public prosecutors had intervened in cases of FGM occurring in their areas although they had been informed in advance.[70] The Federal Minister of Justice wrote letters to the 16 State Ministers of the Interior and of Justice, requesting that they inform law enforcement officers, police, and judicial personnel on FGM in their respective states because of these obvious failings (interview with Herta Däubler-Gmelin, Tübingen 10 April 1999). Whether the respective ministers will do so, and whether this will lead to consequences remains to be seen. The former government also distributed brochures on FGM to public health departments and social workers and provided funding for an information stall of the NGO *TERRE DES FEMMES, Human Rights for Women* (TDF), at the Convention of German Midwives in 1998. It must be noted, however, that these measures do not live up to the expectations expressed in norm 3. Nor was a public information

[70] For example, the Karlsruhe head of the Youth Welfare Department accused the local police of having failed to intervene in a girl's mutilation, although informed by his office's social workers. A further incident happened in Berlin, where a gynecologist mutilated little girls for payment of money. Public prosecutors did not investigate him although a local politician had informed them about the gynecologist's deeds (ARD, 22 March 1999, 21:00h). They only started to take action against him after it was brought before the public (Stuttgarter Zeitung, 25 March 1999).

campaign launched as required by norm 4. The same holds for setting up counseling services (norm 5).

Even though qualified staff could have been employed in already existing services, this staff would still need to be paid. Compared to that, the implementation of the other requirement of norm 4 - the support of NGOs' information campaigns - is relatively inexpensive. An information booklet published by TDF in 1999 was funded with the total sum of DM 15,000 and their brochure in migrants' languages (Arabic, Somali, and so on) was funded with DM 75, 390. The employment of a qualified psychologist would require more than the total of this sum annually. In contrast, the Ministry for Economic-Co-operation and Development has a certain amount for supporting the activities of NGOs in developing countries (norm 6) at its disposal anyway. To allocate these funds differently and take some of the money to support NGOs fighting FGM does not cost any extra. Thus, it comes as no surprise that the former as well as the present governments support local NGOs fighting FGM in Africa.

*(2) For the sake of the norms' implementation only, no measures were taken which would entail long processes of decision-making.* Specifically, steps were avoided that require the change of laws or the introduction of new laws. This is true for the explicit prohibition of FGM (norm 1). The expectation expressed in norm 2, requiring states to grant girls/women fleeing their home countries a refugee status or political asylum, was eventually taken up into a bill on immigration (in autumn 2001) which aims at fundamentally revising the existing asylum laws. It was not in the first draft of the bill, however. It was added to the draft[71] only as a consequence of a political deal between the SPD and the Greens about which I will provide more detailed information below.

In the instance of norm 1, both the former (CDU/CSU and F.D.P.) and the new government (SPD and the Greens) claimed that the norm has already been complied with by existing laws.[72] In the instance of norm 2, the former government refrained from taking any measures at all, while the new government had only planned to resort to measures

---

[71] The draft found a clear majority in the Bundestag (first chamber) but the vote in the Bundesrat (second chamber) remains contested. As of yet (April 2002), it is not clear whether the German President will sign it, which would turn it into a law.

[72] The government pointed out that FGM has been already prohibited because it is a form of physical injury or of grievous bodily harm. As such it is a prosecutable offence. The problem with this approach is, however, that this fact is well-known neither in the population nor among police officers and public prosecutors, as the incidents in Karlsruhe and Berlin show.

that are less demanding[73] since it feared a tremendous loss of political support if it changed the asylum laws to recognize FGM and other sorts of gendered persecution as a just cause (if they had recognized FGM, it would have had to recognize other forms of gendered persecution as well). Therefore, it denied that there was a "protection loop in German asylum laws" for women/girls fleeing FGM and other forms of gendered persecution.

*(3) Measures expected to lead to a loss of political support were avoided as long as they were not linked with other issues that would lead to an even greater loss of support if not dealt with.* This is obvious with regard to norm 2. The issue of asylum-seekers has been strongly politicized in Germany. Many politicians and also the mass media have been stirring up *angst* of being "swamped" by asylum-seekers. Representatives of both big "people's parties", the CDU/CSU and the SPD, were unwilling to loosen the strict asylum laws or to allow for other forms of immigration. However, in 2000 the German IT industry complained that they could not find enough IT specialists and urged the government to allow for immigration of IT specialists. In the resulting discussion, it became obvious that Germany needs immigration of highly qualified professionals in order to sustain its economy. As a result, the government decided to draft a bill on immigration which was to be passed by the cabinet in the end of September 2001. The bill did not provide for refugee status or political asylum for women/girls fleeing FGM or other forms of gendered persecution.

Otto Schily (SPD), Minister of the Interior, made it quite clear that he had no intention of doing so, either, when on the occasion of the celebration of the Refugee Conventions' 50th anniversary, he bawled at the UN High Commissioner for Refugees, Ruud Lubbers, that even if

[73] In fall 1998, the then new foreign minister Joschka Fischer (Green Party) instructed German embassies overseas to conduct serious investigations into gender-specific violations of women's human rights and to report their findings in the Ministry's country reports. Those reports are used by courts in the hearings to determine a person's right to political asylum. The SPD and Bündnis 90/Die Grünen also revised the administrative regulations concerning the asylum proceedings (Verwaltungsvorschriften zur Anwendung des Asylrechts) in order to take account of gender-specific forms of persecution. However, these revisions do not provide girl/women refugees with the right to asylum or the right to refugee status according to the refugee convention. As the revised regulations state only that a judge "may take into account" gender-specific forms of persecution when deciding if a so-called humanitarian deportation obstacle (humanitäres Abschiebungshindernis) exists, they leave it at his/her discretion whether she/he does so. Furthermore, a deportation obstacle is the worst legal status an asylum-seeker may receive and it is usually only issued for 6 months.

frequently repeated, the tale of protection loops for refugees fleeing non-state persecution [which includes gendered non-state persecution, of course] was not true (Knaup and Mestmacher 2001, p. 32). Even though the fear of a significant rise in numbers of refugees is completely unfounded in the case of FGM and other forms of gendered persecution[74], the symbolic force of the current restrictive asylum laws was so high that most politicians refrained from supporting any change that may have conveyed the impression that these laws were being "slackened". Only after the devastating events of September 11, 2001, was the government prepared to change the bill. First of all, as a consequence of the terrorist attacks and the fact that the terrorists had lived in Germany without any interference by the police or other security forces, it decided to re-consider the bill. Furthermore, in order to show citizens that they were reacting to the new global threats, the chancellor and his Minister of the Interior - both SPD - decided to introduce two anti-terrorism bills.

Their Green coalition partner was, however, not readily prepared to agree with the bills, since the Greens feared that they would lead to a severe limitation of civil rights. Because of the public pressure on the Social Democrats to react to the threats of global terrorism, they were in a situation in which their government's standing depended very much on showing a prompt reaction. Otherwise the opposition would have argued that the government was not capable of acting in what was perceived as a threat to German security. The Social Democrats and the Greens went for a deal: The Greens promised not to vote down the anti-terrorism bills. In exchange for their promise, a provision was included in the bill on immigration to provide women/girls fleeing gendered persecution with refugee status in line with the Refugee Convention (interview with Günther Burkhardt Frankfurt, 16 November 2001). Since the result of the Bundesrat's vote on the bill is contested and the opposition has declared that it will sue against it in case the President signs the bill, it remains to be seen whether the bill will ever become a law.

From the state of the implementation of the norms, it is clear that the higher the costs that were attributed to their implementation, the lower

[74] Only 30% of refugees are female. Most of these apply for "family-asylum", that is, they do not claim to be persecuted themselves, but refer to their husband's persecution. Only a marginal number of these women refugees claims to have suffered from gender-specific persecution. Even if a change of law would lead to an increasing number of women refugees fleeing from gender-specific persecution, the Canadian experience shows that the absolute number of women claiming such persecution remains extremely low (UNHCR 1998, p. 8f).

was the willingness of political and administrative actors to adopt national policies in compliance with them. Costs can be understood in rather broad terms here as financial, procedural, or political costs. Only those measures thought to be inexpensive were realized. More expensive measures were not implemented, but did receive some attention because the opposition parties raised them. The findings also suggest that the agreement to an international norm in the framework of international institutions cannot necessarily be expected to lead to a prompt implementation of this norm - at least not in Germany. This finding is in gross contradiction to Germany's self-declared role as a state that carefully complies with international human rights norms and at the same time is prepared to criticize other states' non-compliance.

Thus, the actions of the German state have not been shaped by the international norms. Rather, the international norms formed a framework of the "desirable". Whether parts of this framework were implemented depended on the cost-benefit calculations of the government. However, the fact that the former CDU/CSU + F.D.P. government had agreed to international norms but did *not* demonstrate any willingness to adapt national policies accordingly made it vulnerable to the opposition's efforts to achieve the norms' implementation. Thus, the international norms gave some leverage to the former opposition factions - the SPD and the Green Party. They used the norms as guidelines for the bills they proposed and for questioning the government on this issue. They never failed to name and to quote from the international documents the former government had previously agreed upon and signed.

As a consequence, the former CDU/CSU and F.D.P. government came under pressure to justify its position. It attempted to demonstrate that there was no need for the implementation of the norms, since national policies were already in line with them. The opposition's efforts were therefore regarded not only as unfounded but also as unnecessary. The former government's behavior was thus marked by the urge to show that it actually did comply with the international norms. Hence, the parliamentary factions forming the government (CDU/CSU and F.D.P.) supported the inter-factual resolution on FGM entitled *Genitalverstümmelung ächten, Mädchen und Frauen schützen* (*Proscription against Female Genital Mutilation - Protection of Girls and Women*) (13/10682))[75]

[75] This inter-factional resolution was adopted unanimously by the parliament in June 1998. In the resolution, FGM is denounced as a severe human rights violation. The parliament calls upon the government to commit itself to the protection of girls and women threatened with FGM and suggests a number of measures. Although the resolution reflects the parliament's awareness of the human rights violation and the

and implemented some of the norms partially. Asked why they did so, former Federal Minister of Justice Sabine Leutheusser-Schnarrenberger (F.D.P.) argued that they could not completely ignore existing international norms (interview with Sabine Leutheusser-Schnarrenberger Bonn, 26 January 1999). According to her, the UN-World Conferences have had an "immense impact" on national policies for years (ibid.). From the expert's point of view of the head of the UNHCR's Nuremberg Sub-Office, the parliament's clear denouncement of FGM led to an increased public awareness of the human rights violation and an increased willingness among administrative bodies to support girls and women threatened with FGM (telephone interview with Anna Büllesbach, 29 July 1999).

Since October 1998, the SPD and the Green Party, who exerted pressure on the former government to comply with the international norms, have been in power themselves. Their former role as protectors of the rights of women refugees, including women fleeing FGM, has partially been taken up by the PDS,[76] which has questioned the new government on the topic of women fleeing gendered persecution, including FGM, twice. However, it put forward only "small questions," the responses to which are not discussed in the Bundestag. It has not pursued any activities of a similar scope to that of the SPD and the Green Party during their time in opposition. The SPD + Green government has not at all lived up to the far-reaching demands made when in opposition. Rather, in a similar vein to the previous government, it withdrew to the official position that there was no need for the implementation of the norms since national policies were already in line with them. It introduced no law that explicitly prohibits the practice, nor did it inform professionals dealing with migration and refugee issues on a scope broader than writing letters to some state ministers. Neither did it institutionalize special counseling services or launch a public information campaign. With regard to women/girls fleeing FGM and seeking refuge in Germany, it had no intention to do more than resort to the rather cosmetic measures already mentioned.[77] If September 11 had not happened, no provision would have been added to the bill on immigration to recognize FGM as a just cause for refugee status, despite the fact

---

need for action to eradicate FGM, the resolution itself did not lead to any substantial changes of policies because, unlike a bill, it was not binding and thus amounted only to a declaration of the parliament's opinion on the matter.

[76] The PDS is the succeeding party to the Former Socialist Unity Party (SED), the ruling party of the German Democratic Republic.

[77] See footnote 74.

that the bill changed quite a few other aspects of asylum laws and this would have been an ideal opportunity to include such a change, as the post-September 11 period showed.[78] Thus, it is an irony of history that what can be described as "cultural" globalization à la Boli and Thomas did not have very much influence on Germany's actions with regard to the protection of women/girls fleeing FGM, but the ugly face of globalization, the terror attacks of September 11, ultimately did.

In conclusion, it is clear that the international norms as such have led only to some change of action of the German governments when their implementation was considered to be "cheap" in terms of financial, procedural, and political costs. Thus, world cultural principles are not just assumed by states; they need committed individuals willing to act strategically in order to implement them. The events of September 11 and the subsequent change in the SPD's attitude with regard to women refugees suffering from FGM and other forms of gendered persecution underline this fact.

However, the very existence of the international norms and the fact that German governments have agreed to them in international institutions have given leverage to the activities of parliamentary actors in favor of the norms. The changes of action that occurred with respect to the norms' implementation only came about because of the continuous efforts of these actors.

This brings me to my second argument. The relevant question now is that of the role of NGOs in these actors' efforts. Did they have a role in them at all? And what, if anything, did they do to further the implementation of the norms?

## NGOs and the Implementation of International Norms

In this section, the activities of NGOs concerned with the implementation of the norms are explored. As pointed out in the introduction, NGOs

---

[78] Interestingly, I was told by women politicians of both factions that during the coalition negotiations between the SPD and the Green Party, the (all female) committee on women's issues had agreed to change the asylum laws to recognize gendered persecution as a just cause for asylum Prominent male politicians of the SPD faction, including the current Federal Minister for the Interior, Otto Schily, refused to accept this plan. The only concession this influential group of (male) SPD-politicians made was to revise the enforcement instructions of the asylum laws (as mentioned above) (interviews in Bonn with Maria Brosch, 25 January 1999, and with Christel Hanewinckel, 27 January 1999).

may disseminate information about norms among citizens, aiming at mobilizing the population in order to put pressure on the governments to implement the norms (on the individual level), and they may attempt to raise awareness of the norms among politicians and lobby them to become active in order to further the implementation of the norms (on the national level). As the work of NGOs on the individual level is not considered sufficient to achieve the norms' implementation, the NGOs' activities on the national level are of particular interest. In this section, I first investigate whether the pessimistic account of NGOs' activities on the individual level proves right in my case. Next, I focus on their activities on the national level. As the great majority of activities on FGM were launched by the Green faction and the SPD in the 13th sitting period (1994-1998) of the Bundestag, I focus on this period.[79]

In Germany, only one NGO promotes the implementation of all six identified international norms.[80] This was *TERRE DES FEMMES* (TDF), a women-only NGO, which was founded for the purpose of working towards women's equality in the area of human rights. Prompted by the preparatory work for the World Women's Conference in Beijing, TDF made FGM a special focus of its work.

*Raising Awareness of the Existence of the International Norms among Citizens (Individual Level).* From November 1995 to March 2002, representatives of TDF gave approximately 120 lectures on the "Human Rights Violation Female Genital Mutilation" and the need to change policies in order to address this violation of women's human rights appropriately. These lectures were held in vocational and regular schools, in universities, sometimes by invitation of other NGOs. They were usually advertised in the respective local paper and reported upon afterwards. TDF also started a campaign on FGM, which due to lack of

---

[79] As mentioned above, in the 14th sitting period (1998-2002) the PDS has thus far only put forward two small questions that had no particular focus on FGM but concerned women fleeing gendered persecution in general. They have not introduced draft bills - neither on the topic of women fleeing gendered persecution nor on FGM. Nor have they pursued any activities to put pressure on the new government to implement the other norms on FGM, such as pestering the government with "great questions" on it.

[80] Two other NGOs, PRO ASYL and Der Deutsche Frauenrat, fought for the implementation of norm 2 (the change of asylum laws) and parts of norm 3 (they campaigned for bringing in specifically trained female judges in asylum proceedings whenever a girl/women refugee claims to have suffered from gender-specific forms of persecution). They did so in a broader campaign on the "Protection of persecuted women". In this paper, for reasons of space, I concentrate on the activities of TDF. For those of PRO ASYL and Der Deutsche Frauenrat see: Brabandt 1999.

funding was rather small in scope. It distributed 5,000 posters and 10,000 flyers in the whole of Germany. In 2000 it supplemented this campaign with 20 copies of a short trailer on FGM which has been shown in numerous German cinemas since then.

National papers are more significant for reaching individual citizens than articles in local papers and a small information campaign. TDF representatives have established a network of contacts to national papers (interview with Regina Kalthegener, Bonn, 25 January 1999). Articles on FGM have appeared in a range of them.[81] Besides informing citizens, such articles are also important for the impression they create among members of parliament: They convey the message that FGM is regarded as a significant issue by the public.[82]

However, the number of lectures given and the posters and flyers distributed, even the 20 copies of trailer and the articles in national papers, were not sufficient to inform the bulk of the population. A publication by former super-model Waris Dirie has changed this situation dramatically. The book "Desert Flower" ("Wüstenblume"), in which she recounts her personal experience as a victim of FGM, was number one on the German bestseller lists for weeks in 1999. The German edition of the book lists the address of TDF as a German NGO working on this issue. The number of enquiries reaching TDF's office has increased enormously ever since. However, while the public has been very interested in learning about the issue, no political mobilization has occurred in the form of public pressure on the government to implement the international norms (interview with Regina Kalthegener, Bonn, 25 January 1999 and interview with Gritt Richter, Göttingen, 27 April 2002).

*Raising Awareness of the Existence of the International Norms among Politicians (National Level).* Two TDF representatives attended the World Women's Conference in Beijing (1995), while another representative participated in the NGO-Forum in Huairou. At the NGO-Forum and during their flight home, they came to talk with the representatives of the Green Party who had been delegated to the conference and NGO-Forum (interview with Angelika Köster-Loßack, Bonn, 28 January 1999). Both sides agreed to make FGM their issue and to consider jointly the

[81] For example in the *Frankfurter Rundschau*, the *tageszeitung*, the *Süddeutsche Zeitung* and the weekly paper *Die Zeit*.

[82] For instance, a report in the national paper *Süddeutsche Zeitung* with the title *Frauen-Beschneidung: Eine Folter mitten in Europa* (Female Circumcision: Torture Right in the Middle of Europe) appeared two days before a debate on Human Rights in the Bundestag (12 December 1997), in which bills on FGM by the SPD faction (13/9401) and the Green faction (13/9335) were to be discussed.

political changes necessary in order to deal appropriately with the human rights violation.

In October 1995, shortly after the World Women's Conference, the Bonn local groups of the Green Party and TDF jointly organized a lecture on "Women's Rights After the World Women's Conference" that focused on FGM. TDF also invited Maria Brosch, the coordinator for women's issues of the Green Party, to its workshops on FGM, while the parliamentary faction of the Greens instructed her to signal the party's interest in supporting TDF's cause there. Participants of the workshops discussed how to achieve greater public awareness of FGM and talked about the political steps necessary to better support girls/women who are in danger of being mutilated. As a consequence of this preoccupation with FGM, the Green faction decided to hold a hearing on the topic. It was organized in joint responsibility with TDF. Together they selected the experts to be invited and decided on its structure and on the political demands the experts' lectures should end with (interviews in Bonn with Maria Brosch, 25 January 1999, and with Angelika Köster-Loßack, 28 January 1999; telephone interview with Ines Laufer, 14 June 1999). They diverged only on the question of whether they should demand the explicit prohibition of FGM. While TDF women regarded this as necessary, representatives of the Greens argued that FGM was a criminal offence by existing law already and that it would be too costly (in terms of time and staff) to develop a bill for an individual law prohibiting FGM. The hearing *Ein Schmerz, der die Seele trifft* ("A Pain Striking the Soul") was held in April 1997. After the hearing, the Green faction still did not support the idea of developing such a bill for an individual law. But it drafted a parliamentary bill on FGM in which it adopted all other TDF demands for policy changes in line with the international norms (interview with Angelika Köster-Loßack, Bonn, 28 January 1999).[83] Regina Kalthegener, member of TDF and then chairwoman of the *Forum Menschenrechte* (Forum on Human Rights)[84], counterchecked their bill (13/9335) before it went into parliament (interviews in Bonn with Maria Brosch, 25 January 1999; with Regina Kalthegener, 25 January 1999, and with Angelika Köster-Loßack, 28 January 1999).

TDF also had some contact with SPD members of parliament and contributed to some extent to the SPD's parliamentary bill on FGM

---

83 Instead of requesting a special law prohibiting FGM, the Green faction urged the government to run a campaign informing the public that FGM is a criminal offence (13/9335, p. 11).

84 The Forum on Human Rights is the umbrella organization of all German NGOs working on human rights.

(13/9401). The co-operation between SPD politicians and TDF representatives was not as close as with the Green faction.[85] The contacts with the other factions of the *Bundestag* were marginal. There was only one exception: Sabine Leutheusser-Schnarrenberger, then the speaker of the F.D.P. for Women's Affairs, who belongs to the left-wing minority of her party. She learned about the human rights violation only through TDF (interview with Sabine Leutheusser-Schnarrenberger, Bonn 26 January 1999). The speaker for Women's Affairs of the CDU faction, Anke Eymer, did not have any contact with TDF (telephone interview with Anke Eymer, 27 January 1999), but the head of the concerned desk at the Ministry for Families, Senior Citizens, Women and the Youth, regularly received information from TDF on its activities. She did, however, see no need to propose any activities on behalf of her Ministry (interview with Renate Augstein, Bonn, 29 January 1999).

In sum, although with a different degree of intensity, TDF disseminated information on FGM among politicians and lobbied them. At about the same time, politicians of the Green Party and the SPD made FGM their cause. Concerning the prospects of women's NGOs of exerting influence on national politics, the crucial question is whether politicians of both of these parties did so because of TDF's activities or for other reasons.

*Reasons for Women politicians' commitment.* Politicians of both parties considered the Fourth World Women's Conference in Beijing as decisive for their commitment to the international norms on FGM. Delegates of both parties had attended the conference. Green politicians expressed two reasons for their commitment. First, the Conference's Platform For Action expects states to take action against FGM (and the German government had agreed upon it). They emphasized that the Platform For Action is rather specific about the steps necessary to deal appropriately with FGM, and one MP concluded that "one can ... start up political action on the basis of such norms, demanding their implementation" (interview with Angelika Köster-Loßack, Bonn, 28 January 1999). Second, it was crucial for the Green politicians that African women had approached them personally and requested their support in fighting FGM at the World Women's Conference. Without the African women's request, Green politicians would not have taken up this issue as theirs for fear of "othering" the women concerned (interviews in Bonn with Maria Brosch, 25 January 1999, and with Angelika Köster-Loßack, 28 January 1999).

[85] For the contacts between TDF and the SPD faction see Brabandt 1999.

The World Women's Conference also motivated SPD politicians to fight FGM. Right after the conference they drafted a parliamentary question on what the government planned to do about the human rights violation (13/3270). They soon had the impression that the government was not inclined to implement the international norms it had agreed upon in Beijing (interview with Christel Hanewinckel, Bonn, 27 January 1999). Green politicians came to a similar conclusion (interview with Maria Brosch, Bonn, 25 January 1999). Both factions, therefore, decided to exert some pressure on the government to deal with the issue. Even though TDF was not decisive for politicians' initial commitment to fight FGM, politicians of both factions pointed out that the NGO's activities were important for their own endeavors.

*Politicians' Evaluation of TDF's Influence on Their Activities.* Green politicians evaluated TDF's contribution to their activities as an example of a very close and "successful division of labour..." (interviews in Bonn with Maria Brosch, 25 January 1999, with Angelika Köster-Loßack, 28 January 1999, with Regina Kalthegener, 25 January 1999).

> We would not have achieved as much if Green members of parliament ... had not worked on the subject. However, we also would not have achieved as much if TDF had not provided us with experts' information and put friendly pressure upon us (interview with Maria Brosch, Bonn, 25 January 1999).

Green politicians appreciated the contact with TDF, for it provided them with the opportunity to discuss the necessary political changes with experts: "It's not sensible if we put forward demands and then have the expert organizations saying that the measures we envisage are useless" (ibid). The Green faction had therefore aimed to achieve a consensus with TDF on most issues (ibid). The SPD politicians interviewed also stressed that TDF's expertise had influenced the content of their parliamentary initiatives (interview with Christel Hanewinckel, Bonn, 27 January 1999; telephone interview with Hanna Wolf, 9 July 1999). Furthermore, TDF's lobby efforts supported female politicians of both factions in convincing their male colleagues that FGM was an issue necessary to commit the parties' activities to (interviews in Bonn with Maria Brosch, 25 January 1999 and with Christel Hanewinckel, 27 January 1999). They considered this result of TDF's pressure as important as its impact on their own work.

*Co-operation Between TDF and Politicians of the Green Party and the SPD.* Explaining the close co-operation between her faction and TDF, Maria Brosch points to two factors: (1) Green politicians and TDF women hit it off the first moment they met, and (2) they similarly assessed what to do about the human rights violation, including the necessary political changes (interview with Maria Brosch, Bonn, 25 January 1999). I would argue that their mutual rapport and their common ideas originate in their similar political socialization in the new social movements. The Green politicians dedicated to the implementation of the international norms had joined their party after being active in the women's and/or human rights and/or "Third World" movements. They still belong to these movements through their memberships in NGOs and their honorary activities.

The term "new social movements" stands for political protest groups and social movements which arose in the wake of the extra-parliamentary opposition in the 1960s (Rucht 1997, p. 380). The Green Party has its origin in the new social movements and their membership is distinctive in this respect (Raschke and Hohlfeld 1997, p. 36). Their manifesto covers the new social movements' classic issues: Women's emancipation, environmental protection, peace and disarmament, hunger and misery in the "Third World", and citizen's and human rights (Rucht 1997, p. 380). Against this background, FGM constitutes a classic cross-section topic of the party's issues. At the same time, TDF is part of the women's and the human rights movements. Green politicians like for example Angelika Köster-Loßack were active in TDF local groups before they were elected as members of parliament (interview with Angelika Köster-Loßack, 28 January 1999). Against this background, the close and equal co-operation between Green politicians and TDF representatives seems only logically consistent and based on their common political origins. This implies that women's movements and women's NGOs should look for and aim at establishing co-operative networks with women politicians and, of course, if possible, with women members of the executive who have experienced a similar political socialization. It is this common ground that may be the basis for co-operative efforts aiming at political change.

In contrast to the Green party, the Social Democratic Party (SPD) has its origins in the "old social movement", the labor movement. Nowadays, the SPD is a rather "colorful party" bringing together quite divergent views (Lösche 1997, p. 514). Some SPD members feel a strong affinity for the causes of the new social movements. In fact, the SPD mobilizes the largest share of supporters of new social movements in elections

(Raschke and Hohlfeld 1997, p. 36). The SPD politicians committed to the international focus on women's and human rights as well as on "Third World" issues in their political work have biographies similar to those of Green politicians. In contrast to their Green colleagues, these politicians are a minority within their own party. The majority of SPD politicians do not sympathize with the new social movements' causes. The parliamentary initiatives of the SPD faction did not hurt this majority *when in opposition*. On the contrary, these initiatives facilitated the integration of voters sympathetic to the new social movements' causes. *When in power*, however, it quickly turned out that the implementation of the international norms was not agreed upon by the majority of the faction. This has been in particular the case with regard to the norm expecting states to provide women/girl refugees fleeing FGM with political asylum or refugee status according to the Refugee Convention.

In conclusion, it is clear that TDF played a significant role in the efforts of parliamentary actors to achieve the implementation of the international norms. This is despite the fact that it did not manage to mobilize the public on FGM and that its activities were not decisive in raising the women politicians' interest in the human rights violation. However, TDF's role was significant in that it provided indispensable support for the parliamentary actors willing to work for the implementation of the norms. In particular with the Green faction, TDF engaged in a successful division of labor. In trying to raise awareness of the existence of the international norms among citizens and attempting to mobilize them for its cause, TDF indirectly supported both parliamentary actors working on the issue. Politicians of both the Green faction and the faction of the SPD were thus able to use the information campaign (despite its small scope) and the articles in national newspapers to convince their male colleagues that the issue of FGM is significant and worth being taken up in their political work.[86] This was the same for TDF's lobby efforts. Furthermore, TDF provided the relevant women politicians with the expertise necessary to draft bills on FGM. Thus without TDF's support, these politicians would not have been likely to convince their factions to take the issue into parliament and would also not have had the expertise necessary to draft bills. At the same time, TDF was as dependent on the women politicians as they were on TDF. As an NGO, TDF is not in a position to draft bills and to pester the government with "small" and "great" questions. TDF needed the access to state institutions in order to further the implementation of

[86] The book by Waries Dirie had not been published when the majority of parliamentary activities occurred in the parliament's sitting period from 1994-1998.

the international norms and to lend its expertise. As much as the parliamentary actors would not have been likely to work on FGM without TDF's support, TDF would not have been able to influence politics without the opportunity to cooperate with members of both the Green and the SPD faction. The cooperation between TDF and members of parliament was based on a similar political socialization in the new social movements.

We have to keep in mind, however, that despite the cooperation between TDF and parliamentary actors, the results were rather meager. This is even more the case since after the change in government in 1998, exactly those women politicians who had pushed the issue of FGM into the parliamentary process in the period from 1995-1998 and in doing so, had closely co-operated with TDF, now belonged to the majority-providing factions in parliament. They failed to convince their factions to actually get down to the changes those same factions had been willing to give their name to when in opposition.

## Conclusion

In this contribution, I have focused on the area of cultural globalization, taking the arguments of John Boli and George M. Thomas as a basis for this paper. They argue that (1) globalization has brought about world-cultural principles that shape the actions of states and other subunits and that (2) INGOs play an important role in this process. While Boli and Thomas focus on INGOs in their work, numerous other authors expect this to be also true for NGOs. I have critically assessed these two arguments in the case of the international human rights norms telling states how to deal with FGM as implemented in Germany.

With respect to the first argument, I have shown that in my case, in the period under investigation, both governments were prepared to implement only those norms whose implementation appeared to cause no high financial, procedural, or political costs. In their denouncement of FGM, both governments preferred to focus on its occurrence in *African* countries. While both governments have been clearly fond of the role of self-declared human rights protectors, they have mainly been so when this provided them with a justification to reprimand other, in particular non-Western, countries. World-cultural principles in the form of international human rights norms have clearly shaped their actions when doing so.

With regard to domestic politics, international human rights norms have shaped their actions to a far lesser extent. Neither government has been prepared to explicitly forbid FGM or to inform all professionals who deal with migration and refugee issues on FGM. Nor have they been prepared to initiate a public information campaign or to provide counseling services for those women/girls concerned. Indeed, they had not planned to change the asylum laws to grant women/girls fleeing FGM a secure legal status that would allow them to stay in Germany. Without the terrorist attacks of September 11, the bill on immigration would have passed the cabinet and eventually the Bundestag without any provision to this effect. It is an irony of history that not cultural globalization but the ugly face of globalization, the terrorist attacks, has ultimately brought about this change. Therefore, a double standard between the governments' deeds and rhetoric in international proceedings and their actions at home cannot be ignored.

However, the existence of the international human rights norms has increased the leverage of those actors working for their implementation. It has provided them with a "legitimized" space for their activism. Both groups, NGOs (TDF) and parliamentary actors (the faction of the SPD and the Green Party and later the PDS) utilized the norms as a basis for their work which, they argued, stood on international human rights ground. The fact that Germany had agreed with the international norms in UN-institutions and still continues to do so, at, for example, meetings of the UNHCR-Executive Committee and the Human Rights Commission, put both governments on the defensive. Still, both governments were prepared to implement only those norms under scrutiny whose implementation they considered to be "cheap". In doing so, they clearly followed a logic of cost-benefit-calculations. In particular, the change in the SPD's attitude towards the implementation of the norms underlines this aspect. In the 13th sitting period (1994-1998), the SPD faction had urged the previous government to implement norms it was not willing to implement itself when in power in the 14th sitting period (1998-2002). All interviewees of the Greens and the SPD were unanimous that a leading clique of men within the SPD who considered the resultant costs as being too high hindered a complete implementation of the norms. In the case of the norm concerning refugee status/political asylum for women/girls fleeing FGM, they changed their minds only since the Green faction managed to strike a deal. In linking the implementation of this norm with the Greens' agreement to the anti-terrorism bills, the SPD had to change the calculation of costs. The implementation of this norm became "cheap" compared to the costs the chancellor and his Minister of the Interior would have had to face if their own coalition partner voted down their anti-terrorism bills.

Despite the fact that the implementation of the international norms ultimately depended on the costs attributed to them, it is also clear that no changes at all in the governments' actions would have occurred if there had not been actors willing to make the norms their cause. The parliamentary actors who did so closely cooperated with the NGO TDF. This brings me to the question as to the role of (I)NGOs in the process of the implementation of the international norms.

TDF was the only NGO in Germany that campaigned for the implementation of all of the six identified international norms on FGM. Since TDF did not manage to mobilize the public for the implementation of the international norms, it was of great significance for the NGO to find access to state institutions. If it had not done so, it would not have been able to influence the parliamentary actors working on the issue. Without TDF's support and lobbying efforts, however, the parliamentary actors would have had a far harder time convincing their male colleagues in their factions that FGM is an issue worth being taken up in their political work. Furthermore, the parliamentary actors would have lacked the expertise necessary to draft bills on FGM and pester the government with "small -" and "great questions". Thus, both sides were dependent upon each other. Their cooperation was based on their similar socialization in the new social movements.

While world cultural principles exert some influence on the actions of states in that states like Germany use them to reprimand other states in an international setting and in that they themselves feel that they have to justify non-compliance if confronted with them domestically, such principles do not necessarily shape their actions. However, as in the case of my study with the international human rights norms on FGM, world cultural principles in the form of international human rights norms seem to provide actors interested in their implementation with leverage, with a legitimized space for their activities. IR scholarship has not yet accumulated much knowledge about the process of the implementation of the norms and the exact role of (I)NGOs and political and executive actors in it. It is, therefore, necessary to increase research on this process. Only if international human rights norms are implemented will we be able to speak of a cultural globalization. Even more importantly, only if they are implemented will they have some impact on those for whom they have been designed in the first place.

# Changing Frameworks: 'Exchange' and 'Regulation' instead of 'Markets' and 'States'[87]

Markus Lederer

## Introduction

The debate about globalization raises many important questions: How global is the world? Who wins, who loses? Is it something new? What should we do about it? As these questions very often transcend established borders of academic disciplines, it is of no surprise that scholars of International Political Economy (IPE) have been very active participants in the academic discourse on globalization. IPE defines itself as lying at the crossroads of political science, especially International Relations (IR), and of international economics. From each discipline, methods, concepts, and theories are borrowed and sometimes combined to gain a better understanding of what globalization is all about. The vocabulary which is thereby developed structures any inquiries that are undertaken, and from time to time it is important to take a step back and question whether the right tools are applied. This paper does so by analyzing the contemporary vocabulary of IPE and by assessing its main framework of 'market' and 'state'.

Scholars of IPE have taken the concept of 'state' from political science and that of 'market' from economics, so that the combination of both provides the conceptual baseline of most thinking in the discipline. For example, Robert Gilpin's (1987) classic *The Political Economy of International Relations* states that the "parallel existence and mutual interaction of 'state' and 'market' in the modern world create 'political economy'" (p. 8). The political economist Herman Schwartz (2000) titles his book *States versus Markets,* and for him "international political economy is ... about the essential unity of modern states and capitalist markets" (p. 2). One of Susan Strange's (1994) most important contributions to the study of IPE is titled *States and Markets,* although in the

[87] The chapter benefited from many fruitful discussions with members of the research network Politics-Law-Philosophy (PRP) at the University of Munich - in particular Doris A. Fuchs, Friedrich Kratochwil, Alex Börsch and Philipp Müller - as well as from the financial support of the VW-foundation and the DAAD, which is hereby gratefully acknowledged.

Preface to *Retreat of the State* (1996) she acknowledges that the title of *States and Markets* is problematic and that she wishes she had called it "Markets and Authorities" (p. x). Geoffrey Underhill (2000) thus nicely summarizes the conceptual framework of IPE as trying to understand the "epic struggle between the state and the market" (p. 127).
However, when assessing the framework of 'states' and 'markets' as a whole, Underhill (2000) draws a negative conclusion:

> As long as the system is portrayed as a tug-of-war between the two, then they may be interdependent but not genuinely part of the same dynamics or *political* economy (p. 129).

Similarly, Arvid Lukauskas (1999) argues that the framework of 'states' and 'markets' has reached a condition of "rapidly diminishing returns" (p. 283). This paper takes up this uneasiness and shows that the framework entails four specific assumptions, which taken together, make its use highly problematic. The first is already well known and concerns the problem that markets and states are highly interdependent, but rarely treated as such. The second and more conceptual assumption is that the term 'market' carries a structural bias that makes life unnecessarily difficult for any agent-based modeling. A third section concentrates on the assumptions of the term 'state' and claims that the governance of the international economy is no longer dominated by national governments alone. Last, a fourth section points out that the framework of 'states' and 'markets' also carries a specific liberal bias that is no longer appropriate.

The second part of the paper introduces the alternative framework of 'exchange' and 'regulation'. The section defines the terms and argues that the new dichotomy allows inquiries which are more open to new questions focusing on other instruments, agents, and political spaces than traditional studies of IPE[88]. To illustrate the usefulness of the concept, the example of stock exchanges is discussed because it is exactly such organizational forms, which are at the same time institutions of exchange as well as of regulation, that the framework of 'market' and 'states' does not capture sufficiently. The conclusion briefly raises the question whether the exercise of establishing a new framework is meaningful in any sense and in which issue areas it can be further applied.

---

[88] As my background and interest lies in financial markets, I will primarily focus on the literature and topics discussed in this sub-field, but I believe the general conclusions fit other issue areas of IPE just as well.

The paper does not claim that there is no entity out there which could not be called 'state' or no set of relations which could be described as 'market'. Indeed, for a political scientist, it would be a great mistake not to include the state in his or her studies and of course no economist can exclude markets in his or her analysis, but scholars of IPE should try to develop their own approaches in explaining and understanding globalization.

### States and Markets - a Problematic Baseline
### The Bias of Separateness

A prominent part of the IPE literature comes to the conclusion that 'markets' and 'states' are so intertwined that they cannot be separated. As the mainstream does not fully take those insights into account, a short review seems to be in order.

The most prominent starting point for claiming that markets and states are not only interdependent but constitute each other is still Karl Polanyi's (1957) *The Great Transformation.* Polanyi argues that markets were embedded in non-economic relationships until the rise of a capitalist ideology and that people traded goods because of need, because they wanted to gain prestige, or because reciprocity was good to keep social relations intact. Polanyi sees the defining moment of the market society as when people exchanged goods primarily because they wanted profits, but this market rationale is a historical exception and should not be taken for granted. He points out that national markets are a very late development that was much resisted by local merchants and autonomous towns. The internal markets of early European nation-states were not more than a loose collection of separate municipal markets that resembled the local or long-distance trade of the Middle Ages much more than our modern market economies. National markets did not come into existence until states intervened and introduced competitive principles, especially as they established competition for labor and land. Polanyi states that at least national markets as we know them are structured and enforced by the state. For him, the idea of a separate economic domain is an ideological project that collapsed with the breakdown of the gold standard. Polanyi's discussion is therefore a good reminder to show that 'markets' do not exist in a void.

John Ruggie (1983) builds on Polanyi's insights in his discussion of the "embedded liberalism in the postwar economic order" (p. x). He notes that the established regime allowed a permissive environment for some kinds of transborder transactions, but not for others. A compromise evolved, so that governments enhanced international trade flows through the GATT mechanisms but at the same time established safeguards to cushion negative consequences in the form of capital controls. Ruggie thus shows that political purpose and economic reasoning are again not separable, but to a large extent even constitute each other.

Underhill has a different focus than Polanyi and Ruggie, but arrives at a similar result. He speaks of a "state-market condominium" and stresses less the role of the state in the market than the dominance of market agents in economic governance. His main point is that markets are always created by somebody for somebody:

> The private interests of the market are integrated into the state ... through their close relationship to state institutions in the policy decision-making process and in the ongoing pattern of regulatory governance of market society ...
> What we tend to consider state prerogatives are often delegated to self-regulatory associations of private interests ... (Underhill 2000, p. 129).

Underhill is thus advancing a view that public choice economists have labeled regulatory capture (Stigler 1971, Peltzman 1976). This theory argues that public institutions, especially when they enjoy some independence from the legislative oversight, are easily captured by the very same private interests that they are supposed to regulate. In such a view the term 'state' becomes problematic and almost as much an ideological project as the term 'market'.

The studies mentioned show that markets and states cannot be conceptualized as being separated. The following three sections will argue that an even more critical perspective of the relationship is in order and that it is necessary to question the terms themselves.

*The structural bias*

The social sciences are witness to a debate between those who think that political and economic actors are autonomous agents and others who believe that actors are deeply embedded in certain structures. The following section explains that the term 'market' implies a structural view of the world that cannot be justified a priori and claims that many studies of IPE explicitly or implicitly make structures their most important independent variable.

The structural dominance of the term 'market' is especially prominent in descriptions of the international financial system, where capital markets are described as a structural feature that determines the policies of states (Webb 1991, Goodman and Pauly 1993, Cohen 1993). The conclusion that in a time of high financial integration, states can no longer pursue an independent monetary policy builds on the Mundell-Fleming model that exchange rate stability, private capital mobility, and domestic monetary independence cannot all be achieved simultaneously. The reason for this loss of interdependence is that with capital being mobile, real interest rates are constrained to be more or less the same in all countries, and states will no longer be able to affect them. For many of these authors, increasing capital mobility is forcing international convergence across countries towards similar policies with less governmental influence.

Even in studies that are explicitly trying to avoid such reasoning and that focus on actors, the structural bias becomes dominant due to the connotation of the term 'market'. An illustration is Benjamin Cohen's (1998), *The Geography of Money,* in which the author describes the deterritorialization of monetary relations. Cohen captures new hierarchical relationships between different currencies and their respective "domains of authority". Following Strange, he tries to appreciate the rising importance of non-state actors, which are "*interacting with* societal forces in the social spaces created by money's transnational networks" (Cohen 1998, p. 25f). However, Cohen does not identify which actors are really important and which win or lose, as he speaks only of "markets" and "societal actors". At one point in the book Cohen even asks, "*Who* in the market governs?" (p. 146), but then turns away to discuss how money is supplied or demanded. Supply and demand are of course extremely important, but again the question of who governs is only halfway answered, as Cohen does not analyze which market actors are doing what. The 'market' is thus again not perceived as having independent agents.

The problem with this narrative as with many others is that they are often deterministic and thus do not analyze which actors are critical, which preferences they have, and what channels they use:

> Much recent research underspecifies which private or state actors are central to financial policy making, what their preferences are with respect to key issues and what policy choices they face. (Lukauskas 1999, p. 283).

An alternative, which for example Lukauskas offers, is a rational-choice analysis of the intentions and actions of individual persons. However, such a return to a purely positivistic framework can be avoided by conceptualizing actors as agents[89]. Talking of agents allows scholars to analyze individual decisions and avoids the abstractness of structural explanations. It does not, however, exclude the possibility that ideas or other structural forces cause actors to do certain things Such an agent-based approach is thus open to the idea that a slave and a master constitute each other or might even be constituted by a third force (for example the relationship between the productive forces), but it nevertheless will focus on what the individual slave or master does. Otherwise it will be very hard to analyze when and why an individual slave starts to revolt. Scholars of IPE should thus emancipate themselves from the implied structural determinism of the term 'market' and should focus more on who does what.

*The national bias*

A third problem of the framework of 'markets' and 'states' is that the latter term is blind to interventions and control mechanisms that are not based on national governments. This becomes explicit in the debate about global governance, which discusses the challenge of how to govern an ever more internationalized economy when the tools of governance were developed within and for the territory of national states.

This debate reaches back at least to the 1970s. After the oil crisis, many in the developed as well as in the developing countries had a sense of increased interdependence (the classical discussion is Keohane and Nye 1977) and thought that only international organization(s) could cope with the rising problems of the global village earth. During the 1980s, increased cooperation of states was debated under the term 'regime'. While many interesting discussions were centered around the concept - as for example if states cooperate because of relative or absolute gains or if regimes are independent or intervening variables (for a good overview of the debate see Baldwin 1993) - some authors in the

---

[89] Building on the work of Anthony Giddens, several IR scholars are trying to bridge the gap between structural accounts and actor centered analysis by focusing not so much on the one or the other, but on the interplay between agents and structures. How far such structuration approaches (for example by Wendt 1999) are successful or if there are, for ontological as well as for epistemological reasons, still two stories to be told (Hollis and Smith 1994) can not be fully discussed here.

early 1990s turned away from the concept and tried to replace it with the notion of global governance. Several reasons can be found for such a shift.

The most important reason is probably that the regime discussion has become too academic and does not have the same normative implications as authors of global governance would like it to have. For the mainstream of IR theory, regimes are perceived from a neo-institutionalist perspective, which defines itself as a positivistic approach. The attempt to broaden the regime approach to include critical or constructivist perspectives (for example Keohane 1988 or Hasenclever 1997) has for the most part been rejected. Another reason for the shift away from regimes to the global governance concept is that regimes are considered to exist only in one issue area (for example Young 1994, p. 26). However, global governance includes all problems of "global order" (Rosenau 1992, p. 8f). Last but not least, the discussion about regimes is state-centric, although there are some attempts to include private regimes as well (for example Haufler 1993). Global governance, however, is explicitly trying to include new forms of governance without governments (Rosenau and Czempiel 1992). Thus, in a rather eclectic way, network analysis, multilateralism, multi-level analysis, questions of subsidiarity, informal control mechanisms, and discussions about steering are combined.

That the global governance approach does not fulfill the criteria of parsimony or elegance is obvious, but some more serious challenges have been raised as well. Like planning in the 1950s, the concept implies a certain order and security, which is actually not given. Furthermore, it does not account for the possibility that political fights with winners and losers will occur, and thus governance can be judged as a "postpolitical phenomenon" that has no "starting point for asking important questions about domination and resistance in global perspective" (Latham 1999, p. 25, p. 35). Similarly, some scholars ask who is in control of global governance and how far it is democratically legitimized (Messner and Nuscheler 1996b, p. 24f) or how far the debate really contributes to the development of a stable global order (Rosenau 2000, p. 189). All these criticisms, however, never question the principle argument that it is not only normatively wishful, but also has become empirically true that the government or even one state alone never does all the governance necessary on its territory. It is therefore time to abandon the state-centrism of IPE on the conceptual as well as on the empirical level.

*The liberal bias of the separation of public and private*

The framework of 'markets' and 'states' has as a last assumption a clear divide between private and public. The former section has shown that governance can no longer be attributed only to the sovereign state. This part of the paper adds that the involvement of formerly private actors also changes the concept of the state itself, as the state can no longer be thought of as representing the public sphere. Private actors have established themselves as political agents and can make decisions in specific issue areas, which formerly had been exclusively in the domain of the Leviathan (Zürn 1998, p. 166f).

Non-state agents have of course always been influential, especially in the domain of international finance, as the examples of the large bankers like Fugger, Rothschild, or J. P. Morgan nicely show. In the seventies, Lindblom (1977) is already arguing that the distinction between private and public modes of organization does not hold. He compares state-directed systems and market systems and concludes that one feature they all have in common are bureaucracies, no matter if they are the US postal system, a Chinese state farm, or General Motors (p. 11). However, the important change many see today is that private actors are not only powerful, but also have acquired authority, that is, their actions are perceived as being legitimate. Companies always had means to dominate the political decision-making process, but these days this dominance is more and more accepted as being the most effective and best one - a process which questions the old dichotomy of public and private:

> According to liberal and democratic theory, only the public sphere is empowered and entitled to prescribe behavior for others, for only public authorities are accountable through public institutions. (Cutler, Haufler, and Porter 1999, p. 18).

It is thus something more than the often quoted "Power Shift" (Mathews 1997) from the state to civil society; it is more fundamentally a "shift of authority" (Florini 2000, p. 15) which blurs the distinction between private and public, thus raising questions of legitimacy.

Illustrative examples of such a new private authority are the role business plays in the regulation of the Internet, in the governance of the insurance industry, or in the regulation of intellectual property rights. The most prominent example in international finance is the role of bond-rating agencies like *Moody's Investors Service* or *Standard & Poor's*, which have "moved from influence to authority" (Sinclair 1999b, p. 159). These agencies evaluate the credit standing of corporate as well as public institutions and are perceived to be the objective evaluators of whole sectors or countries, as it is the ultimate aim of any emerging economy to reach an investment grade status. These examples show that private authority is gaining importance and thus challenging the old public-private divide, that is a part of the framework 'market' and 'state'.

Claire Cutler (1997) is therefore right in claiming that it is a liberal myth that the market is only in the domain of the private and is thus apolitical. Similarly, Paul Hirst argues that modern societies are no longer clearly divided along a public-private distinction that was central to the liberal view as it has developed in the economic mainstream in the Western hemisphere for the last decades:

> In fact it would be better to see the state as a part of an 'organizational society', with large hierarchically controlled institutions on both sides of the public-private divide that are either unanswerable to or only weakly accountable to citizens. (Hirst 2000, p. 20).

Of course these developments also raise problems when large areas of social life are regulated by private companies. These "public simulacra of private governments" are autonomous in their decision-making procedures and only rarely accountable to their stakeholders (Hirst 1997). For Hirst, the nightmare of Weber and Kafka that bureaucracies are no longer controlled is becoming a real possibility. Such a negative view is also shared by Friedrich Kratochwil (1997), who speaks of the "Disappearance of Publics" and fears that those networks of private authority no longer have a place for citizens who actively participate in their polity. Others, as for example Wolfgang Reinicke (1998), view private authority much more positively and as the only way to regain control over complex problems. Reinicke argues that non-state actors will be useful to provide "horizontal subsidiarity" and that they "have better information, knowledge and understanding of complex, technology-driven, and fast-changing public policy issues" (Reinicke 1998, p. 90). However, no matter how one judges these new forms of governance, one has to concede that private and public are no longer as clearly divided as economic liberalism and the mainstream of IPE perceive it to be. This again raises doubts about a framework that takes such a separation as one of its starting points.

Overall, one can say not only that the framework of 'markets' and 'states' has the ontological problem of being so interconnected that any useful separation is hardly possible, but that it also puts too much stress on structure, narrows governance to the state, and carries with it a certain liberal understanding which might no longer be appropriate for today's world. Whether the alternative of 'exchange' and 'regulation' is better suited as a conceptual framework and thus allows a better or at least a different understanding of globalization is examined now.

## Exchange and Regulation: A New Framework Applied

The new framework of 'exchange' and 'regulation' focuses first of all on the question of who does what. It thus explicitly rejects the structuralism as well as the state-centrism of 'markets' and 'states'. It is furthermore a much broader framework that includes more actors and issues than the old framework.

### *Why exchange and what is it?*

In its broadest sense almost all human interaction is exchange. For example, when in a conversation words are directed at somebody and a reaction of some kind is given, an exchange takes place. Exchange is thus a relation between two or more persons, each of whom offers a benefit in order to induce a response (Blau 1964). Exchange relations are therefore common in all forms of social life. In the following, however, the analysis is narrowed down to economic exchange in the way modern economics uses the term. The *International Encyclopedia of the Social Sciences*, for example, defines exchange as the "transactions of labor, resources, products, and services within a society" (Codere 1968, p. 239). For exchange to take place, people must have some extra goods to trade with each other; thus a certain economic development is a prerequisite for economic exchange to exist. The history of exchange therefore depends on the history of the division of labor (Lindblom 1977, p. 34). Another condition for the possibility of economic exchange is that both parties gain from it or at least think they do (Greif 2000, p. 251). The famous gun at the head and the following exchange of wallet against life will therefore not be considered.

Taking exchange as a starting point of economic analysis is not self-evident, as it is only one part of economic life, along with consumption and production. Marx and Engels (1983, p. 19f), for example, believe it is foolish to start with exchange because the way the forces of production are related already determines the way exchange can take place. Thus, they critique the freedom to choose with whom one exchanges whatever one wants as a freedom open only to the bourgeois that is built upon the surplus the bourgeois extracts from the naked labor of its workers. For Marx and Engels, every analysis therefore has to start with the conditions under which the production of goods takes place. Class relations and the situation of the poor do indeed not get into the focus of 'exchange', but power structures within an exchange relation are important as well. Contrary to a Marxist analysis, the framework can thus illuminate *how* power is used, while the question of *why* power is applied is indeed neglected.

An important point is to differentiate between 'exchange' and 'market', an exercise too often neglected, so that markets are seen everywhere and the term becomes rather hollow. First, the framework stresses that 'market' is a subcategory of 'exchange'. Markets are thus a form of exchange that is characterized by the use of money and by the signaling effect of supply and demand made transparent through prices, in contrast to other modes of exchange like reciprocity and redistribution. Reciprocity is exchange, as an obligatory gift exchange, in which goods are exchanged not only for their economic value, but also for social or moral reasons. Redistribution is the form of exchange that occurs when taxes or other exactions are collected and reallocated (Polanyi 1957, p. 44f). An illustrative example for the latter is the old Persian empire, where not even market-places existed, but all distribution was centrally organized by the king's bureaucracy.

Most people would probably subscribe to the view that markets are the most important form of exchange today because the forces of supply and demand are the most reliable mode of providing an efficient and regular allocation of scarce values (Lindblom 1977, p. 34). Of course there is no such thing as a perfect market, and thus one can probably always find an example in a market that has not been priced 'right', but nevertheless it seems justified to claim that many contemporary economic transactions are determined by price signals. This is of course a functional definition of the market and has been at the center of modern economics and especially its theoretical core: general equilibrium theory. However, functions also have a history. Markets thus arose from simple exchange relations but could establish a life on their own and start to develop certain institutions like the trader or the entrepreneur.

Nevertheless, even in our day redistribution and reciprocity are important modes of exchange. One example is bribery or a very modern form of it - campaign donations. Nobody would deny that an exchange takes place which to a large part depends on price signals, as the price of a donation will for example regulate how close one might sit to the President at a White House dinner. However, reciprocity itself is also important ("I give you a gift, you do me a political favor and think positively about me and my business"). As prices are only part of the story and often not even the most important one, it seems rather odd to speak of a market for campaign donations. Another illustration is modern marriages, which are no longer arranged by price signals either (for a contrary view and the most prominent case of claiming that all social relations including marriages are governed by markets see Becker 1976). Feminist scholars point to another example that highlights the huge sphere of unrecorded economic activity going on each day performed primarily by women involving the care of children, the aged, or the disabled. Such an "economy of care" again does not involve markets (Helleiner 2001, p. 246). Herbert Simon (1991) summarizes all these examples nicely when he claims that if a Martian had to describe the structure of economic life on earth, he would point out that organizations of various sizes and forms dominate and that markets are of minor importance. Thus, everybody who applies too broad a definition of 'market' and subsumes everything under it just gives it the same connotation as 'exchange' and hence makes the term 'market' redundant (Rosenbaum 2000, p. 462).

The second and more important aspect that differentiates 'exchange' and 'market' concerns the agents as well as spaces of exchange and refers to the fact that the term 'market' is hardly ever considered in relation to agents (Rosenbaum 2000, p. 459). However, markets as we know them could establish a life of their own only within the economic freedom the towns of the 15th and 16th century were starting to provide (Braudel 1986). During the Middle Ages, all modes of exchange were so heavily regulated that no reliable price signals were produced. The concept of a 'just price' stood contrary to the development of independent signals, as all market participants had the deeply entrenched understanding that the prices negotiated were those in which neither party's economic status was altered (Brown 1999, p. 696). The establishment of markets can furthermore not be separated from the rise of an independent trader class, who traveled to the big fairs and festivals in which traditional exchange was slowly replaced through the forces of supply and demand. Similarly, the development of national markets during the 19th century cannot be understood without the consolidation of the nation-state, and terms like 'welfare state' or 'competition state' point by themselves to the role of a specific actor.

Especially, when we talk of financial markets like the interbank money market or the foreign exchange market today, there will probably be no associations with certain places. Saskia Sassen (1991), however, shows that even these exchanges, which to a large part are nothing but digital transactions, are bound to certain places and institutions. She points out that the global spaces of finance are concentrated in a few cities or even in certain districts like New York's downtown, London's City or Tokyo's financial center. Only in such centralized places is there a critical mass of technological infrastructure, knowledge, and networking, so that diverse forms of exchange can take place.

One can therefore conclude that 'exchange' has a broader meaning than 'market' even if one only points out that markets are a subcategory of exchange. In a broader view, 'exchange' highlights spatial characteristics, certain agents, and power structures that the term 'market' does not encompass.

*Stock exchanges instead of securities markets*

There is a discrepancy between the role stock exchanges play in modern economic systems and their treatment in IPE. On the one hand, stock exchanges are seen as "epitomizing capitalist free markets" (Porter 1994, p. 22), as they are increasing their importance in the industrialized world and are spreading their influence to countries that have traditionally relied on credit markets like Japan, France, and Germany. In former socialist economies like Russia or in most states of Eastern Europe, the establishment of stock exchanges is seen as an important step to becoming integrated in the capitalist world economy, and it is more than just symbolic that in Poland the Warsaw Stock Exchange occupies the former headquarters of the Communist Party. The number of developing countries with stock markets has doubled during the 1990s, and even in China and Vietnam stock markets have become popular ways of financing as well as of investing. There can thus be no doubt that stock exchanges are important agents of globalization.

On the other hand, although the development of stock *markets* has received attention in some extraordinary studies (Lütz 1998, Moran 1994, Porter 1994, Simmons 2001, Sobel 1994, Weber and Posner 2000), the IPE literature on international finance neglects stock *exchanges*, as it is in general more interested in exchange rate regimes, questions of debt and balance of payments, central and commercial banking, and fiscal or monetary policy. It focuses less on members of the financial service industry, and if it does so it is more concentrated on the role of banks and their relation to individual states (Michie 1992, p. 662). The claim is made that this neglect is due to the fact that exchanges are not taken as what they are - economic actors with a history, with internal structures, and with political ambitions as well as a specific set of preferences. Stock exchanges are simply subsumed under stock markets, but in reality they have been as far away from a market as the election of the pope from democracy. This tradition of stressing that stock exchanges are nothing else but markets is often even reflected in political decisions, as for example the *American Securities Exchange Act* of 1934 or the EU's *Investment Service Directive* of 1993, both of which define exchanges simply as markets. Stock exchanges are, however, important agents in their own right and should be considered as such. This concerns their history, their economic as well as political functions, and their contemporary ownership structure.

The world has known the issuing of stocks and their trading since Roman times, but the institution of stock exchanges did not develop until the 17th and 18th century. The establishment of stock exchanges is interpreted from various historical perspectives, and although all explanations give different independent variables why stock exchanges exist, they never claim that stock markets and stock exchanges were simply one and the same. One view stresses the developing nation-state's need to find new means of financing the expensive wars, especially of England and France from the turn of the 17th to the 18th century. One of the methods used was the creation of permanent funded debt in contrast to the usual indebtedness all governments had known before. These durable debts only became interesting for investors when the yield was guaranteed by the state and more important when the debt became transferable as well as tradable, which could best be done through the creation of permanent places of exchange (Michie 1992, p. 662). A second perspective focuses on the role of private agents who needed to finance risky business ventures, as for example the Dutch and English East India Companies (founded in 1612 and 1623 respectively). In a third view, which analyzes the development of modern capitalism, Braudel (1986) compares the establishment of stock exchanges to the setting up of permanent stores. He points out that before stock exchanges were established permanently, traders met regularly at the big fairs of Lyon, Frankfurt, or Antwerp during the 16th century. However, once stock exchanges were established, the high times for fairs were over and it was no longer necessary to meet once a year, as it had become customary to be at the market constantly (p. 25f).

The different historic interpretations partly result from the fact that stock exchanges have to perform a wide range of functions and are neither simply markets nor 'one-purpose-vehicles'. Economically, in a model world where all commodities and all prices were completely specified for free, information would be symmetric, and all contracts would be enforced at no cost. Thus, there would actually be no need for exchanges to exist. However, as institutional economics has pointed out again and again, in the real world it is costly to specify attributes, profound information asymmetries exist, and parties have incentives to cheat on their contracts, and therefore institutions which address these problems are needed (Pirrong 1998, p. 433). Politically, exchanges are symbols of successful financial developments or of dominant financial centers. The establishment of stock exchanges is thus often a political decision, especially as they are hard to control once they are established and as there are certain political reasons a government might not want to promote them. It is for example not possible for the state to gain easy revenue through a capital-based system as easily as it can through a credit-based system, as exchanges have always been more independent than banks.

IPE should therefore ask why individual exchanges exist and what their political importance is. One way of doing so is by focusing on the ownership structure of stock exchanges because until recently exchanges were oligopolistic enterprises that set the prices for the services they offered and did not face any national or transnational competition. Brokers or market makers were thus not used to the forces of supply and demand, and it is no exaggeration to claim that in the US for a long time the public health service knew more competition and was more market-oriented than the New York Stock Exchange (NYSE). This is changing, and stock exchanges have to adapt more and more to a competitive market environment. A result of this trend is that exchanges all over the world are transforming their ownership structures. Within the last couple years, stock exchanges have become less and less organized as public enterprises having public functions. They are now comparable to private companies and are even following the example of the Australian Stock Exchange, which in 1998 was the first exchange that became listed on itself (Di Noia 2001, p. 46 Fn. 15). This entails a change in the power structure of the exchange, as it is now common that the owners of an exchange are also its customers. This can lead to the situation in which the management of an exchange might not want to maximize its profits anymore because this would increase the prices for its owner-customers. As an example, one can consider the Deutsche Bank, which owns a large part of Deutsche Börse, and thus as an owner should be interested in a high revenue gained through trading fees or information services. However, the Deutsche Börse also is a customer that likes prices to be as low as its traders are active buying and selling on the floor. These details, which are of importance because they determine who has a voice in the exchange and thus in an important segment of the financial structure of a country, are lost when stock exchanges are not taken as agents which have an internal dimension to look at, but just as black boxes that are part of the market.

Stock exchanges should therefore be perceived as just financial intermediaries that behave like standard firms (Lee 1998, Di Noia 2001, p. 46). Within such an approach, questions of monopolization and competitiveness come into focus. This becomes especially true as stock exchanges are busy forming alliances or merging with competitors. Although the attempted merger of the London Stock Exchange and the Deutsche Börse failed, Euronext - an alliance between the Paris bourse, the Amsterdam and the Brussels stock exchanges - is alive and gaining market share as are about a dozen other formal and informal forms of cooperation. Such alliances do not make sense between markets, but only between specific agents. They raise doubts to what extent national stock markets still exist or question the ability of national states to protect their national exchanges and regulate them. As many important aspects of financial globalization will be determined by such transnational agents, it is time that IPE focuses on them. This, however, will not happen when scholars are busy looking only for market structures and keep forgetting that there are agents out there who do politics.

### *Why regulation and what is it?*

Regulation has several meanings and the only consensus existing is that there is no overall definition accepted by all (Baldwin and Scott, Hood 1998, p. 2f). For a long time the term was limited to a specific governmental control of services provided by private enterprises in transport, communication, electricity, or other utility services. In this sense, regulation was perceived as an American institution because elsewhere these industries were for the most part owned and operated by the respective governments (a typical example for such a view is Wilcox 1968). Today's economists and political scientists see this perspective as being too narrow, although much discussion about the validity of the concept of 'natural monopolies' is still centered around such an understanding.

Regulation, especially from the 1980s on, was used more broadly as political intervention of the government in the economic realm. For example, for *The New Palgrave: A Dictionary of Economics*, regulation "consists of governmental actions to control price, sale and production decisions of firms in an avowed effort to prevent private decision-making that would take inadequate account of the 'public interest'" (Breyer and MacAvoy 1987, p. 128). *The New Palgrave Dictionary of Economics and the Law* argues that regulation "is the imposition of economic controls by government agencies on (usually) private agencies" (Keeler 1998, p. 213), and for White it is "any nonfiscal intervention (i.e. excluding specific taxes or subsidies) in the operation of private-sector markets" (White 1996, p. 208f). Thus, regulation in this sense is government involvement in the private sphere, and it encompasses all controls that government imposes on business except income redistribution or macroeconomic stabilization. This view is, however, still too narrow, as it does not include non-governmental forms of regulation and because it narrows regulation to technical interference.

Regulation in its broadest sense - often referred to as 'social regulation' (Ogus 1994, part III) - is not simply a question of technical or instrumental dimensions, but has a stronger political component as well. This becomes obvious when one considers that regulation always entails control by a superior entity, or as Friedman (1985) states, regulation "can cover all attempts by authority to control behavior" (p. 111). This is very similar to classical definitions of politics as they are offered for example by David Easton (1971): "the authoritative allocation of values for a society" or by Harold Lasswell (1958): "Who gets what, when and how?". Regulation in this perspective is characterized by the setting of rules, the monitoring of how far these rules are observed, and the enforcement of rules in case of noncompliance (Baldwin 1995, p. 5f, Baldwin and Scott, Hood 1998, p. 3, Lütz and Czada 2000, p. 15). Regulation is nothing particularly new, as all economic exchange relations were from their very beginning subject to detailed rules. For example, in the very first market places, regulators were concerned that no middle men would buy and resell at the market and increase the general price level. Today product as well as process regulation can be found on every level of governance.

Some warn that such a broad use of the term also brings about the danger of

> intellectual over-extension, the loss of disciplinary focus and coherence, and consequent lack of immunity to academic fads and

fashions ... After all, if regulation is everything, perhaps it is nothing more than another naked emperor? (Baldwin and Scott, Hood 1998, p. 36).

It seems, however, possible to avoid such a mistake without giving up the broad political meaning of regulation by pinning down which forms of regulation actually exist and how they can be differentiated. It is thus time to reflect on the various clothes the emperor still has at his disposal in order to stress the political implications specific regulatory modes have. Comparing the different forms, one notices that they involve different regulatory agents, which again have different aims and instruments. Furthermore, the actors involved face a variety of conflicts and base their regulation on specific forms of legitimacy. The four most important forms of regulation and their differences are summarized in the following chart:

| | **Regulation through public ownership** | **Cooperative regulation** | **Self-regulation** | **Statutory regulation**[90] |
|---|---|---|---|---|
| **Agents** | Government, parties, bureaucracy | Unions, business, parliament | Self-regulatory organi-zations (SRO) | Agencies, ex-perts, judges, single-issue movements |
| **Aims** | Macro-economic growth and stability | Macro-economic stability and growth | Efficiency | Correction of market failures |
| **Instru-ments** | Nationalization, planning | Redistribution, taxation, nationalization | Privatization | De- and Re-regulation, privatization |
| **Conflicts** | Budgetary allocations | Budgetary allocations | Extent of regulatory scope | Review and control of rules |
| **Legitimacy** | Majoritan, input-oriented, hierarchical | Majoritan, input-oriented, decentralized | Majoritan within SRO, output-oriented | Non-majoritan, pluralistic, output-oriented |

There is neither space nor necessity to describe each regulatory mode in detail or to analyze how far combinations and overlaps have to be considered. Nevertheless, the usefulness of focusing on regulation

90 The term 'statutory' regulation has been popularized by Majone (1994, 1997) and derives its meaning from the fact that in this regulatory mode public agencies of all kinds are involved and most of them are initiated by statute.

becomes obvious when one considers that many forms of governance are almost never highlighted in any detail. For example, self-regulation is often not accounted for in traditional policy analysis, as no visible government agent is included. This leads some scholars to argue that self-regulation is a result of market forces and not a conscious process. Adam Smith's famous phrase that an individual is "led by an invisible hand to promote an end which was no part of his attention" suggests that in many instances order comes about automatically. Benjamin Cohen (1998, p. 103) refers to Mandeville's *Fable of the Bees* as an example of an unplanned spontaneous model that can become very authoritative. Today such perceptions can be found in a popularized neo-liberal discourse which argues that the market will regulate itself once nobody intrudes on it and that the product of such a development would then be "government by the market" (Self 1993). However, the decision to let an economic agent take care of its own business and to set the rules of the game is by itself a political decision and a form of regulation just as much as any other. It is therefore important to see that in most cases in which people claim regulation by the market is happening, self-regulation by private actors and/ or a deliberate form of non-regulation by official actors is actually taking place.

Furthermore, such a focus stresses the role of agents, as they differ significantly from one form to another. With statutory regulation, for example, the involvement of public agencies or private-public commissions of all kinds becomes visible. Some point to the increased role of the Judiciary (Jayasuriya 2001, p. 103), while others focus more on new pluralist single-issue groups (Majone 1997, p. 158). Concerning the latter, it is important to note that they differ from the corporate interest groups because these groups do not speak for an entire sector or an economy as unions or most business associations do.

It is therefore no exaggeration to claim that 'regulation' allows a new perspective on who governs. This all is of course nothing spectacular for the student of comparative politics, who in one form or the other always focuses on different forms of governance which are performed by a variety of state and non-state actors. Scholars of IPE, however, are very often still entrapped in the Realist legacy of IR and thus treat the state as a black box. Focusing on the question of who regulates avoids such reductionism and allows scholars to highlight new actors and issues, which are of importance for today's globalized world as well.

*Stock exchanges regulating and regulating stock exchanges*

Concerning the regulation of financial markets, surprisingly little attention is paid to the institutional structure of who regulates what (Goodhart et al 1998, p. 142). This again is due to the assumptions the terms 'market' and 'state' carry with them, as other regulatory institutions are not considered in their own right. In the context of globalization, the framework implies that markets by themselves are now governing financial markets, a fact more assumed than analyzed and then either defended or taken as a reason to call for new state involvement. However, when the focus is shifted to the actual agents of regulation, a different picture emerges. The following section thus briefly highlights that stock exchanges have been active regulators themselves for as long as they have existed. This has partly changed, as the US introduced statutory regulation during the 1930s, and is about to change in the Member States of the EU. Such developments are, however, missed in an analysis that simply focuses on 'states' and 'markets'.

Stock exchanges rely on certain constitutive rules established through contract law to come into existence at all. But once they are established, stock exchanges are very active in the regulation of capital markets and perform many of the functions that the traditional framework considers to be in the preserve of the state. Exchanges, for example, harmonize and implement common standards. They are active in attempting to reduce market power as well as fraud, and they help to secure transactions by avoiding defaults on contracts. This was especially important in the early years of stock trading, as there were huge time lags between the date the stock trading took place and the actual settlement of the transaction. Trading on exchanges was thus only permitted between the members, which of course reduced the number of players. Those members who were getting in trouble or were defaulting were suspended of their trading privileges. Later on, exchanges established clearing and settlement institutions in order to ensure that trades which were agreed on also took place. Since then, clearing houses themselves as private institutions have started to set capital standards as well as limits on position risk or have set standards for the amounts a member can owe to others individually or collectively (Herring and Litan 1995, p. 55).

There are several reasons why such self-regulation can be considered very effective. First, market participants themselves have a strong interest in compliance, as they profit from the regulation. Second, regulation is perceived to be more efficient due to the high knowledge regulators have when they are also participants in the exchange. Third, regulation done by peers enjoys a high degree of legitimacy (Lee 1998, p. 190f). However, even today's proponents of the concept of self-regulation acknowledge that problems can arise and of course they did. The greatest challenge is that exchanges again and again operate the market only in favor of their members, which leads to noncompetitive situations. It is thus no surprise that historically exchanges were not only self-regulatory, but also cartel-like and introduced high entry barriers for any newcomers (Pirrong 1998, p. 436). Thus, at certain moments when self-regulation was no longer feasible, a change in the regulatory mode took place.

The situation in the US is a good example of such a change, as stock exchanges were the only serious regulators until the 1930s, but then had to share power with a newly created institution. From the very beginning, the NYSE used the building of cartels and price-fixing as a means of guaranteeing the dominance of their members over the stock market. Although the government was involved, it only became an important agent when the exchange itself failed, as it did most spectacularly in 1929 (for a good historical overview see Geisst 1997). After the big Wall Street crash of the late 1920s, a Senate investigation uncovered "institutional failure and abuse of the public interest for private gain under the guise of self-regulation" (Sobel 1994, p. 25). President Roosevelt consequently pushed for full public disclosure in securities sales, 'letting in the light', and established the core of today's regulatory structure. This was done by two legislative acts - the *Securities Act of 1933* and the *Securities Exchange Act of 1934*. These laws provide the foundation for the *Securities Exchange Commission* (SEC), and thus started statutory regulation in the financial market of the US. Since then, the SEC has been one of the most interdependent and powerful public institutions, and there have rarely been comments that it is captured by the interests of the financial service industry (Grundfest 1998). This shift from one form of regulation to another is one of the most important events in the development of the US financial market and might provide an important lesson for today. It is, however, rarely considered in the globalization literature because it does not fit into the category of more state, less market or the other way round.

With Europe, especially with the Member States of the EU[91], a similar picture emerges, only within a certain time lag. In the UK, the 'old boys network' of the London Stock exchange was setting the rules of the game until 1986, when the 'big bang' that did away with the fixed commissions and the established cartels not only liberalized trading, but started to change the regulatory structure as well:

> The regulatory changes devised a system more similar to that of the United States in its requirements, with expectations that increased transparency, reporting requirements, and other regulation that provides investors with adequate protection against negligence, unethical behavior, and unprofessional activities. (Sobel 1994, p. 42).

In 1997 the new Labor government also changed regulatory oversight by concentrating all supervisory tasks in the *Financial Services Authority* (FSA). This move finally ended the heavy reliance on a mixture of statutory legislation and a quasi-private system of self-regulatory organizations. The FSA has rule-making power and cooperates with exchanges and clearing houses and is now the most "powerful financial watchdog" in the world (FT 14. 6. 2000, p. 10).

Something similar happened in Germany during the 1990s, which until then was the definite "laggard" in the modernization and re-regulation of its financial service industry (Lütz 1998, p. 159). The German government became an active player in creating a new regulatory structure when in 1994 it established a new supervisory body, the *Bundesaufsichtsamt für den Wertpapierhandel*. Since 2001 the Ministry of Finance has been considering plans to follow the UK example to establish a mega-regulator that will oversee all aspects of financial regulation in Germany. The regulatory changes in the UK and in Germany are thus at least as profound as they were in the US in the 1930s.

These changes should, however, not be interpreted as a power shift from the markets to the state, but as a regulatory shift from self-regulation in the UK and cooperative regulation in Germany towards statutory regulation. Especially in the case of Germany, claiming that the 'state' has regained control is incorrect because first, the government only shifted power from the Länder level to the federal level, and thus although the state's role has increased, there is an internal change

[91] The thesis that the EU itself is becoming a regulatory state in the issue area of finance is analyzed in my dissertation. Here, only the developments within two Member States are briefly described.

accompanying it. Second, pressure from IOSCO, the organization responsible for the international coordination of securities regulators, motivated the government[92]. Third, many changes of the German securities law, for example the fact that insider trading is no longer legal, directly result from legislation at the EU level. Again, a focus on regulation and its different modes highlights such details which are left out by looking at 'states' and 'markets'.

We can therefore conclude that stock exchanges have had an important role in self-regulation, but that their role has been changing lately. That such important transformations are rarely considered (for an exception see Lütz 1998, 2000) results from the emphasis most studies place on securities markets and state bureaucracies. The new framework of 'exchange' and 'regulation', however, allows IPE to raise these issues and to show their political importance for the discussion of globalization.

## Conclusion

Several options are now open to the reader. First, he or she might consider the exercise to have failed, because 'markets' and 'states' are not so bad after all and IPE has done a good job in trying to establish the interdependencies between the two. 'Exchange' and 'regulation' have no value added whatsoever and are thus no alternative. Case lost.

Second, he or she agrees that the terms 'market' and 'states' are problematic for the reasons given, but does not believe that the alternative is any better. First, the argument could be made that one framework based on a dichotomy is simply replaced by another and maybe there is more than white and black out there. Second, the new framework does not yet allow for hypotheses of how 'exchange' and 'regulation' relate to each other. Third, the terms themselves also carry their own biases. This is especially true for 'regulation', which sounds rather apolitical and entails a functional or technical bias, similar to governance or management. It is thus of no surprise that scholars who believe that 'the regulatory state' is becoming the dominant form of governance (especially Majone 1996, 1997) are often criticized for a very one-

[92] IOSCO itself is a case in point that the term 'state' does not do justice to who regulates. As Underhill has shown in a prize-winning study, IOSCO is a hybrid regime primarily made up of government regulators, but it considers itself an NGO (Underhill 1995, 251, fn. 42). It is thus a prime example that 'public' and 'private' are a lot harder to differentiate than the traditional framework suggests.

dimensional view of power. As a defense, it could however be said that the purpose of the paper was not to test a theory and thereby "kill" another in the way Popper thought of falsification, nor was it to explain everything the old framework can and a little more, as Lakatos would have proposed. The paper was only an exercise in applying a new framework and thereby questioning traditional assumptions and bringing up new issues. An exercise, which political science and IPE should consider worthwhile in itself. Case dismissed, but appeal is possible.

Third, he or she agrees that the new framework is useful and maybe even better than the old one, but wonders what to do next. Focusing on stock exchanges has of course been the easy part, as they were not a critical case. However, there are other issues and agents that the new framework could be applied to. Banking regulation is a case in point, as Basle II will increase the role of banks as regulatory agents, but the same is true for Internet providers, who are the focal points of exchange as well as regulation. The privatization of public utility providers, which will increase dramatically through the pressure of GATS, might also be discussed under the question of who regulates and exchanges. Case won, but more work ahead.

# Transformative Change and Global Order: Lessons Learned

Doris A. Fuchs and Friedrich Kratochwil

In this final chapter, we want to pull together the strings of the information and ideas developed by the contributors to this volume and other scholars in the globalization and global governance debates. Thereby, we hope to identify what we have learned about the transformative changes occurring and provide a more detailed and sophisticated analysis of them than the first wave of globalization studies.

As demonstrated in several contributions to this volume, globalization and global governance function as shorthands, as terms that lump together various processes and practices. Early analyses of globalization used this shorthand, in particular, as a vehicle for suggesting a stage model of history. Such a model with its implications of different epochs succeeding each other - an image beholden to notions of a philosophy of history as "unfolding" or reaching the end of history - in turn fostered images of the inevitability of the transformative changes, as Müller has so aptly demonstrated in his contribution. By employing the epic of narrative to fill in the gaps that exist between the various transformations which we subsume under the concept of globalization, these early analyses were able to suggest an overall uniform development or overarching trend towards a predetermined goal. Thus, globalization, like "history" before it, became an actor and often relieved the authors from inquiry into the very processes and their interactions that constituted this phenomenon. In this context, the piece by Lebow and Stein can be read as a suggestion for raising, via the method of counterfactual reasoning, a new awareness of alternative plausible paths for historical developments, showing the contingent character of "overall developments." At the same time, their analysis allows a critical assessment of globalization trends and processes, separating "globalization" from either the triumphalism of "Americanization" or from the fears such a picture of inevitability might engender.

In the same manner, as Harris and Yunker (1999) show, early analyses of global governance purveyed images of harmony, the development of a global civil society, and global common problem-solving, reflecting a faith in the enlightenment tradition with its beliefs in reason and progress, rationality and consensus, and humankind's ability to learn. These beliefs also had been underlying the modernization discourse, so that the global governance discourse postulates a repetition of the 'modernisation' of states and societies on a global scale (Björklund and Berglund 2001). Here, the stages model of history allowed early global governance advocates to present it as an apolitical, functional process, promising efficient problem-solving and order and security, allowing the unmasterable, turbulent changes associated with globalization to become governable (Latham 1999).[93] At the same time, a new type of international professionalism developed a lingua franca that was presumably helpful not only for identifying problems but also for facilitating solutions. But as Kennedy suggests, that approach overestimated the influence such an internationalist framework can exert on problem-solving and underestimated significantly the opportunities for finding solutions on the "local" or subordinate levels. His suggestion to focus on the assessment of distributional outcomes rather than on the conceptual tools per se is a useful reminder of the need to re-introduce "politics" into the otherwise largely technocratically-oriented debates. As long as the perception of global governance as harmonious apolitical problem-solving prevails, claims of critical observers that global governance means nothing but a decline in democratic practices and legitimacy, and the shaping of the world according to neoliberal beliefs and economic interests, need to be taken seriously as a corrective.

With more attention paid to the transformative processes themselves, a finer grained analysis has now become possible, shifting the center of attention from the macro-historical process to issues of governance. In this context, Berari´s contribution shows particularly vividly how effective international financial institutions have been in shaping domestic institutions of transition countries by implementing the political project underlying the Washington consensus that had emerged in the 80s. That this strategy was neither as unproblematic and "technical" as often suggested, and that the hegemony of certain ideas and concepts often prevented more adequate responses to the social and economic problems at hand, will not be lost on the attentive reader. Likewise, Finger delineates convincingly the instrumentalization of the state (and the World Bank) by public services transnational corporations. At the same time, Brabandt shows that the reach and diffusion of institutions of global governance, such as women's human rights norms,

[93] As Lederer shows in his contribution, such a bias was also reflected in the planning approach of the 50s and 60s.

is neither as automatic nor as comprehensive as frequently argued, even in the case of the industrialized world.

The shift in focus from the macro-trends subsumed under globalization to specific issues of governance has alerted us to the changing nature of politics, well brought out by debates about new actors, new forms of organization(s), and the need for new conceptual tools. As the old conceptual distinctions between public and private, or between state and market have lost their purchase, new conceptual tools have become necessary, particularly in the post-globalization debate. In consequence, Lederer's plea for a shift from the old vocabulary that worked with the crucial distinction of "state vs. market" to a different one emphasizing the difference between "exchange and regulation" is especially apt. Likewise, Kennedy's admonition concerning the conceptual blinders of the "new international style" of choosing an apolitical technical stance and thereby misdiagnosing the practical problems hits its mark.

Finally, the shift in focus has allowed us to regain the space for political action. All authors in this volume share a concern for returning attention to politics and for identifying possibilities for shaping future developments. The consequences of globalization, according to the main debates, concern three areas in particular: (in)equity, (in)security, and (a lack of) democratic legitimacy. Globalization and global governance as shorthands allow neither the identification of specific consequences in these areas nor the development of appropriate political responses. The stage model of history implied by early analyses, in particular, with its suggestion of overall trends and predetermined outcomes, fails to account for the complexity of the implications of globalization and global governance. In the following, we will delineate the shortcomings of this model using the issue area of security as an example. Then, we will illustrate the existence of various types of implications of globalization and global governance for all of the three core areas of concern: (in)equity, (in)security, and (a lack of) democracy.

## Security and the Shortcoming of Shorthands

The analyses in this volume have hinted at the complexity of creating order in an arena that is progressively spanned by networks, even though these networks will not be entirely decentralized but still have hubs and nodes at which influence can be exerted. It is perhaps this aspect that increasingly has worried analysts after the attack of

September 11. Not only do we now have largely invisible opponents that cannot be deterred, a fundamental building block for both domestic and international order, but attacks by terrorist networks also do not need to address the traditional state structures as entry points for their influence attempts but can focus on objects of high symbolic value.[94] But the rapidly increasing interconnection of our information infrastructures and the growing reliance on them to "steer" other infrastructures, ranging from energy flows to financial data and water supplies, also exponentially increase the vulnerability of our information-based societies. Under these circumstances, computers need not be tampered with physically, dams need not actually be destroyed, or water supplies need not be physically contaminated as long as some hackers can get behind the usual and easily penetrated "fire walls" that "secure" our data, energy supplies, and water. From such a perspective on security, the triumphalism of the first wave of globalization studies is particularly inappropriate. Likewise, the more careful analyses of the second wave of globalization studies dealing with opportunities and limitations for robust regimes in global governance are now increasingly supplanted by chilling prospects concerning the vulnerabilities created by networks and the activities in virtual spaces.

Such reflections also provide ample food for thought about the typical interpretation of the "re"-emergence of ethnic conflicts and "failed" states. While it is conventional wisdom to identify in the former the cause for the latter and while certainly some cases may fit that pattern, the bitter truth might very well be that things are much more complicated and dangerous. The notion that ethnic conflicts are based on "age-old enmities" that re-emerge in the absence of effective performance of both the public institutions and of the economy – a malaise that has to be cured by further "development" in order to overcome these atavistic tendencies – has been too easily accepted. We ought to entertain the thought that such an explanation, notwithstanding its popularity and the comfort it offers by reaffirming our prejudices, gets the story quite wrong.

After all, this conventional interpretation in the end is based on the stages model of history, that is, ideas of a linear development from the tribe to the state to a cosmopolitan global order. If anything has been shown by the globalization debate in its first and second stages, how-

[94] The latter has often been explained in terms of the actual weakness of terrorists who thereby attempt to make up for their lack of strength in terms of the traditional indicators of military strength.

ever, it is the phenomenon that integrative as well as disintegrative tendencies are equally part of the "globalization" picture. In this regard, the presumption of a linear development leading to an automatic end of ethnic conflict is more than naïve. Moreover, the virulent "ethnic" conflicts of today are usually not based on "ancient" hatreds but are of quite recent origins, even if frequently historical claims are utilized in order to justify present actions. The thesis of atavism thus fails to inquire into the role of political entrepreneurs that are able to mobilize their followers through the modern media (tapes, transistors, television) and that escalate conflict. The inflammatory transmissions by radio stations in Rwanda before the genocide have to be mentioned in this context, as do the rock groups and football clubs that exacerbated the tensions in Yugoslavia and that created flashpoints at which the previously unthinkable suddenly became not only thinkable but was executed in orgies of violence. Violence in turn creates "scores" that have to be settled and that can be as easily projected back into the past as into the future.

Finally, precisely because of the much denser information and transportation networks, potential warlords competing with the state by establishing a protection racket can plug into "networks" of mercenaries, weapons purveyors, drug distributors, and smugglers, thereby gaining access to resources - earning their money by selling drugs or even engaging in slavery - or raising funds in the various diasporas abroad. Instantaneous global information, the inaccessibility of certain regions to modern means of transport (or of reducing some of them relatively easily to such a status by blowing up bridges or creating stone avalanches), and the simultaneous existence of an extensive network for modern mass transport that no longer can be easily controlled by a few "points of access[95]" give such groups an advantage of mobility similar to that which nomads have traditionally enjoyed. However, while formerly substantive advantages could be gained by shifting from nomadisim - which sometimes consisted of little more than raiding of the settled areas and living from plunder - to a more sedentary life style, globalization has made it possible to reap many of these benefits while not forgoing the advantages of mobility. In other words, precisely because of the communications revolution and the inability to track transmissions effectively in the digital age, the marauding "nomads" of today have access to economic and financial networks while "being on the run" and thus are able to disappear in different places among members of the

[95] For example, earlier sea ports or border stations.

diaspora or other groups of sympathizers that know each other through the chat rooms and web pages of the internet.

Thus, both the phenomenon of increasing war-lordism in many regions of the world – in which by relatively small means entrepreneurs can extort resources from the unwitting population and utilize them worldwide - and the new profile of the "modern" terrorist who is as easily at home in the communities created by atavistic fantasies as he is in cyberspace or in the hot spots of the "modern" world, are a troubling reminder that our conventional understanding and interpretation of ethnic and civil conflict is woefully inadequate. Here the utopian character of the globalization debate, representing the latest example of an unwavering faith in progress, definitely has taken on some characteristics of a "dystopia" familiar from some science fiction novels.

## The Controversial Effects of Globalization and Global Governance

The reality of globalization and global governance is much more complicated, then, than popular uses of these shorthands suggest. Overly optimistic evaluations regarding the effects of globalization and global governance, suggested by early studies, can be counterbalanced by rather pessimistic assessments. This is the case for all three areas of concern: (in)equity, (in)security, and (a lack of) democracy.

In the (in)equity debate, some participants argue that globalization has a positive impact on social equity as it provides previously marginalized groups and disadvantaged individuals with new opportunities. Likewise, trade liberalization and the availability of foreign investment are supposed to help the poorer countries in particular to catch up (the old convergence argument). Similarly, globalization optimists point to the diffusion of technological innovations, the global spread of the communications infrastructure, and the pursuit of global economic efficiency as potential sources of worldwide economic growth and welfare.

At the same time, however, other scholars and practitioners tell us that we need to be concerned about both the national and the global distribution of income and welfare. For years, scholars and practitioners have reported a trend with fewer and fewer people owning more and more of the world's resources: "Across the world, resource distribution now resembles the form of a pear rather than an egg" (Scholte 2000a, p. 238). While acknowledging that globalization is not the original or only source of social injustice, they argue that there is sufficient evidence that in many cases it appears to be increasing inequality, perpetuating and strengthening social hierarchies, and widening gaps in income and welfare (Biersteker 2000, Scholte 2000a). In this perspective, entire regions are being left behind, in particular due to a lack of access to global markets and communications infrastructures that would allow them to take advantage of opportunities provided by globalization. Within countries, scholars draw attention to growing income gaps between economic and social elites benefiting from the increase in opportunities by globalization and those parts of the population lacking the necessary resources and skills to do so. Moreover, we have been witnessing a mounting pressure on social welfare systems in Western developed countries. In fact, the evidence of increasing social inequity is sufficiently strong that even the World Economic Forum, generally not a suspect for leftist leanings, perceives the major challenge for globalization to be the provision of evidence that the new global capitalism can function to the benefit of the majority and not only of corporate managers and investors.

With respect to (in)security, evaluations cover a similarly broad spectrum. On the positive side, scholars argue that security threats from international warfare are on the decline, at least for some parts of the global population, due to increasing trade linkages and the diffusion of democracy. The latter phenomenon and the associated decline in authoritarian regimes also are frequent referents for claims of an increase in individual security. Other observers highlight the contribution of the diffusion of human rights norms and global communication to the protection of ethnic minorities, cultural traditions, and civil liberties. For the individual, observers see the greater freedom and liberty and protection from cultural and social coercion due to an increasing choice among cultural norms, societal bonds, and individual roles.

Referring to a privatization of security, a number of scholars report a decline in various dimensions of security due to globalization and global governance, however, similar and in addition to the issues raised above. According to them, the decline in threats to bodily safety arising from international warfare is more than made up by an increase in internal violence and disorder due to the social costs of economic restructuring (Harvey 1995) and the rule of private "security forces" in some countries (Volkow 2000). Likewise, feminist scholars highlight the need to consider particular threats to the bodily safety of women created by the global sex trade, for instance (Pettman 1996, Kempadoo and Doezema 1998). Moreover, debates center on the implications of globalization for material security[96] (poverty, a reduction in job security[97]) and challenges to cultural and societal foundations of personal security (identity formation, sense of belonging), which can be linked to experiences of stress, heightened everyday competition, and a lack of control.

Finally, the democratic potentials and challenges of global governance have received a lot of attention in the literature. This debate originated in discussions about a decline of the nation state and a reduction in the authoritative decision-making capacity of the state, the traditional locus of democratically determined authority. However, scholars and practitioners disagree not only about whether the state is losing political capacity, but also about the potential implications of such a development for democratic legitimacy. Thus, some scholars do not perceive a decline of the state as a challenge to democracy but argue that the institutions and processes of global governance, the increasing participation of non-state, supra-state, and sub-state actors, in fact strengthen the democratic legitimacy of global policy-making. They emphasize that the participation of civil society and/or supra-national institutions in political decision-making is a highly desirable phenomenon in a time of the "crisis of the nation state." In this perspective, the possibility that governance would be carried out not just by governments and intergovernmental institutions but also by NGOs and MNCs, as well as academia and the media, for instance, suggests democracy is being placed on a broader base. Observers applaud a "cosmopolitan democracy" through transworld institutions (Held 1995, Archibugi et al. 1998) and the promotion of the public good through global civil society and multilateral governance from below (Smouts 1999).

From the perspective of critical observers of global governance, however, such optimism is turning out to be premature. They argue that the abilities of the various actors to replace the state and strengthen the democratic basis of global governance are severely limited. Scholars emphasize, in particular, that hopes based on civil society ignore the lack

---

[96] Threats to material security in the extreme cases also mean threats to bodily safety, of course. Moreover, the debate on material security is closely linked to the one on (in)equity.

[97] Fundamentally, trends have meant the availability of more and more labor in the world on the one side and more and more concentrated and flexible capital on the other. As one may argue, the social bargain has been reconstructed at the expense of workers. Basic laws of supply and demand thus would suggest falling prices of labor worldwide unless they are mediated by major global employment fostering economic growth, which, however, the global ecological system may not be able to sustain

of necessary resources and access of large parts of the global population and the associated imbalances within the NGO community. They also draw attention to an underestimation of the imbalance in resources between NGOs and powerful states and corporations and underline the lack of democratic credentials of many powerful civil society actors themselves. Moreover, scholars and practitioners postulate that relying on supra-national public authority for the promotion of democracy is likely to remain illusionary at this point. After all, IGOs increasingly are under criticism themselves for lacking democratic legitimacy. Furthermore, observers stress that the imbalance in influence of IGOs on countries and of countries on IGOs, as well as the neglect of crucial social issues by the most powerful IGOs, have undermined claims of IGOs representing the global population in pursuit of global public goods. Increasing global opposition to IGOs further shows that removed officials and bureaucratic institutions making fundamental decisions do not look like legitimate representatives in a democratic decision-making process to the majority of citizens. In addition, skepticism towards the democratic promise of global governance has arisen to the extent that the reliance of its advocates on the assumption of a global harmony of interests and consensus in solution-finding mechanisms has been revealed. According to critical observers of global governance, current governance efforts at the global level have a club quality that reinforce rather than improves existing hierarchies and imbalances on political decision-making (Björklund und Berglund 2001) and should be viewed as a "politics of disempowerment" rather than a superior democratic practice (Ake 1999).

## Disaggregating Trends

In order to explore the implications of globalization and global governance, resolve the above controversies, and recapture the space for political action, then, the processes and practices summarized with these shorthands need to be disaggregated. Thereby, we can show that globalization and global governance have fundamentally different faces and therefore may require different responses in different parts of the world or sectors of society. Likewise, such a differentiated analysis demonstrates that certain claims about globalization and global governance can be maintained only if specific conceptualizations of processes and actors are applied. The following discussion briefly presents a few examples of this influence of foci and conceptualizations on globalization and global governance accounts.

Differences in geographic and social impacts illustrate most clearly why overly simplistic evaluations of globalization and global governance as uniform trends and overarching developments are highly questionable. In industrialized countries, for instance, we can witness a level of consumption unknown before by the majority of the population. The economic and social elites in these countries are benefiting from a vast range of opportunities provided by globalization. This part of the picture fits well with the stages of history scenario and its notion of progress. At the same time, however, more than a billion people around the globe are still living on less than $1 a day, and statistics indicate that global poverty has been increasing in the last decades, often combined with decreasing opportunities for many individuals and groups to improve their welfare. A significant part of the populations in developing countries is not experiencing a satisfying or even sufficient level of consumption and welfare yet, and it does not have the means to make use of globalization. Globalization may carry significant benefits, but they will accrue to those with access while equally significant losses are imposed on those without it (Langhorne 2001). As Kratochwil points out in his contribution to this book, entire regions of the globe are being reduced to practical irrelevance for the 'global' economy, while we observe the concentration of economic activity within and between OECD countries. Thus, our assessment of the potential welfare benefits of globalization and its implications for social equity, in particular, depend on whether we look at developed or developing countries, at individuals and groups with access and resources or without.[98]

Similarly, the implications of globalization and global governance for questions of government capacity are not uniform across the globe. As the analyses by Finger and Berari have shown, government choice and impact diverge across states. Thus, the US and other industrialized countries have played a crucial role in determining the shape of globalization and have been able to create some buffers (Brand et al. 2000, Woods 2000). These countries are less susceptible to influence of IGOs pushing a neoliberal liberalization agenda, for instance, while at

[98] The creation of material and institutional infrastructures, financial systems, and an "efficient" domestic administration, the basis for being able to use the opportunities provided by globalization in terms of financial investment, for instance, often proves to be an unconquerable hurdle for developing countries.

the same time they have more influence on IGO policies.[99] Likewise, NGO activism tends to strengthen the influence of interests and values of developed countries while further marginalizing developing countries and weakening their governments (O'Brien et al. 2000).[100]

Similar to the need to distinguish between the implications of globalization and global governance for different geographic areas and social strata, differentiated analyses need to be aware of the foci and blindspots created by the application of given conceptual lenses. The dimension of security provides an illustrative example in this case. Most scholars would agree that security when defined in traditional terms, that is, as military security, for the majority of people in developed countries has at minimum not been reduced by globalization. If we conceptualize security more broadly, however, to include facets such as bodily safety, material welfare, ecological security, identity, social cohesion, and cultural preservation, as well as the threats to all of these described above, the picture is much less uniform.

Likewise, evaluations of the democratic potential of global governance fundamentally depend on conceptualizations of the various actors involved and the associated foci of analysis. Differences in conceptualization are particularly visible and consequential in the case of civil society, as pointed out in the introductory chapter to this volume. Scholars and practitioners attributing a significant democratic potential to global governance tend to base this evaluation on notions of increased participation by a civil society composed of a large number of societal organizations, transnational collaborations, networks, and collective efforts in pursuit of common goals. Moreover, they generally associate a benign character with these groups and assume that the joint pursuit of the various interests of these groups will lead to outcomes reflecting societal preferences.

If we use a broader conceptualization of civil society and include both traditional market actors such as businesses and business associations, as well as criminal networks, however, we will perceive the

---

[99] Moreover, these countries exhibit increasing rather than decreasing state activism in some areas such as *Standortpolitik* (Brand et al. 2000).

[100] Differences in focus are often related to (if not a function of) the choice of indicators applied. In consequence, rather different assessments of globalization and global governance exist even when a similar geographic focus has been chosen. In terms of increases in inequity within (industrialized) countries, for instance, scholars have arrived at very different results depending on whether they have looked at individual incomes or household incomes. As people with limited financial resources are more inclined to share households, trends towards increasing income gaps tend to become much weaker when the latter indicator is used.

potential of this "civil society" to enhance the democratic legitimacy of global governance much more critically.[101] One cannot count on the ability of citizens and NGOs to provide democratic legitimacy to the participation of civil society in global governance, if economic and illegal interests outweigh societal ones due to better financial and informational resources, if networks of private authority prevail with little if any participation by citizens (Kratochwil 1997).

As this section has briefly indicated, then, the implications of globalization and global governance differ according to the geographical and societal foci of analyses, conceptual lenses applied, and the blindspots created by these choices. In this respect, the debates on the implications of globalization and global governance are not very different from the debates on their nature and extent, discussed in the introductory chapter in this volume. As in the case of our present assessment, the requirement to be aware of the complexity and various dimensions of these phenomena and the dangers of simple generalizations as well as the need to be explicit about conceptualizations and assumptions emerge as constant themes.

## Conclusions

The starting point for the post-globalization debate has to be that both concepts, globalization and global governance, are shorthands lumping together a variety of processes and phenomena while, at the same time, claiming to provide a universal frame for orientation and the derivation of meaning. As such narratives, globalization and global governance describe and analyze the ongoing and fundamental changes in the world at a highly aggregated level. However, as argued and demonstrated by the contributions to this volume, such a focus on the macro level not surprisingly hides rather than reveals the politics of globalization and

[101] Overly optimistic evaluations of the potential of civil society to increase the democratic legitimacy of global governance need to be questioned even in the case of narrower conceptualizations of global governance. Not all politically active NGOs pursue objectives in line with democratic ideas. The Arian Nation, for instance, is also part of that civil society. Other large NGOs pursuing objectives commonly evaluated as benign, such as environmental and human rights NGOs, do not always have sufficient transparency and accountability within their own structures. A broader conceptualization of civil society, however, captures a place of social and economic conflict that is dominated by business interests and increasingly penetrated by criminal networks. Attributing the ability to increase the democratic potential of global governance to this actor clearly should raise some eyebrows.

global governance as well as potential intervention points for shaping the changes occurring. The significant social, spatial, and contextual differences in the nature and implications of these changes wash out when we look at them from the mountain top.

This does not mean that we stop at the finding that any implications of globalization and global governance are simply a function of the discursive uses of these terms. As both contributions to this volume and numerous other scholarly efforts have shown, globalization and global governance have real material implications that need to be addressed. As long as there is a potential that human beings will suffer those consequences of globalization and global governance discussed above, we cannot be content with theoretical discussions but need sophisticated empirical analyses. The implications debates, more than anything, highlight political and research needs for developing viable options. After all, even if globalization and global governance can carry significant benefits, there is increasing evidence of the potentially serious negative consequences of the associated processes and phenomena for a substantial part of the global population.

Potential increases in inequity and insecurity and a decline in democratic capacity deserve our attention. Both the harvesting of the potential benefits provided by globalization and global governance and the prevention of social, political, and economic disorder require that potential negative consequences are reduced if not avoided. Globalization critics, visible at Seattle, Genoa, and other WTO and G7 meetings, have been gaining in number. ATTAC, the most prominent conglomeration of groups and individuals critical of globalization, today has groups around the world and a membership that is growing by leaps and bounds. Admittedly, the combination of the sometimes conflicting goals of anti-globalization activists, which include everything from an equitable income distribution to stricter regulation of capital and corporations, improved environmental stewardship, and a global tax regime, shows that this grouping is more a protest movement against globalization in its current shape than a unified pursuit of an alternative model. Still, the concerns of these protesters and activists as well as other critical observers of globalization and global governance should not be ignored.

As our analyses have shown, however, we need to dissect globalization and global governance in order to derive strategies for political action and intervention. While the macro level of observation favored by these shorthands does reflect identifiable trends and tendencies in the ongoing changes in the world, it is not useful for the identification of steering needs and instruments. These need to be developed at the micro-level, as only contextual analyses will pinpoint political levers and opportunities for action. Disaggregation, then, is a necessary requirement for politics, shaping and directing the processes and practices captured with the terms globalization and global governance.

More fundamentally, however, the debates on globalization and global governance should also remind us of the dangers of attempts to construct universalistic accounts of history, of which global governance and especially globalization are serving as the latest examples. This is why the globalization debate replaced the one on the "End of History." Such narratives direct our attention towards certain core themes while pushing others to the side and hiding the lack of a systematic assessment. With respect to globalization, the "necessary" structural adjustment of the economy and the opportunities of the information society have been core themes in political debates in developed countries. With respect to global governance, the decline of the political capacity of the state and the increasing participation of non-state actors in governance have similarly functioned as core themes. Questions of structural changes in society and their implications for community have been pushed to the side. Not surprisingly, the same has happened to the issue of security, the traditional core task of the state, a focus on which would have led to rather different evaluations of the transformative changes under way.

With the wisdom of hindsight, we can see that the issue of security, in particular, should have concerned us as a group and the profession as a whole a bit more during the last decades. But if it is any comfort, the security discourse itself frequently showed the same ethereal quality as the first wave of globalization studies. It took leave from the analysis of practical political problems and disappeared into the virtual spaces opened up by technology. Aside from the more and more complex scenarios of the electronic battlefield with real-time information on the enemies' every movement (whose phantasmagorical qualities were exposed by NATO's battle experiences in Kosovo), the never-ending debates concerning a National Missile Defense system clearly indicated that mainstream security analysis limited itself to conventional threats and their presumptive technological "solutions" while at the same time neglecting or discounting the emergent dangers of terrorist networks.

At least insofar as this book is about governance problems largely in the area of international politics and the international political economy, we have tried to come back to earth and address real world issues that have emerged from the previous debates about regimes, international institutions, and organizational forms. The issues largely concern those that had been neglected by traditional structural analyses of world politics and by the unfounded enthusiasm concerning the "end of history". Both orientations proved of little help for understanding the problems of order under conditions of rapidly increasing interdependencies and externalities in which the traditional steering mechanisms could no longer deliver what was expected from them.

# Bibliography


Ake, C. (1999). Globalization, Multilateralism, and the Shrinking Democratic Space. In M. Schechter *Future Multilateralism: the Political and Social Framework*. Tokyo: United Nations Press.

Albert, M., D. Jacobson, Y. Lapid, eds. (2001). *Identities, Borders, Orders*. Minneapolis: University of Minnesota Press.

Alter Chen, M. (1996). Engendering World Conferences: The International Women's Movement and the UN. In *NGOs, the UN & Global Governance*, edited by T. G.

Anderson, B. (1983). *Imagined Communities*. London: Verso.

Anheiner, H., M. Glasius, M. Kaldor, eds. (2001). *Global Civil Society*. Oxford: Oxford University Press.

Archibugi, D., D. Held, and M. Kohler (1998). *Re-imagining Political Community: Studies in Cosmopolitan Democracy*. Cambridge: Polity Press.

Arendt, H. (1966). The Concept of History. In *Between Past and Future: Six Exercises in Political Thought*, edited by H. Arendt. Cleveland and New York: Meridian.

Arrow, K. (1974). *The Limits of Organization*. New York: Norton.

Baker, G. (2000). Wittgenstein in Metaphysical/Everyday Use. Working Paper. Oxford University.

Baldwin, D. A. (1979). Power Analysis and World Politics: New Trends versus Old Tendencies, *World Politics* 31 (1):161-94.

Baldwin, D. A. (1993). Neoliberalism, Neorealism, and World Politics. In *Neorealism and Neoliberalism: The Contemporary Debate*, edited by D. A. Baldwin. New York: Columbia University Press.

Baldwin, R. (1995). *Rules and Government*. Oxford: Clarendon Press.

Baldwin, R., C. Scott, C. Hood (1998). Introduction. In *A Reader on Regulation*, edited by R. Baldwin, C. Scott and C. Hood. New York: Oxford University Press.

Baran, P. (1964). *On Distributed Communications*. Santa Monica, CA: Rand.

Barber, B. R. (1995). *Jihad vs. McWorld*. New York: Times Books.

Barlett, C.A., and S. Goshal (1998). *Managing Across Borders: The Transnational Solution*. London: Random House.

Bauman, Z. (1998). *Globalization: The Human Consequences*. New York: Columbia University Press.

Baylis, J., and S. Smith (2001). *The Globalization of World Politics*. 2nd ed. Oxford: Oxford University Press.

Beck, U. (1995). *Risikogesellschaft: Auf dem Weg in eine andere Moderne*. Frankfurt: Suhrkamp.

Beck, U., ed. (1998a). *Perspektiven der Weltgesellschaft*. Frankfurt: Suhrkamp.

Beck, U., ed. (1998b). *Politik der Globalisierung*. Frankfurt: Suhrkamp.

Beck, U. (1999a). *What is Globalization?* Oxford: Polity Press.

Beck, U. (1999b). *World Risk Society*. Cambridge: Polity Press.

Becker, G.S. (1976). *The Economic Approach to Human Behavior*. Chicago: Chicago University Press.

Beetham, D. (1991). *The Legitimization of Power*. Atlantic Highlands: Humanities Press International.

Biersteker, T. (2000). "Globalization as a Mode of Thinking in Major Institutional Actors." In Ngaire Woods (ed.). *The Political Economy of Globalization*. New York: St. Martin's Press.

Björklund, J., and S. Berglund (2001). From the Canterbury Tales to the Canterbury Conference. The Governance Perspective: What It Has Been, What It Is and What It Could Be. Paper read at the ECPR Conference, September 8-10, 2001, at Canterbury.

Blau, P. (1964). *Exchange and Power in Social Life*. New York, Wiley.

Boli, J. (2001). Sovereignty from a World-Polity Perspective. In *Problematic Sovereignty, Contested Rules and Political Possibilities*, edited by S. D. Krasner. New York: Columbia University Press.

Boli, J., and G.M. Thomas (1999). INGOs and the Organization of World Culture. In *Constructing World Culture: International Nongovernmental Organizations Since 1875*, edited by J. Boli and G. M. Thomas. Stanford, CA: Stanford University Press.

Bordo, M.D., B. Eichengreen, D. Klingebiel, and M. Martinez-Peria (2001). Is the Crisis Problem Growing More Severe?, http://emlab.berkely.edu/users/eichengr/EconomicPolicy.pdf.

Boughton, J.M., and K.S. Lateef, eds. (1995). Fifty Years after Bretton Woods. The Future of the IMF and World Bank. Proceedings of a Conference Held in Madrid, Spain, September 29-30, 1994. Washington, D.C.: International Monetary Fund and World Bank.

Brabandt, H. (1999). VN, NGOs und nationale Frauenpolitik in Deutschland: Die Umsetzung der internationalen Normen zum Umgang mit der Problematik der genitalen Verstümmelung. unpublished M.A.-thesis, Tübingen.

Brand, U., A. Brunnengräber, L. Schrader, C. Stock, and P. Wahl (2000). *Global Governance. Alternative zur neoliberalen Globalisierung?* Münster: Westfälisches Dampfboot.

Braudel, F. (1986). *Die Dynamik des Kapitalismus*. Stuttgart: Klett Cotta.

Breyer, S., and P.W. MacAvoy (1987). Regulation and Deregulation. In *The New Palgrave: A Dictionary of Economics*, edited by J. Eatwell, M. Milgate and P. Newman. London: Macmillan.

Brooks, S.G., and W.C. Wohlforth (forthcoming). American Primacy in Perspective, *Foreign Affairs*.

Brown, D.M. (1999). Markets and Exchange in Pre-Modern Economies. In *Encyclopedia of Political Economy*, edited by P. A. O'Hara. London: Routledge.

Buelens, J., ed. (1999). *Globalisation and the Nation-State*. Cheltenham: Edward Elgar.

Burki, S.J., and G.E. Perry (1998). *Beyond the Washington Consensus: Institutions Matter*. Washington, D.C.: World Bank.

Burns, T., ed. (1994). *After History: Francis Fukuyama and His Critics*. Lanham, MD: Rowman and Littlefield.

Camdessus, M. (1999). "Second Generation Reforms: Reflections and New Challenges". Opening Remarks to IMF Conference on Second Generation Reforms by Managing Director of the International Monetary Fund, Washington, D.C., November 8., http://www.imf.org/external/np/speeches /1999/110899.HTM.

Carr, E.H. (1946). *The Twenty Years Crisis*. New York: Harper.

Castells, M. (1996). *The Rise of the Network Society*. Oxford: Basil Blackwell.

Cerny, P. (1990). *The Changing Architecture of Politics*. London: Sage.

Cerny, P., ed. (1993). *Finance and World Politics: Markets, Regimes and States in the Post-hegemonic Era*. London: Edward Elgar.

Cerny, P. (1995). Globalization and the Changing Logic of Collective Action, *International Organization* 49:595-625.

Cerny, P. (1999). Globalization, Governance, and Complexity. In *Globalization and Governance*, edited by A. Prakash and J. Hart. London: Routledge.

Cerny, P. (2000). Embedding Global Financial Markets. In *Private Organizations in Global Politics*, edited by K. Ronit and V. Schneider. London: Routledge.

Clark, I. (1999). *Globalization and International Relations Theory*. Oxford: Oxford University Press.

Clarke, R. (1971). *La Course à la Mort ou la Technocratie de la Guerre*. Paris: Seuil.

Clegg, S. (1989). *Frameworks of Power*. London: Sage.

Codere, H. (1968). Exchange and Display. In *International Encyclopedia of the Social Sciences*, edited by D. L. Sills. London: Macmillan.

Cohen, B. (1993). The Triad and the Unholy Trinity: Lessons for the Pacific Region. In *Pacific Economic Relations in the 1990s: Cooperation or Conflict?*, edited by R. A. Higgott, R. Leaver and J. Ravenhill. London: Allen and Unwin.

Cohen, B. (1998). *The Geography of Money*. Ithaca and London: Cornell University Press.

Cohen, B. (2000). Marketing Money: Currency Policy in a Globalized World. In *Coping with Globalization*, edited by A. Prakash and J. Hart. London: Routledge.

Coméliau, C. (2002). *The Impasse of Modernity. Debating the Future of the Global Market Economy*. London: Zed Books.

Commission on Global Governance (1995). *Our Global Neighborhood*. Oxford: Oxford University Press.

Connor, W. (1994). *Ethnonationalism: The Quest for Understanding*. Princeton: Princeton University Press.

Connors, J. (1996). NGOs and the Human Rights of Women at the UN. In *"The Conscience of the World": The Influence of Non-Governmental Organizations in the U.N. System*, edited by P. Willets. London: Hurst & Company.

Cowhey, P., and J. Richards (2000). Dialing for Dollars: Institutional Designs for the Globalization of the Market for Basic Communication Services. In *Coping with Globalization*, edited by A. Prakash and J. Hart. London: Routledge.

Cox, R.W. (1987). *Production, Power, and World Order. Social Forces in the Making of History*. New York: Columbia University Press.

Cox, K., ed. (1997). *Spaces of Globalization: Reasserting the Power of the Local*. New York: Guilford Books.

Creveld, M., van. (1999). *The Rise and Decline of the State*. Cambridge: Cambridge University Press.

Crozier, M. (1987). *Etat modeste, Etat moderne*. Parsi: Seuil.

Cutler, C.A. (1997). Artifice, Ideology and Paradox: The Public Private Distinction in International Law, *Review of International Political Economy* 4 (2):261-85.

Cutler, C.A., V. Haufler, T. Porter, eds. (1999). *Private Authority and International Affairs*. New York: State University of New York Press.

Czempiel, E.-O. (1992). Governance and Democratization. In *Governance without Government*, edited by J. N. Rosenau and E.-O. Czempiel. Cambridge: Cambridge University Press.

Dahl, R.A. (1973). *Die politische Analyse*. München: Paul List Verlag.

Deacon, B., with M. Hulse, and P. Stubbs (1997). *Global Social Policy. International Organizations and the Future of Welfare*. London, Thousand Oaks, New Delhi: Sage Publications.

Deibert, R.J. (2000). International Plug N'Play: Citizen Activism, the Internet, and Global Public Policy, *International Studies Perspectives* 1:255-72.

Di Noia, C. (2001). Competition and Integration among Stock Exchanges in Europe: Network Effects, Implicit Mergers and Remote Access, *European Financial Management* 7 (2):39-72.

Dorsey, E. (1997). The Global Women's Movement: Articulating a New Vision of Global Governance. In *The Politics of Global Governance*, edited by P. F. Diehl. Boulder, CO: Lynne Rienner.

Drake, W., ed. (1995). *The New Information Infrastructure*. New York: Twentieth Century Fund.

Dunne, T., M. Cox, K. Booth, eds. (1998). *The Eighty Years Crisis*. Cambridge: Cambridge University Press.

Easterly, W. (2001). *The Lost Decade: Developing Country Stagnation In Spite of Policy-Reform 1980-88*. Washington, D.C.: The World Bank.

Easton, D. (1971). *The Political System. An Inquiry into the State of Political Science*. 2nd ed. New York: A. Knopf.

Eatwell, J. (1998). *Understanding Globalization: The Nation-State, Democracy, and Economic Policies in the New Epoch*. London: Almquist.

Eichengreen, B. (1996). *Globalizing Capital: A History of the International Monetary System*. Princeton, NJ: Princeton University Press.

Eichengreen, B. (1999). *Toward a New International Financial Architecture: A Practical Post-Asia Agenda*. Washington, D.C.: Institute for International Economics.

Eichengreen, B., and C. Ruehl (2000). Bailing-In: Systemic Goals, Ad-Hoc Means, http://elsa.berkeley.edu/users/eichengr/bailinchristof7.pdf.

Evans, P. (1997). The Eclipse of the State? Reflections on Stateness in an Era of Globalization, *World Politics* 50:62-82.

Everard, J. (2000). *Virtual States: The Internet and the Boundaries of the Nation State*. London: Routledge.

Falk, R. (1999). Liberalism at the Global Level. In *Toward Genuine Global Governance*, edited by E. E. Harris and J. A. Yunker. Westport: Praeger.

Fauconnier, G. (1997). *Mappings in Thought and Language*. Cambridge: Cambridge University Press.

Filipovic, M. (1997). *Governments, Banks and Global Capital: Securities Markets in Global Politics*. Aldershot: Ashgate.

Finger, M., and J. Allouche (2002). *Water Privatisation: Transnational Corporations and the Re-Regulation of the Water Industry*. London: SPON Press.

Finger, M., and B. Ruchat (eds.) (1997). *Pour une Nouvelle Approche du Management Public. Réflexions autour de Michel Crozier*. Paris: Seli Arslan.

Finger, M., and L. Tamiotti (forthcoming). The Emerging Linkage between the WTO and the ISO: Implications for Developing Countries. In: Newell, P. (ed). *Development and the Challenges of Globalisation*. London: Intermediate Technology Publications.

Finnemore, M. (1996). *National Interests in International Society*. Ithaca: Cornell University Press.

Florini, A.M. (2000). Who Does What? Collective Action and the Changing Nature of Authority. In *Non-State Actors and Authority in the Global System*, edited by R. A. Higgott, G. R. D. Underhill and A. Bieler. London: Routledge.

Foster, C., and F. Plowden (1996). *The State under Stress*. Buckingham: Open University Press.

Freud, S. (1991). Die analytische Therapie, 28. Vorlesung. *Vorlesungen zur Einführung in die Psychoanalyse*. Frankfurt.

Friedman, L.M. (1985). On Regulation and Legal Process. In *Regulatory Policy and the Social Science*, edited by R. G. Noll. Berkeley, CA: University of California Press.

Friedman, T.L. (1999). *The Lexus and the Olive Tree: Understanding Globalization*. London: Harper Collins.

Fuchs, D. and S. Lorek (2001). Sustainable Consumption Governance in a Globalizing World, *Global Environmental Politics* 2(1):19-45.

Fukuyama, F. (1992). *The End of History and the Last Man*. London: Penguin.

Gamble, C. (1994). *Timewalkers: The Prehistory of Global Colonization*. Cambridge, MA: Harvard University Press.

Gamble, A. (2000). Economic Governance. In *Debating Governance*, edited by J. Pierre. Oxford: Oxford University Press.

Garrett, G. (1998). Global Markets and National Politics: Collision Course or Virtuous Cycle, *International Organization* 52:149-76.

Garrett, G. (2000). Globalization and National Autonomy. In *The Political Economy of Globalization*, edited by N. Woods. New York: St. Martin's Press.

Geisst, C. (1997). *Wall Street: A History*. New York: Oxford University Press.

George, S., and F. Sabelli (1994). *Faith and Credit: The World Bank´s Secular Empire*. London, etc.: Penguin Books.

Giddens, A. (1984). *The Constitution of Society*. Cambridge: Polity Press.

Giddens, A (1985). *The Nation-State and Violence*. London: Polity Press.

Giddens, A. (1994). *The Constitution of Society: outline of the theory of structuration*. Cambridge: Polity Press.

Giddens, A. (1999). *Runaway World: How Globalization is Reshaping Our Lives*. London: Profile Books.

Gill, S. (1990). *American Hegemony and the Trilateral Commission*. Cambridge: Cambridge University Press.

Gilpin, R. (1975). *US Power and the Multinational Corporation: The Political Economy of Foreign Direct Investment*. New York: Basic Books.

Gilpin, R. (1987). *The Political Economy of International Relations*. Princeton: Princeton University Press.

Gilpin, R. (2000). *The Challenge of Global Capitalism: The World Economy in the 21st Century*. Princeton: Princeton University Press.

Gilpin, R. (2001). *Global Political Economy. Understanding the International Economic Order*. Princeton: Princeton University Press.

Glaubrecht, S. (1995). Genitalverstümmelung, Teil 1, *Rundbrief* 3/1995:19-22.

Goodhart, C., Bank of England, L. Rojas-Suarez, P. Harmann (1998). *Financial Regulation. Why, How, and Where Now?* London: Routledge.

Goodman, J.B., and L. Pauly (1993). The Obsolence of Capital Controls? Economic Management in an Age of Global Markets, *World Politics* 46:50-82.

Goldblatt, D., D. Held, A. McGrew, and J. Perraton. (1997). Economic Globalization and the Nation-State: Shifting Balances of Power. *Alternatives*, 22 (3): 269-85.

Grande, E. (2001). Die neue Unregierbarkeit: Globalisierung und die Grenzen des Regierens jenseits des Nationalstaats. Working Paper No. 2/2001. München: Technische Universität München, Lehrstuhl für Politische Wissenschaft.

Grant, R.T., and E.B. Reeve (1944). Observations on the General Effects of Injury in Man: With Special Reference to Wound Shock, Special Report No. 277. London: Medical Research Council.

Gränzer, S., A. Jetschke, T. Risse, and H.P. Schmitz (1998). Internationale Menschenrechtsnormen, transnationale Netzwerke und politischer Wandel in den Ländern des Südens, *Zeitschrift für Internationale Beziehungen* 5 (1):5-41.

Greif, A. (2000). The Fundamental Problem of Exchange: A Research Agenda in Historical Analysis, *European Review of Economic History* 4 (3):251-84.

Griffin, D.R. (1999). Global Government: Objections Considered. In *Toward Genuine Global Governance*, edited by E. E. Harris and J. A. Yunker. Westport: Praeger.

Gross Stein, J., J. Fitzgibbon, M. MacLean, R. Stren (2001). *Networks of Knowledge: Collaborative Innovations in International Learning*. Toronto: University of Toronto Press.

Grundfest, J.A. (1998). Securities Regulation. In *The New Palgrave Dictionary of Economics and the Law*, edited by P. Newman. London: Macmillan.

Guitian, M. (1992). *The Unique Nature and the Responsibilities of the International Monetary Fund*. Washington, D.C.: International Monetary Fund.

Güttner, T. (1995). Frau, warum weinst du? Genitale Verstümmelung von Mädchen/Frauen in Afrika, *Rundbrief* 1/1995:4-8.

Habermas, J. (1973). *Legitimationsprobleme im Spätkapitalismus*. Frankfurt: Suhrkamp.

Habermas, J. (1984). *Vorstudien und Ergänzungen zur Theorie des kommunikativen Handelns*. Frankfurt am Main: Suhrkamp.

Hacker, P. (1999). *Wittgenstein*. London: Routledge.

Hafner, K. (1996). *Where Wizards Stay Up Late*. New York: Simon and Schuster.

Hall, R. and T. Biersteker, eds. (forthcoming). *The Emergence of Private Authority in the International System*. Cambridge: Cambridge University Press.

Harris, E.E., and J.A. Yunker, eds. (1999). *Toward Genuine Global Governance*. Westport: Praeger.

Harvey, R. (1995). *The Return of the Strong: The Drift to Global Disorder*. London: Macmillan.

Hasenclever, A., P. Mayer, and V. Rittberger (1997). *Theory of International Regimes*. Cambridge: Cambridge University Press.

Haufler, V. (1993). Crossing the Boundary between Public and Private. In *Regime Theory and International Regimes*, edited by V. Rittberger. Oxford: Clarendon Press.

Held, D. (1995). *Democracy and the Global Order*. Stanford: Stanford University Press.

Held, D., and A. McGrew (1993). Globalization and the Liberal Democratic State, *Government and Opposition* 28 (2):261-85.

Held, D., A. McGrew, D. Goldblatt, and J. Perraton (1999). *Global Transformations: Politics, Economics, and Culture*. Cambridge: Polity Press.

Helleiner, E. (1994). *States and the Reemergence of Global Finance: From Bretton Woods to the 1990s*. Ithaca: Cornell University Press.

Helleiner, E. (1998). Electronic Money: A Challenge to the Sovereign State?, *Journal of International Affairs* 51 (2):387-410.

Helleiner, G.K. (2001). Markets, Politics, and Globalization: Can the Global Economy Be Civilized?, *Global Governance* 7 (3):243-63.

Herring, R.J., and R.E. Litan (1995). *Financial Regulation in the Global Economy*. Washington, D.C.: The Brookings Institutions.

Hewson, M., and T.J. Sinclair, eds. (1999). *Approaches to Global Governance Theory*. Albany: SUNY Press.

Hirst, P. (1997). *From Statism to Pluralism. Democracy, Civil Society and Global Politics*. Bristol: UCL-Press.

Hirst, P. (2000). Democracy and Governance. In *Debating Governance*, edited by J. Pierre. Oxford: Oxford University Press.

Hirst, P., and G. Thompson (1995). Globalisation and the Future of the Nation State, *Economy and Society* 24 (3):408-42.

Hirst, P., and G. Thompson (1996). *Globalization in Question: The International Economy and the Possibilities of Governance*. Oxford: Polity Press.

Hollis, M., and S. Smith (1994). Two Stories about Structure and Agency, *Review of International Studies* 20:241-51.

Holton, R.J. (1998). *Globalization and the Nation-State*. London: MacMillan.

Holthaus, I. (1996). Frauenmenschrechtsbewegungen und die Universalisierung der Menschenrechte, *Peripherie* 61:6-23.

Huntington, S. (1996). *The Clash of Civilizations and the Remaking of World Order*. New York: Simon and Schuster.

Hurrell, A., and N. Woods (1999). *Inequality. Globalization and World Politics*. Oxford: Oxford University Press.

IMF (1997). The Role of the IMF in Governance Issues: Guidance Note, Approved by the IMF Executive Board, July 25, http://www.imf.org/external/pubs/ft/exrp/govern/govindex.htm.

IMF (1999). Codes of Good Practices on Transparency in Monetary and Financial Policies: Declaration of Principles. Adopted by the Interim Committee of the IMF on September 26, 1999, http://www.imf.org/external/np/mae/mft/code/index.htm.

IMF (2000). Report of the Managing Director to the International Monetary and Financial Committee on Progress in Strengthening the Architecture of the

International Financial System and Reform of the IMF. September 19, 2000, http://www.imf.org/external/np/omd/2000/02/report.htm.

James, H. (1996). International Monetary Cooperation Since Bretton Woods. Oxford: Oxford University Press.

Jayasuriya, K. (2001). Globalization and the Changing Architecture of the State: The Regulatory State and the Politics of Negative Coordination, *Journal of European Public Policy* 8 (1):101-23.

Jessop, B. (1997). Die Zukunft des Nationalstaates - Erosion oder Reorganisation? Grundsätzliche Überlegungen zu Westeuropa. In *Jenseits der Nationalökonomie? Weltwirtschaft und Nationalstaat zwischen Globalisierung und Regionalisierung*, edited by S. Becker, T. Sablowski and W. Schumm. Hamburg: Argument-Verlag.

Kalathil, S., and T.C. Boas (2001). The Internet and State Control in Authoritarian Regimes: China, Cuba and the Counterrevolution, Working Paper. Washington, D.C.: Carnegie Endowment for International Peace.

Kaufmann, D., A. Kray, and P. Zoido-Lobaton (1999). *Governance Matters*. Washington, D.C.: World Bank.

Kaufmann, D., A. Kray, and P. Zoido-Lobaton (2000a). Improving Governance and Controlling Corruption: New Empirical Frontiers and the Case for Collective Action, Background Paper for the Maastricht Conference. Washington, D.C.: World Bank.

Kaufmann, D., A. Kray, and P. Zoido-Lobaton (2000b). *Aggregating Governance Indicators*. Washington, D.C.: World Bank.

Keck, M.E., and K. Sikkink (1998). *Activist Beyond Borders: Advocacy Networks in International Politics*. Ithaca and London: Cornell University Press.

Keeler, T.E., and S.E. Foreman (1998). Regulation and Deregulation. In *The New Palgrave Dictionary of Economics and the Law*, vol. 3, edited by P. Newman. London: Macmillan.

Kempadoo, K., and J. Doezema (eds.). (1998). *Global Sex Workers: Rights, Resistance, and Redefinition*. London: Routledge.

Kenny, A.. (1973).*Wittgenstein*. London: The Penguin Press.

Kenny, A. (1984). *The Legacy of Wittgenstein*. Oxford: Basil Blackwell.

Keohane, R.O., and J.S. Nye (1977). *Power and Interdependence: World Politics in Transition*. Boston: Little and Brown.

Keohane, R.O. (1988). International Institutions: Two Approaches, *International Studies Quarterly* 32 (4):379-96.

Kickert, W. (ed.) (1997). *Public Management and Administrative Reform in Western Europe*. Cheltenham: Edward Elgar.

Knaup, H., and C. Mestmacher. (2001). Zuwanderung, Beinharte Linie. *Der Spiegel*, 27/2001, 32-33.

Koselleck, R. (1985). *Futures Past: On the Semantics of Historical Time*. Cambridge, MA: MIT Press.

Köhler, H. (2000). The IMF in a Changing World, http://www.imf.org/external/np/speeches/2000/080700.htm.

Kratochwil, F. (1989). *Rules, Norms, and Decisions. On the Conditions of Practical and Legal Reasoning in International Relations and Domestic Affairs*. Cambridge: Cambridge University Press.

Kratochwil, F. (1997). International Organization: Globalization and the Disappearance of Publics. In *Global Governance: The Role of International Institutions in the Changing World*, edited by J.-Y. Chung. Seoul: Sejong.

Kratochwil, F. (2000). The Politics of Place and Origin: An Inquiry into the Changing Boundaries of Representation, Citizenship and Legitimacy. In *Confronting the Political in International Relations*, edited by M. Ebata and B. Neufeld. London: Macmillan-Millennium.

Kristof, N. (1998). Experts Question Roving Flow of Global Capital. *New York Times*, September 20.

Krugman, P. (1994). Competitiveness, A Dangerous Obsession, *Foreign Affairs* 73:28-44.

Langhorne, R. (2001). *The Coming of Globalization. Its Evolution and Contemporary Consequences*. Houndsmills and Basingstoke: Palgrave.

Lapid, Y., and F. Kratochwil (1996). Revisiting the "National": Towards an Identity Agenda in Neorealism? In *The Return of Culture and Identity in IR Theory*, edited by Y. Lapid and F. V. Kratochwil. Boulder, CO: Lynne Rienner.

Lasswell, H.D. (1958). *Politics: Who Gets What, When, How*. New York: Meridian Books.

Latham, R. (1999). Politics in a Floating World. In *Approaches to Global Governance Theory*, edited by M. Hewson and T. J. Sinclair. Albany: State University of New York Press.

Leatherman, J., R. Pagnucco, et al. (1994). International Institutions and Transnational Social Movement Organizations: Challenging the State in a Three-Level Game of Global Transformation. Paper read at the 35th Convention of the International Studies Association, 30 March - 2 April 1994, at Washington, D.C.

Lebow, R.N., and T. Risse-Kappen, eds. (1995). *International Relations Theory and the End of the Cold War*. New York: Columbia University Press.

Lebow, R.N. (2000). What's So Different About a Counterfactual?, *World Politics* 52:550-85.

Lebow, R.N. (2000/2001). Contingency, Catalysts and International System Change, *Political Science Quarterly* 115:591-616.

Lee, R. (1998). *What is an Exchange? The Automation, Management and Regulation of Financial Markets*. Oxford: Oxford University Press.

Lenin (1939). *Imperialism, the Highest Stage of Capitalism.* 2nd ed. New York: International Publishers.

Lindblom, C. (1977). *Politics and Markets.* New York: Basic Books.

Lipietz, A. (1992). *Towards a New Economic Order: Postfordism, Ecology and Democracy.* Translated by M. Slater. Oxford: Polity Press.

Lipnack, J., and J. Stamps (1986). *The Networking Book: People Connecting with People.* New York: Routledge and Kegan Paul.

Lipschutz, R. (1999). From Local Knowledge and Practice to Global Environmental Governance. In *Approaches to Global Governance Theory,* edited by M. Hewson and T. J. Sinclair. Albany: State University of New York Press.

Lösche, P. (1997). SPD - Sozialdemokratische Partei Deutschlands. In *Handwörterbuch des politischen Systems der Bundesrepublik Deutschland,* edited by U. Andersen and R. Woyke. Bonn: Bundeszentrale für politische Bildung.

Luhmann, N. (1999). *Die Gesellschaft der Gesellschaft.* 2 vols. Frankfurt: Suhrkamp.

Lukauskas, A.J. (1999). Review Essay. Managing Mobile Capital: Recent Scholarship on the Political Economy of International Finance, *Review of International Political Economy* 6 (2):262-87.

Lütz, S. (1998). The Revival of the Nation-State? Stock Exchange Regulation in an Era of Globalized Financial Markets, *Journal of European Public Policy* 5 (1):153-68.

Lütz, S. (2000). From Managed to Market Capitalism? German Finance in Transition, Max-Planck-Institut für Gesellschaftsforschung Discussion Paper 00/2.

Lütz, S., and R. Czada (2000). Marktkonstitution als politische Aufgabe: Problemskizze und Theorieüberblick. In *Die politische Konstitution von Märkten,* edited by S. Lütz and R. Czada. Wiesbaden: Westdeutscher Verlag.

Majone, G. (1994). The Rise of the Regulatory State in Europe, *West European Politics* 17 (3):77-101.

Majone, G. (1996). Regulation and its Modes. In *Regulating Europe,* edited by G. Majone. London: Routledge.

Majone, G. (1997). From the Positive to the Regulatory State: Causes and Consequences of Changes in the Mode of Governance, *Journal of Public Policy* 17 (2):139-67.

Martin, B. (1993). *In the Public Interest. Privatization and Public Sector Reform.* London: Zed Books.

Marx, K., and F. Engels (1983). Einleitung zu den "Grundrissen der Kritik der Politischen Ökonomie". In *Marx-Engels-Werke (MEW),* vol. 42, edited by I. f. M.-L. b. Z. d. SED.

Mathews, J.T. (1997). Power Shift, *Foreign Affairs* 76 (1):50-66.

McNeely, C. (1995). *Constructing the Nation-State: International Organization and Prescriptive Action.* Westport, Conn.: Greenwood.

McNeill, W. (1963). *The Rise of the West.* Chicago: University of Chicago Press.

McNeill, W. (1982). *The Pursuit of Power. Technology, Armed Force, and Society since 1000 AD*. Chicago: University of Chicago Press.

Meinecke, F. (1957). *Die Idee der Staatsräson*. München: Oldenbourg Verlag.

Messner, D., and F. Nuscheler (1996a). Global Governance. In Policy Paper 2. Bonn: SEF, Development and Peace Foundation.

Messner, D., and F. Nuscheler (1996b). Global Governance, Organisationselemente und Säulen einer Weltordnungspolitik. In *Weltkonferenzen und Weltberichte*, edited by D. Messner and F. Nuscheler. Bonn: Dietz.

Meyer, J., J. Boli, G.M. Thomas, and F.O. Ramirez (1997). World Society and the Nation-State, *American Journal of Sociology* 103 (1):144-81.

Meyer, J., and B. Rowan (1977). Institutionalized Organizations: Formal Structure as Myth and Ceremony, *American Journal of Sociology* 83 (2):340-63.

Michie, R.C. (1992). Development of Stock Markets. In *The New Palgrave Dictionary of Money & Finance*, vol. I, edited by P. Newman, M. Milgate and J. Eatwell. London: Macmillan.

Milner, H. (1988). *Resisting Protectionism: Global Industry and the Politics of International Trade*. Princeton: Princeton University Press.

Monk, R. (1991). *Ludwig Wittgenstein: The Duty of Genius*. London: Pengiun.

Moran, M. (1994). The State and the Financial Services Revolution: A Comparative Analysis, *West European Politics* 17 (3):158-77.

Mürle, H. (1998). Global Governance. Literaturbericht und Forschungsfragen. In *INEF-Report 32*. Duisburg: Institute for Development and Peace.

Naisbitt, J. (1994). *Global Paradox: The Bigger the World Economy, the More Powerful Its Smallest Players*. New York: W. Morrow.

Nef, J. (1954). *La Naissance de la Civilisation Industrielle*. Paris: Armand Colin.

Ogus, A. (1994). *Regulation. Legal Form and Economic Theory*. Oxford: Clarendon Press.

Ohmae, Kenichi. (1990). The Borderless World. Power and Strategy in the Global Market Place. London: Harper Collins.

Ohmae, K. (1995). *The End of the Nation State: The Rise of the Regional Economies*. New York: Free Press.

O'Brien, R., A.M. Goetz, J.A. Scholte, M. Williams (2000). *Contesting Global Governance*. Cambridge: Cambridge University Press.

Parker, B. (1996). Evolution and Revolution: From International Business to Globalization. In *Handbook of Organization Studies*, edited by S. R. Clegg, C. Hardy and W. R. Nord. London: Sage.

Pauly, L. (1997). *Who Elected the Bankers? Surveillance and Control in the World Economy*. Ithaca: Cornell University Press.

Pauly, L., and S. Reich (1997). National Structures and Multinational Corporate Behavior: Enduring Differences in the Age of Globalization, *International Organization* 51:1-30.

Peltzman, S. (1998). Toward a More General Theory of Regulation. In *Political Participation and Government Regulation,* edited by S. Peltzman. Chicago: University of Chicago Press.

Pettman, J.J. (1996). "An International Political Economy of Sex?" in E. Kofman and G. Youngs (eds.). *Globalization: Theory and Practice.* London: Pinter.

Pijl, K. van der (1984). *The Making of an Atlantic Ruling Class.* London: Verso.

Pijl, K. van der (1998). *Transnational Classes and International Relations.* London and New York: Routledge.

Pirrong, S.C. (1998). Self-Regulation of Private Organized Markets. In *The New Palgrave Dictionary of Economics and the Law,* vol. 3, edited by P. Newman. London: Macmillan.

Polany, K. (1957). *The Great Transformation.* Boston: Beacon Press.

Pollitt, C. (1990). *Managerialism and the Public Services.* Oxford: Blackwell.

Porter, T. (1994). *States, Markets and Regimes in Global Finance.* New York: St. Martin´s Press.

Putnam, R., and N. Bayne (1987). *Hanging Together. Cooperation and Conflict in the Seven-Power Summits.* Cambridge, MA: Harvard University Press.

Quinn, D. (1997). The Correlates of Change in International Financial Regulation, *American Political Science Review* 91:531-51.

Raschke, J., and C. Hohlfeld (1997). Bündnis 90/Die Grünen. In *Handwörterbuch des politischen Systems der Bundesrepublik Deutschland,* edited by U. Andersen and R. Woyke. Bonn: Bundeszentrale für politische Bildung.

Reich, R. (1993). *The Work of Nations: Preparing Ourselves for the 21st Century.* London: Simon Schuster.

Reinicke, W. (1995). *Banking, Politics and Global Finance: American Commercial Banks and Regulatory Change.* Cheltenham and Brookfield, VT: Edward Elgar.

Reinicke, W. (1998). *Global Public Policy: Governing Without Government?* Washington, D.C.: Brooking Institution.

Robertson, R. (1992). *Globalization: Social Theory and Global Culture.* London: Sage.

Rodrik, D. (1999). Institutions for High-Quality Growth. What They Are and How to Acquire Them. Paper read at the IMF Conference on Second Generation of Reforms, November 8-9, at http://www.imf.org/externals/pubs/ft/seminar/1999/reforms/rodrik.htm.

Rorty, R. (1989). The Contingency of Language. In *Contingency, Irony, and Solidarity,* edited by R. Rorty. Cambridge: Cambridge University Press.

Rosenau, J.N. (1992). Governance, Order, and Change in World Politics. In *Governance Without Government: Order and Change in World Politics,* edited by J. N. Rosenau and E.-O. Czempiel. Cambridge: Cambridge University Press.

Rosenau, J.N. (1997). *Along the Domestic-Foreign Frontier. Exploring Governance in a Turbulent World.* Cambridge: Cambridge University Press.

Rosenau, J.N. (1999). Toward an Ontology for Global Governance. In *Approaches to Global Governance Theory*, edited by M. Hewson and T. J. Sinclair. Albany: State University of New York Press.

Rosenau, J.N. (2000). Change, Complexity, and Governance in a Globalizing Space. In *Debating Governance*, edited by J. Pierre. Oxford: Oxford University Press.

Rosenau, J.N., and E.-O. Czempiel, eds. (1992). *Governance Without Government: Order and Change in World Politics*. Cambridge: Cambridge University Press.

Rosenbaum, E.F. (2000). What is a Market? On the Methodology of a Contested Concept, *Review of Social Economy* 58 (4):455-82.

Rucht, D. (1997). Neue soziale Bewegungen. In *Handwörterbuch des politischen Systems der Bundesrepublik Deutschland*, edited by U. Andersen and R. Woyke. Bonn: Bundeszentrale für politische Bildung.

Ruggie, J.G. (1982). International Regimes, Transactions, and Change: Embedded Liberalism in the Postwar Economic Order, *International Organization* 36 (2):379-415.

Ruggie, J.G. (1983). International Regimes, Transactions, and Change: Embedded Liberalism in the Postwar Economic Order. In *International Regimes*, edited by S. D. Krasner. Ithaca: Cornell University Press.

Ruggie, J.G., ed. (1993a). *Multilateralism Matters*. New York: Columbia University Press.

Ruggie, J.G. (1993b). Territoriality and Beyond: Problematizing Modernity in International Relations, *International Organization* 47 (1):139-47.

Ruggie, J.G. (1996). *Winning the Peace: America and World Order in the New Era*. New York: Columbia University Press.

Ruigrok, W., and R. van Tulder (1995). *The Logic of Restructuring*. London: Routledge.

Sassen, S. (1991). *The Global City: New York, London, Tokyo*. Princeton: Princeton University Press.

Sassen, S. (1996). *Losing Control: Sovereignty in an Age of Globalization*. New York: Columbia University Press.

Scharpf, F., and V. Schmidt, eds. (2000). *Welfare and Work in the Open Economy*. 2 vols. New York: Oxford University Press.

Schmidt-Häuer, J. (1998). Feministische Herausforderungen an das herkömmliche Menschenrechtsparadigma. In *Lokal bewegen - global verhandeln, Internationale Politik und Geschlecht*, edited by U. Ruppert. Frankfurt: Campus Verlag.

Scholte, J.A. (2000a). *Globalization: A Critical Introduction*. Houndsmills and Basingstoke: Palgrave.

Scholte, J.A. (2000b). Global Civil Society. In *The Political Economy of Globalization*, edited by N. Woods. New York: St. Martin´s Press.

Schwartz, H. (2000) *States versus Markets. The Emergence of a Global Economy*. London: Palgrave Macmillan.

Scott, J. (1998). *Seeing like a State*. New Haven: Yale University Press.

Searle, J. (1995). *The Construction of Social Reality*. London: Penguin.

Self, P.J.O. (1993). *Government by the Market?* Basingstoke: Macmillan.

Sell, S.K. (1999). Multinational Corporations as Agents of Change: The Globalization of Intellectual Property Rights. In *Private Authority and International Affairs*, edited by C. A. Cutler, V. Haufler and T. Porter. New York: State University of New York Press.

Shaw, M. (2000). *Theory of the Global State*. Cambridge: Cambridge University Press.

Simmons, B.A. (2001). The International Politics of Harmonization: The Case of Capital Market Regulation, *International Organization* 55 (3):589-620.

Simon, H.S. (1991). Organizations and Markets, *Journal of Economic Perspectives* 5 (2):25-44.

Sinclair, T.J. (1999a). Synchronic Global Governance and the International Political Economy of the Commonplace. In *Approaches to Global Governance Theory*, edited by M. Hewson and T. J. Sinclair. Albany: State University of New York Press.

Sinclair, T.J. (1999b). Bond-Rating Agencies and Coordination in the Global Political Economy. In *Private Authority and International Affairs*, edited by C. A. Cutler, V. Haufler and T. Porter. New York: State University of New York Press.

Smith, A. (1995). *Nations and Nationalism in a Global Era*. Cambridge: Polity Press.

Smith, J., R. Pagnucco, and C. Chatfield. (1997b). Social Movements and World Politics: A Theoretical Framework. In *Solidarity Beyond the State, The Dynamics of Transnational Social Movements*, edited by J. Smith, C. Chatfield and R. Pagnucco. Syracuse, NY: Syracuse University Press.

Smith, J., R. Pagnucco, G. Lopez (1998). Globalizing Human Rights: The Work of Transnational Human Rights NGOs in the 1990s, *Human Rights Quarterly* 20:379-412.

Smouts, M.-C. (1999). Multilateralism from Below: a Prerequisite for Global Governance. In M. Schechter *Future Multilateralism: the Political and Social Framework*. Tokyo: United Nations Press.

Sobel, A.C. (1994). *Domestic Choices, International Markets, Dismantling National Barriers and Liberalizing Securities Markets*. Ann Arbor: University of Michigan Press.

Soros, G. (1998). *The Crisis of Global Capitalism. Open Society Endangered*. New York: Public Affairs.

Soros, G. (2001). *Draft Report on Globalization*. New York: Public Affairs.

Spar, D., and D. Yoffie (2000). A Race to the Bottom, or Governance from the Top. In *Coping with Globalization*, edited by A. Prakash and J. Hart. London: Routledge.

Stairs, D. (1999). Global Governance as a Policy Tool: The Canadian Experience. In *Globalization and Global Governance*, edited by R. Väyrynen. Lanham: Rowman & Littlefield.

Stern, D. (1995). *Wittgenstein on Mind and Language*. Oxford: Oxford University Press.

Stigler, G.J. (1971). The Theory of Economic Regulation, *The Bell Journal of Economics and Management Science* 2 (1):3-21.

Stiglitz, J.E. (1998a). More Instruments and Broader Goals: Moving toward the Post-Washington Consensus. World Institute for Development Economics Research (WIDER) Annual Lectures 2, http://www.worldbank.org/html/extdr/extme/js-010798/wider.htm.

Stiglitz, J.E. (1998b). Towards a New Paradigm for Development: Strategies, Policies, and Processes. Prebisch Lecture, UNCTAD, http://www.worldbank.org/html/extdr/extme/jssp101998.htm.

Strang, D. (1990). From Dependence to Sovereignty: An Event History Analysis of Decolonization, *American Sociological Review* 55:846-60.

Strange, S. (1986). *Casino Capitalism*. Oxford: Basil Blackwell.

Strange, S. (1994a). States and Markets: An Introduction to International Political Economy. 2nd ed. London: Pinter.

Strange, S. (1994b). Wake Up Krasner! The World Has Changed, *Review of International Political Economy* 1 (2):208-20.

Strange, S. (1994c). From Bretton Woods to the Casino Economy. In *Money, Power and Space*, edited by S. Corbridge, R. Martins and N. Thrift. Oxford: Basil Blackwell.

Strange, S. (1995). The Defective State, *Daedalus* 124 (2):55-74.

Strange, S. (1996). *The Retreat of the State. The Diffusion of Power and Wealth in the World Economy*. Cambridge: Cambridge University Press.

Strange, S. (1998). *Mad Money. When Markets Outgrow Governments*. Ann Arbor: University of Michigan Press.

Swank, D. (1998). Funding the Welfare State: Globalization and the Taxation of Business in Advanced Market Economies, *Political Studies* XLVI:671-92.

Tetlock, P.E., and A. Belkin (1996). *Counterfactual Thought Experiments in World Politics*. Princeton: Princeton University Press.

Tetlock, P.E., R. N. Lebow, and G. Parker,, eds. (forthcoming). *Unmaking the West: Counterfactual Histories of Alternative Worlds*.

Tetzlaff, R. (1998). Afrika zwischen Demokratisierung und Staatszerfall, *Aus Politik und Zeitgeschichte* 21:3-15.

Thomas, G.M., J. Meyer, et al. (1987). *Institutional Structure: Constituting State, Society and the Individual*. Beverly Hills, CA: Sage.

Thomas, G.M. (1993). U.S. Discourse and Strategies in the New World Order. In *Old Nations, New World: Conceptions of World Order*, edited by D. Jacobson. Boulder, CO: Westview.

Thomas, C. (2000). *Global Governance, Development and Human Security*. London: Pluto Press.

Thrift, N. (1994). On the Social and Cultural Determinants of International Financial Centres: The Case of the City of London. In *Money, Power and Space*, edited by S. Corbridge, N. Thrift and R. Martins. Oxford: Blackwell.

Tocqueville, A. de (1970). *Democracy in America.* 2 vols. Vol. 2. New York: Schocken Books.

UNCTAD (2002). *Trade and Development Report*. Geneva: UNCTAD.

Underhill, G.R.D. (1995). Keeping Governments out of Politics: Transnational Securities Markets, Regulatory Cooperation, and Political Legitimacy, *Review of International Studies* 21:251-78.

Underhill, G.R.D. (2000). Global Money and the Decline of State Power. In *Strange Power. Shaping the Parameters of International Relations and International Political Economy*, edited by T. C. Lawton, J. N. Rosenau and A. C. Verdun. Aldershot: Ashgate.

UNHCR (1998). *Berücksichtigung von frauenspezifischen Verfolgungsgründen in westlichen Asylländern*. Bonn: UNHCR.

Väyrynen, R., ed. (1999). *Globalization and Global Governance*. Lanham: Rowman & Littlefield.

Volkow, V. (2000). Gewaltunternehmer im postkommunistischen Russland, *Leviathan* 28 (2):253-79.

Waismann, F. (1968). *How I see Philosophy*. London: Macmillan.

Walker, R.B.J. (1993). *Inside Outside: International Relations as Political Theory*. Cambridge: Cambridge University Press.

Waltz, K. (1970). The Myth of National Interdependence. In *The International Corporation*, edited by C. Kindleberger. Cambridge, MA: MIT Press.

Wapner, P. (1997). Governance in Global Civil Society. In *Global Governance, Drawing Insights from the Environmental Experience*, edited by O. Young. Cambridge: MIT Press.

Wapner, P. (1995). Politics Beyond the State: Environmental Activism and World Civil Politics, *World Politics* 47:311-40.

Webb, M. (1991). International Economic Structures, Government Interests, and International Coordination of Macroeconomic Adjustment Policies, *International Organization* 45 (3):309-42.

Weber, M. (1922). *Wirtschaft und Gesellschaft*. Tübingen: J.C.B. Mohr.

Weber, S., and E. Posner (2000). Creating a Pan-European Equity Market: The Origins of EASDAQ, *Review of International Political Economy* 7 (4):529-73.

Webster, N., (P. Babcock Gove, ed. in chief) (1993). *Webster´s Third New International Dictionary*. Springfield: Merriam-Webster.

Wellman, B., and S.D. Berkowitz, eds. (1988). *Social Structures: A Network Approach*. Cambridge: Cambridge University Press.

Wendt, A. (1999). *Social Theory of International Politics*. Cambridge: Cambridge University Press.

Werle, R., and V. Leib (2000). The Internet Society and Its Struggle for Recognition and Influence. In *Private Organizations in Global Politics*, edited by K. Ronit and V. Schneider. London: Routledge.

White, L.J. (1996). International Regulation of Securities Markets: Competition or Harmonization. In *The Industrial Organization and Regulation of the Security Industry*, edited by A. W. Lo. Chicago: University of Chicago Press.

Wilcox, C. (1968). Regulation of Industry. In *International Encyclopedia of the Social Sciences*, vol. 13, edited by D. L. Sills. London: Macmillan.

Willets, P. (1996). Introduction. In *"The Conscience of the World": The Influence of Non-Governmental Organisations in the U.N. System*, edited by P. Willets. London: Hurst & Company.

Willets, P. (2000). Representation of Private Organizations in the Global Diplomacy of Economic Policy-Making. In *Private Organizations in Global Politics*, edited by K. Ronit and V. Schneider. London: Routledge.

Williamson, J. (1990). What Washington Means by Policy Reform. In *Latin American Adjustment: How Much Has Happened?*, edited by J. Williamson. Washington, D.C.: Institute for International Economics.

Wittgenstein, L. (1958). *Philosophical Investigations*. 2nd ed. Oxford: Basil Blackwell.

Wittgenstein, L. (Rush Rhees, ed.). (1969). *Philosophische Grammatik [Philosophical Grammar]*. Oxford: Basil Blackwell.

Wolfensohn, J. (2001). The Challenges of Globalization: The Role of the World Bank, http://www.worldbank.org/html/extdr/extme/jdwsp040201a-en.htm.

Woods, N. (2000). *The Political Economy of Globalization*. New York: St. Martin´s Press.

World Bank. (1989). *Africa – From Crisis to Sustainable Growth*. Washington D.C.: World Bank.

World Bank (1992). *Governance and Development*. Washington, D.C.: World Bank Task Force Report.

World Bank (1994). *Governance: The World Bank´s Experience*. Washington, D.C.: The World Bank.

World Bank (1997a). *World Development Report 1997: The State in a Changing World*. Washington, D.C.: Oxford University Press for the World Bank.

World Bank (1997b). *The Private Sector in Infrastructures: Strategy, Regulation, and Risk*. Washington: World Bank.

World Bank (1998). *The 1998/1999 World Development Report: Knowledge for Development*. Washington, D.C.: Oxford University Press for the World Bank.

World Bank (1999). *The 1999/2000 World Development Report: Entering the 21st Century*. Washington, D.C.: Oxford University Press for the World Bank.

World Bank (2000a). *The 2000/2001 World Development Report: Attacking Poverty*. Washington, D.C.: Oxford University Press for the World Bank.

World Bank (2000b). *Reforming Public Institutions and Strengthening Governance. A World Bank Strategy*. Washington, D.C.: The World Bank.

World Bank (2000c). *Helping Countries Combat Corruption. Progress at the World Bank since 1997.* Washington, D.C.: The World Bank.

Young, O. (1994). *International Governance. Protecting the Environment in a Stateless Society. Ithaca*: Cornell University Press.

Yunker, J.A. (1999). A Pragmatic Route to Genuine Global Governance. In *Toward Genuine Global Governance*, edited by E. E. Harris and J. A. Yunker. Westport: Praeger.

Zacher, M. (1999). Uniting Nations: Global Regimes and the United Nations System. In *Globalization and Global Governance*, edited by R. Väyrynen. Lanham: Rowman & Littlefield.

Zürn, M. (1998). *Regieren jenseits des Nationalstaates. Globalisierung und Denationalisierung als Chance*. Frankfurt am Main: Suhrkamp.


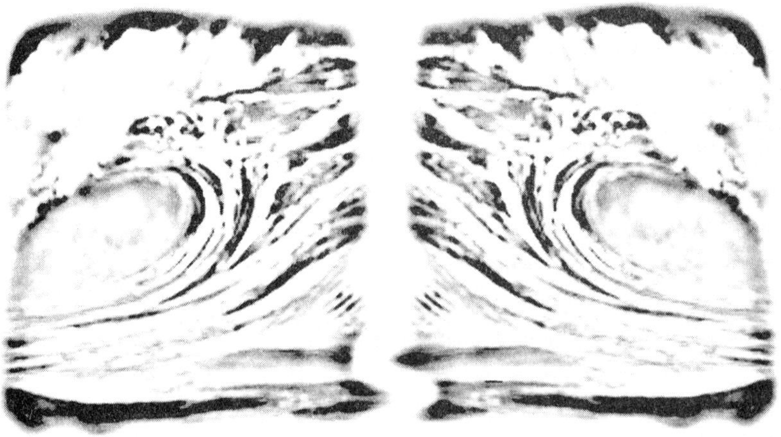

## Fragen politischer Ordnung in einer globalisierten Welt

herausgegeben von Prof. Dr. Friedrich Kratochwil (Universität München)

Alexander Mutschler
**Eine Frage der Herrschaft**
Betrachtungen zum Problem des Staatszerfalls in Afrika am Beispiel Äthiopiens und Somalias
Insbesondere in Staaten der sog. Dritten Welt kommt es immer wieder zu Fällen von Staatszerfall, die im Extremfall, wie etwa in Somalia, zum Verschwinden von staatlichen Strukturen führen. In dieser Arbeit wird Staatszerfall mit Hilfe politischer Begriffe und Faktoren analysiert. Zum einen wird nach der Funktionalität und Legitimität der Herrschaft des Staates, zum anderen nach der Rolle von in Konkurrenz zum Staat stehender Herrschaftsverbände gefragt. Vor diesem Hintergrund wird in zwei Fallstudien, Äthiopien und Somalia, die Entwicklung dieser Staaten seit Ende des zweiten Weltkriegs bis zum Niedergang der Militärdiktaturen zu Beginn der 90er Jahre betrachtet.
Bd. 1, 2002, 360 S., 25,90 €, br., ISBN 3-8258-6138-4

Doris A. Fuchs; Friedrich Kratochwil (eds.)
**Transformative Change and Global Order**
Reflections on Theory and Practice
The world at the beginning of the 21st century is fundamentally different from what it was only 50 years ago – or so it seems. In the political realm, scholars identify deep changes in organization. What are the new institutions and qualities of political order? Debates on this question have focused on two concepts in particular: globalization and global governance. Using these concepts as entrance points, therefore, the contributors to this volume explore theory and practice of political organization in a transformed/ing world with the aim of shaping the post-globalization discussion.
Bd. 2, Herbst 2002, ca. 272 S., ca. 20,90 €, br., ISBN 3-8258-6374-3

## Wissenschaftliche Paperbacks

Politikwissenschaft

Hartmut Elsenhans
**Das Internationale System zwischen Zivilgesellschaft und Rente**
Bd. 6, 2001, 140 S., 12,90 €, br., ISBN 3-8258-4837-x

Klaus Schubert
**Innovation und Ordnung**
Bd. 7, Herbst 2002, ca. 248 S., ca. 19,90 €, br., ISBN 3-8258-6091-4

## Politik: Forschung und Wissenschaft

Klaus Segbers; Kerstin Imbusch (eds.)
**The Globalization of Eastern Europe**
Teaching International Relations Without Borders
Bd. 1, 2000, 600 S., 35,90 €, br., ISBN 3-8258-4729-2

Hartwig Hummel; Ulrich Menzel (Hg.)
**Die Ethnisierung internationaler Wirtschaftsbeziehungen und daraus resultierende Konflikte**
Mit Beiträgen von Annabelle Gambe, Hartwig Hummel, Ulrich Menzel und Birgit Wehrhöfer
Bd. 2, 2001, 272 S., 30,90 €, br., ISBN 3-8258-4836-1

Theodor Ebert
**Opponieren und Regieren mit gewaltfreien Mitteln**
Pazifismus – Grundsätze und Erfahrungen für das 21. Jahrhundert. Band 1
Bd. 3, 2001, 328 S., 20,90 €, br., ISBN 3-8258-5706-9

Theodor Ebert
**Der Kosovo-Krieg aus pazifistischer Sicht**
Pazifismus – Grundsätze und Erfahrungen für das 21. Jahrhundert. Band 2
Bd. 4, 2001, 176 S., 12,90 €, br., ISBN 3-8258-5707-7

## Einführungen: Politik

Jürgen Bellers
**Bildungspolitik**
Strategien, Verwaltung, Recht und Ökonomie. Ein Kompendium für Lehramts-Examenskandidaten, Lehrer, Hochschulen und Weiterbildungseinrichtungen
Bd. 1, 2001, 192 S., 20,90 €, br., ISBN 3-8258-5624-0

Jürgen Bellers; Claudius Rosenthal (Hg.)
**Die gesellschaftliche Basis von Außenpolitik**
Internationale Wirtschaft, Umwelt, Ideologien, Regional- und Entwicklungspolitik, internationaler Klientelismus
Bd. 2, 2001, 512 S., 30,90 €, br., ISBN 3-8258-5625-9

Jürgen Bellers
**Politische Ökonomie der Medien**
Bd. 3, 2002, 128 S., 20,90 €, br., ISBN 3-8258-5867-7

LIT Verlag Münster – Hamburg – Berlin – London
Grevener Str. 179 48159 Münster
Tel.: 0251 – 23 50 91 – Fax: 0251 – 23 19 72
e-Mail: vertrieb@lit-verlag.de – http://www.lit-verlag.de

Preise: unv. PE